# How to Land Your First Paralegal Job

# How to Land Your First Paralegal Job

By
Andrea
Wagner

Foreword by
Therese A. Cannon

EP ESTRIN PUBLISHING

First printed January 1992.
        10 9 8 7 6 5 4 3 2 1
Manufactured in the United States of America.


Library of Congress Catalog Number 91-76097
ISBN  0-9630112-1-9

*Dedicated to my family—parents,
husband, sisters and children—for
their support.*

*Thanks to my publisher, Chere Estrin,
for having the faith that I could complete
this project.*

# Table of Contents

# List of Illustrations

# Foreword

Since the inception of the paralegal profession just over twenty years ago, about 100,000 aspiring legal assistants have started new careers in this dynamic field. Many of these legal assistants were fortunate enough to have received help from their schools' placement offices, or from one of the growing number of placement counselors who specialize in legal assistants. But many more have struggled along on their own — trying to put together a resumé that shows their background in the most favorable light; trying to locate positions that will offer them the chance to do interesting work for decent pay in a pleasant environment;  and trying to interview effectively so that they get the job offer and learn whether it's the job they want.

Finally, here is a book designed to help a new legal assistant to do all those things. This fine publication tells the inside story of how legal assistants can best go about finding their first positions. The author, Andrea Wagner, has gained exceptional insight into this career through ten years in the field, first as a paralegal program placement director, and then as one of the first and most successful paralegal recruiters and placement counselors working with a specialized employment agency. In addition to this hands-on experience, Andrea has a formal paralegal education and experience working in the field.

This book is a complete guide to that first, all-important job search. It tells the reader in the greatest detail how to prepare a resumé that will get the interview—focusing on the legal assistant's strengths and most marketable skills. It prepares the reader for the difficult and sometimes trying experience of the job interview, providing tips on dress and attitude, as well as sample questions and ideas on developing the best responses. It covers, in step-by-step style, all aspects of finding a job, from preparing a cover letter to negotiating salary. The Buzzwords section and the Hot Tips are especially practical and helpful to the novice legal assistant.

Use this book well, and best of success with your first job search and your career.

Therese A. Cannon, Dean
School of Paralegal Studies
University of West Los Angeles

# Acknowledgements

I am grateful to the following people for their assistance with the completion of this book.

Molly George for a superb editing job, and Tony Polk for great advice on editorial questions.

Bill Sorkin and Tom Keville, along with the staff at Sorkin & Associates, for allowing me the time to complete this project.

Cristina Kotsovolos for inputing the book so quickly and accurately.

Rachel Wagner, my daughter, for allowing me to use the word processor that I bought her!

Dana L. Graves for her assistance with the "Buzzwords" section.

The National Federation of Paralegal Associations for allowing me to use their list of associations.

The National Association of Legal Assistants for letting me use their membership list.

The American Bar Association for the use of their paralegal and legal assistant schools list.

# Introduction

The purpose of this handbook is to assist new paralegals in finding satisfying and fulfilling jobs. Whether you are a paralegal student beginning your career, a recent college graduate searching for a career, or a person changing careers, my goal is to give you that extra competitive edge to get the job you want in the paralegal market.

Because paralegals are a relatively new profession, there are still a wide array of entreés into the marketplace. During my eight years as a legal assistant recruiter and placement director, I have placed all kinds of paralegals with all kinds of backgrounds. I have placed people in the largest law firms in the nation and in one-lawyer firms that had never employed a paralegal before. I know which approaches work, and which don't. I've seen the successes and the failures. Over the years I have developed a keen awareness of how successful job searches work and what law firms and corporate employers of paralegals look for in successful applicants—from what kinds of resumés and cover letters work, to how to conduct yourself successfully in an interview.

This book is designed to share what I know with you. It is designed to be a practical handbook to be used again and again. In it you will find step-by-step procedures to follow when you look for a job. Included are samples of cover letters, resumes, and interview questions, as well as a suggested reading list and employment reference sources.

I have also included convenient checklists for your use with each subsequent job hunt. Special "Hot Tips" sections will give you insiders' information about this marketplace. You will find these sections very helpful.

Best of luck in your job hunting. You are entering the most dynamic and fastest growing profession in the nation!

# 1

# The Paralegal Field

**An Emerging Profession with Great Opportunities**

If you are serious about landing a job as a paralegal, this book is a "must" read for you! It is a **simple, clear guidebook** that will tell you what kinds of jobs are available, what kinds of law firms and companies have jobs, and how you can get them. If you use this book conscientiously, you will be **way ahead of your competition** in pursuit of your first paralegal position.

One of the beauties of the paralegal profession is that it's in its infancy. Although many paralegals are doing high-level, fascinating work—in big, important cases—the field still has **enormous entrance flexibility.** Described as the fastest growing profession of the 1990s by the U.S. Department of Labor, the paralegal field is expanding so rapidly that there are as yet no "etched in stone" standards for entering it. While most paralegals have trained at one of the nation's 600+ paralegal schools and programs, others enter fresh out of college with no paralegal training whatsoever. Others get their start in the profession from different fields, and still others jump into the field from their positions inside law firms—particularly legal secretaries whose jobs are being outdated by computerized word processing.

Even though the economic downturn of the early 1990s has caused widespread economic turmoil in the legal industry, there is widespread consensus that the field and **role of paralegals will only continue to expand in the next decade.** If the legal industry as a whole is going to be forced to become more efficient and businesslike, the reasoning goes, paralegals will become more important because they are extremely cost effective—and billable to clients.

Moreover, the paralegal field offers the unique opportunity to do important work on interesting matters without the commitment to years of additional education for a law degree. Many new college graduates are becoming paralegals so they can taste a career in the law before committing themselves to three difficult years of law school. Many other professionals—teachers, for instance—are becoming paralegals because the work seems more interesting and the compensation is comparable or better.

Whatever your present position, whatever your motivations for wanting to enter the profession, **this book can be your ticket inside**. It will not only give you practical, step-by-step guidance about how to seek your first job, it will tell you where the jobs are and what special requirements exist for different specialty areas. It will tell you what kinds of jobs are available for your qualifications and how qualifications for entry-level positions differ from region to region in the United States.

If you are presently a paralegal student, you are learning about the tasks of your chosen profession. But knowing how to do a job and knowing how to land one are two very different skills. This book will help you package yourself and your knowledge so that you can land the entry-level job you want that will take you to the career you envision. It will provide you with invaluable information about how to gather strategic information about potential employers and how to network to get your job, and then how to negotiate for an appropriate salary.

By the time you complete your job search, this book should be worn and dog-eared. But by that time, you also should have begun a career that can fascinate and reward you as few others can. Good hunting!


## WHO ARE THESE PEOPLE? THE PARALEGAL DEFINED

Paralegals perform a wide assortment of tasks in a broad range of legal matters. Some are engaged in high-level work that was once the province of associate level lawyers; others are doing work of less sophistication. They are all paralegals, however. Because the concept of the paralegal is new, it is still in the process of being defined. That gives enormous flexibility in the profession—you can start out doing rudimentary work and then quickly migrate into sophisticated, fascinating endeavors. Because of the flexibility of activity and entrance requirements—and the speed with which the profession is growing—

there are **great opportunities available for people with a wide assortment of backgrounds.** In short, the field is wide open; you can make of it almost what you want.

The National Federation of Paralegal Associations (NFPA), an umbrella group of local paralegal associations, defines the position as follows:

> A paralegal/legal assistant is a person qualified through education, training or work experience to perform substantive legal work that requires knowledge of legal concepts and is customarily, but not exclusively, performed by a lawyer. This person may be retained or employed by a lawyer, law office, governmental agency or other entity or may be authorized by administrative, statutory or court authority to perform this work.

The terms "paralegal" and "legal assistant" are fairly synonymous. These words will be used interchangeably throughout this handbook, hopefully without confusion. The two terms have essentially the same meaning; they refer to people who assist attorneys with all forms of substantive legal work except those tasks that, by law, require a lawyer. This means that paralegals cannot give legal advice, appear in court, or independently represent a client. Virtually all other forms of legal work are open to paralegals, and some state legislatures are currently revising statutory restrictions on the profession.

## BIRTH OF THE PROFESSION

Paralegals first appeared in the mid-1960s as part of President Lyndon Johnson's "War on Poverty." Federally funded lawyers in poverty law programs used the first paralegals to reduce the cost of helping low-income clients. After that, innovative private attorneys, realizing that legal assistants could help them offer more efficient legal service at a lower cost, began hiring them. In the early 1970s, the use of paralegals spread as more conservative firms realized that they would have to use paralegals to remain competitive.

Many of the early paralegals were trained on the job by attorneys. These attorneys acted as mentors to their legal assistants, who learned only the procedures of that particular office. These newly minted paraprofessionals were taught the "hows" (legal procedures) of law, but not the "whys" (substantive law). From among this early group, forward-thinking paralegals established the first schools to provide formal legal assistant training. The classes were designed to provide a comprehensive legal foundation and to make the students more proficient in their tasks. In-house training, combined with a thorough educational program, gives the best legal assistant training possible. Some schools, recognizing the value of practical experience, have instituted internship programs.

The paralegal educational system is developing rapidly. Although some law firms hire new paralegals directly out of college and train them in-house, most legal assistants now attend paralegal programs that range in length from several months to several years. A number of colleges and universities throughout the nation now offer four-year legal studies bachelor's degrees. Many institutions offer students training in legal procedures and the substantive foundation of law.

In the early 1970s, the American Bar Association (ABA) began an approval process for paralegal programs to help standardize the training. Institutions desiring ABA approval must initiate contact and pass ABA scrutiny. Some schools have not sought ABA approval, but still offer quality programs. It is up to each person to decide which program is appropriate. Considerations include cost, location, length of the program, and requirements for acceptance.

---

**HOT TIP:** Many employers confuse **certified** with **certificated**. When you see an advertisement requiring a "certified" candidate, the firm may mean, "must have a certificate," or vice versa. In either case, send your resumé! The law firm may never understand the difference, enabling you to land a good job.

---

Upon completion of a program, a student has earned a certificate or diploma. The student is **certificated**. The National Association of Legal Assistants (NALA) offers a two and one half day examination program through which a paralegal can become a **certified** legal assistant (CLA). This is the only nationwide test available (at this writing) that enables successful participants to describe themselves as "certified." However, the CLA designation may not be for everyone. Many people with legal experience but no paralegal training seek to become "certified" to give themselves an advantage in securing a paralegal job. The importance of CLA certification varies from state to state. Each paralegal should check with the local legal assistant association where she or he will be working.

According to the U.S. Department of Labor, the paralegal career has been the fastest growing profession and will remain so until the year 2000. To keep pace with this boom, the number of paralegal schools is increasing rapidly, graduating paralegals by the thousands. In California alone, there are over sixty institutions on the current list of schools compiled by the Los Angeles Paralegal Association. Even though paralegal jobs are plentiful, the **number of candidates vying for these positions has made entry-level competition challenging**.

As an employment counselor specializing in paralegal placement, I have received hundreds of paralegal resumés for entry-level positions. Sifting through the pile is a tedious and tiring process. I know that I may be missing some good people who are buried in the pile. The **objective of this book** is to pull you out of the stack and differentiate you from the other candidates. You want to be unique. You want to be remembered.

There are over **85,000 paralegals in the United States**. Most work for law firms or corporations. Some are independent contractors hired by lawyers on a temporary basis for specific projects; some work directly with the public. In a few states these independent contractors are called **legal technicians or independent paralegals**. These independent contractors are allowed to represent clients in areas of the law that are relatively procedural and uncomplicated, such as bankruptcy, family law, landlord/tenant disputes, and immigration.

Independent paralegals are highly controversial in the legal community. In those states where independent paralegal is still highly restricted, many legislators are sponsoring bills which would allow paralegals to provide certain low-cost legal services directly to the public. Texas has passed such a law. Several states already allow paralegals to represent clients in municipal court.

The paralegal field is exciting because it is always changing. Paralegals were first hired to do the tedious busy work of attorneys. Now, experienced paralegals perform associate level work. The profession attracts all types of

5

people, from recent college graduates to retirees who are too young at heart to retire. Many people enter the field from other careers because they are interested in law but do not want to go through the rigors of law school. Others, like teachers, are attracted by the higher pay.

---

**HOT TIP:** Age should **not** be a factor in the decision to become a legal assistant. According to the most recent Los Angeles Paralegal Association salary survey, the average age of paralegals is 37.

---

**Entry-level salaries** are in the low to mid twenties, varying by region. The Northeast and Pacific Coast have the highest pay scales, while the Midwest and Southeast are at the bottom. Larger cities tend to pay more, because the cost of living is higher. Experienced senior paralegals in specialty areas can earn between $60,000 and $80,000 in some areas. Your local paralegal association will have access to both local, regional and national compensation studies that you can consult.

The issue of **"exempt"** versus **"nonexempt"** compensation policies has been a hot topic. Although many firms pay their paralegals salaries that are exempt from overtime (for "exempt" employees), an increasing number of firms are paying hourly/overtime rates (for "nonexempt" employees). This method of compensation can be quite lucrative, because paralegals are often required to work overtime, especially before and during trial, or at corporate and real estate closings. However, some people—like Dana L. Graves, former Legal Assistant Manager at a prestigious firm in Los Angeles—view overtime pay as a diminishment of the professional status of legal assistants.

This controversy is generally revisited each year at raise and bonus time, because there are many arguments for and against paid overtime. A few of the major firms in the country have developed a **two-tier track system** to address the arguments on both sides of the issue. In such systems, senior legal assistants are not paid overtime. However, their bonuses are significantly higher than those who are paid overtime. (See **Chapter 14**, "Getting Paid What You're Worth," for salary negotiation strategies.) Generally, however, paralegals are paid for the time they work in either overtime pay of compensatory time off, or in a year-end bonus.

## SO MANY INTERESTING OPTIONS—WHAT PARALEGALS DO

### The Beginning Paralegal

There are **four general specialties** paralegals can train for: litigation, real estate, corporate, and probate. Within these areas there are many highly specialized subcategories. For example, litigation can be broken down to bankruptcy, business law, environmental law, family law, personal injury and products liability, to name a few. A corporate paralegal may specialize in mergers and acquisitions, securities or corporate financing. (See below for additional categories.)

Another way to enter the paralegal field is by starting out as a litigation **case clerk** or **paralegal assistant**. This position is very popular with mid-size and larger firms. Generally, you do not need a paralegal certificate. Your assignments will include assisting a paralegal in large scale litigation with such duties as organizing and indexing documents, summarizing simple depositions and performing assignments which enhance the overall organization of the case. Many firms promote from within and after a certain length of time, can promote you from paralegal assistant to paralegal.

Listed below are **some of the duties an entry-level paralegal** may be expected to perform:

### Litigation Paralegal
- ▶ Assist attorneys at trial
- ▶ Prepare for trial
- ▶ Digest or summarize depositions
- ▶ Index or organize documents
- ▶ Prepare simple pleadings and discovery such as interrogatories

### Real Estate Paralegal
- ▶ Prepare loan documents
- ▶ Oversee transactions from beginning to end
- ▶ Draft and review leases
- ▶ Work closely with escrow and title companies
- ▶ Review surveys
- ▶ Prepare closing binders

*Corporate Paralegal*
- ▶ Draft minutes
- ▶ Form and dissolve corporations
- ▶ Work with the Securities and Exchange Commission (SEC)
- ▶ Review Blue Sky laws
- ▶ Oversee mergers and acquisitions
- ▶ Assist with leveraged buy outs

*Probate Paralegal*
- ▶ Oversee probate proceedings from beginning to end
- ▶ Prepare federal tax forms
- ▶ Assist at the sales of assets
- ▶ Draft wills and trusts

### Computing Your Future

Though computers have been used in business for years, law firms have just recently started using them extensively for practice support. If you know a variety of computer applications, you will have an appreciable advantage in competing for paralegal positions. A savvy legal assistant will **seize the opportunity to acquire computer skills** and become more valuable in the job market.

Computer applications in each area of law are so complex that they merit an entire book. With that in mind, I will give you just a brief overview of how computers are generally used in each area.

All areas of law are supported by **word processing** for secretarial help in drafting documents. If you have been a student, you probably are already very familiar with a few word processing programs—sweating out term papers over WordPerfect or Microsoft Word. In order to organize and draft documents, word processing is becoming a standard requirement for many paralegals. If you prefer word processing to dictation, you can give your secretary letters and documents on disk rather than on tape.

**Database technology** plays an important role in document-intensive litigation. Documents are indexed for search and retrieval on computer. Full-text databases are also used for storing deposition and trial transcripts. The software indexes every word, so the legal assistant can quickly find relevant testimony.

**Document assembly software** is used extensively in real estate and probate law where many standard forms are used. The legal assistant drafts documents by pulling up the master form and "marking it up" for the specific work at hand. This form then goes to the attorney, who makes the final edit.

**Spreadsheet** programs are used in any legal work that must compute numbers. This is particularly important in tax law. Knowledge of a good spreadsheet program is invaluable to the probate paralegal who must track estate taxes.

Finally, database systems are used to **create commercial legal research banks**. **Lexis** and **Westlaw** are large research databases created by Mead Data Central and West Publishing Company. The law firm or corporate legal department's unique research needs rely on these major data banks.

---

**HOT TIP:** If you know computers but don't know their applications in the legal profession, a single paralegal course about using computers in litigation, for instance, can make you a valuable potential employee. With one course, you may become **instantly more employable**—even landing jobs over more experienced paralegals who don't have your computer knowledge!

---

### Legal Specialties and Subspecialties

Each major discipline of the law has subspecialties. For example, you may litigate a case in the areas of bankruptcy, family law or products liability. Listed below are some of the subspecialties for legal assistants working in each major discipline.

*Litigation*
- bankruptcy
- environment
- workers' compensation
- personal injury
- collections
- commercial litigation
- computerized litigation support

▶ administrative law
▶ criminal law
▶ family law
▶ government law
▶ health care
▶ immigration and naturalization
▶ insurance law
▶ labor/employment discrimination
▶ medical malpractice
▶ products liability
▶ social security

*Corporate*
▶ banking
▶ business/finance
▶ taxation
▶ copyright
▶ trademark
▶ patent
▶ entertainment
▶ ERISA
▶ pension plans
▶ government contracts
▶ international
▶ mutual funds
▶ securities
▶ Blue Sky

*Real Estate*
▶ eminent domain
▶ environment
▶ landlord/tenant
▶ land use
▶ development

## PARALEGAL JOB DESCRIPTIONS

### *Litigation Paralegal*

Some of the typical assignments that litigation paralegals may perform are:

*Processing the Case and Commencement of Action*
- initial client interview
- organization of client file
- ascertaining and analyzing the facts
- investigation
    interviewing witnesses
    subsequent client interviews
    investigating court records, corporate records, titles and deeds
    investigating medical reports, wage analysis, loss of income, etc.
    visiting the scene; taking photographs, measurements
- determining legal issues
- formulating a plan of research
- researching the law; briefing cases
- drafting a memorandum of law
- correspondence
- drafting complaints or answers
- service of process

*Discovery*
- drafting requests for admissions and responses
- drafting requests for production and responses
- drafting interrogatories and responses
- depositions
    setting up depositions; notice; subpoena; reporter
    preparing questions
    taking notes on testimony
    preparing digest of testimony
- document organization and analysis

*Pretrial Duties*
▶ locating and selecting expert witnesses
▶ preparing witnesses
▶ drafting trial brief
▶ preparing questions for jury selection
▶ preparing evidence
▶ drafting pretrial motions
▶ drafting opening statements
▶ settlements
    drafting releases
    drafting and filing motions for dismissal
▶ maintaining the client case docket and tickler system
▶ preparing trial notebooks

*Trial*
▶ organizing trial exhibits and handling exhibits at trial
▶ coordinating witnesses' appearances
▶ coordinating and organizing trial settings
▶ taking notes at trials

*Post-Trial Duties*
▶ summarizing trial testimony and drafting motions
▶ maintaining appellate timetables
▶ satisfying judgments and collection work, i.e., garnishment, levies

**Probate Administration Paralegal**
Some of the typical assignments handled by probate paralegals are:

*General*
▶ prepare composites of wills
▶ petitions for probate
▶ proofs of subscribing witness to will
▶ order admitting will to probate
▶ letters testamentary
▶ estate inventories

- creditors' claims for family members
- petitions and orders for family allowance consents to transfer
- stock powers
- affidavits of domicile
- inheritance tax declarations
- estate tax returns
- petitions for final account
- distributee's receipts
- petitions for appointments of conservator
- letters to and interviews with beneficiaries
- opening, maintaining and reconciling of estate checking and savings accounts
- obtaining inheritance tax referees
- opening safe deposit boxes
- obtaining appraisals
- documentation for sales and transfers of assets
- assistance to beneficiaries in filing of life insurance claims
- obtaining employer ID numbers for estates

*Estate Planning*
- drafting wills and trusts
- application to IRS for taxpayer ID number for trusts
- checking on asset transfers for trusts
- maintaining savings account records
- letters to client explaining will or trust
- drafting agreements regarding ownership of property
- changes in beneficiary designations and titles to property
- maintaining records of wills
- updating will and trust form books

## Corporate Paralegal
Typical assignments given to corporate legal assistants include the following:

*Organization of a Corporation*
- initial client interview
- opening the client file

13

▶ preparing and filing documents relative to incorporation
    pre-incorporation subscriptions
    reserving corporate name
    pre-incorporation agreements
    articles of incorporation
▶ drafting bylaws
▶ notices for incorporating a going business
▶ organizational meetings

*Routine Operation of a Corporation*
▶ issuance of shares
▶ drafting buy-sell agreements
▶ drafting resolutions
▶ drafting documents required for registration of securities
▶ drafting notices of securities exemptions
▶ drafting Subchapter S elections
▶ drafting termination of Subchapter S elections
▶ notice of director's meeting; waivers; minutes
▶ drafting amendments to the bylaws
▶ drafting amendments and restatements of articles
▶ drafting changes in capital structure
▶ drafting dividend resolution; declaration

*Basic Organizational Changes*
▶ mergers and acquisitions
▶ consolidation
▶ reorganizations
▶ request for tax rulings

*Dissolution of Corporations*
▶ drafting dissolutions
▶ sales of assets

*Preparation of Corporate Tax Returns*

*Formation of Close Corporations*

14

### Real Estate and Property Law Paralegal

Some typical duties for legal assistants in this legal specialty area include:

*Drafting and Reviewing Documents Relative to Real Estate*

▶ brokers and agents contracts (listing agreements)
▶ options to purchase
▶ sales contracts
▶ exchanges
▶ real property security transactions
▶ drafting deeds
    general warranty
    special warranty
    quit claim
▶ deeds of trust
▶ promissory notes
    installment
    all-inclusive (wrap-around)
▶ interim construction loans
▶ closing sales of real property
▶ restrictions on land use
▶ permanent loans
▶ dedication of homestead
▶ real property leases
▶ subdivision contracts
▶ construction agreements
▶ mechanics' and materialmen's liens
▶ property management contracts
▶ real estate syndication

Now you've gotten a feeling for the different areas of the law practice, and the types of responsibilities delegated to paralegals in each area. The next step is figuring out how legal assistants and paralegals fit into law firm and corporate organizational structures, and determining the likely places to find jobs. These topics are both addressed in the next chapter.

15

# 2

# Where Do You Fit In The Organization?

## Finding the Decision Makers in Law Firms & Corporations

It is crucial in seeking your first paralegal job that you **determine who makes the hiring decisions** in the law firm or corporation. This also includes finding out what is the accepted process of interviewing and hiring. In nonlegal work, being referred to a personnel or human resources department may sound a death knell to your job aspirations: successful applicants often find that going directly to the person making the hiring decision is most productive.

However, the direct approach may not be appropriate in seeking a paralegal job. Law firms and corporate counsels' offices are **often very formal**, and this means following established procedures. While it will ultimately be necessary to meet with the hiring authority, it may be inappropriate to seek to do so at first. You initially want to determine who is the first person in a firm or corporation you need to contact about employment. Once that contact is made, you can determine through questioning who makes the final decision. With that knowledge, you will have a better understanding of who you're meeting and why, and you can modulate your behavior accordingly. You may, for instance, seek to establish a personal rapport while interviewing with an associate who may later be your boss. For the firm's managing partner, who is the ultimate hiring authority in a number of firms, you may want to be more formal.

## LAW FIRM STRUCTURES

Law firms and corporations are structured quite differently. Most large firms have a **managing partner or management committee** made up of the senior partners who are responsible for managing the firm. The hiring authority could be any one of the following persons: partner, associate, director of administration, office manager, recruiting coordinator, paralegal manager or paralegal.

Usually there is an office administrator, sometimes called the **director of administration** (DOA) or the office manager. This person is in charge of the day-to-day operations of the firm, from overseeing its financial organization to figuring out what kind of computer system to purchase. Sometimes this person is in charge of hiring paralegals, and you may need to meet with the administrator first. Then again, there may be a personnel department that handles this initially, and then reports to the administrator.

Some firms are structured so that the paralegals are managed by a **paralegal supervisor** (also called a legal assistant manager in some firms). All managers are good sources of information about the firm's structure, work flow and hiring process. Smaller firms usually have one office manager who may be the first contact in the hiring process. Call the firm initially and ask the receptionist who is the appropriate person to contact about employment. Once that contact is made, you can begin gathering the additional information you need about the firm.

Many large firms (over fifty attorneys) have a formal, **structured paralegal department** (sometimes called "program"), headed by a paralegal manager or coordinator. Paralegal managers have become such important figures in the paralegal world that they have founded the Legal Assistant Management Association (LAMA) with chapters around the nation.

Some large firms have also created a **legal assistant career ladder** frequently called the "paralegal program" that you can climb as you gain position. Legal assistant levels I, II and III may exist, all with different levels of pay and degrees of responsibility. Some firms will also utilize case clerks, document clerks or paralegal assistants who also fall within the program.

These clerks are below the paralegal position. It's a great way for those of you without a certificate to enter the field and work your way up the ladder. At some point, however, you may be required to obtain a certificate or take certain courses in order to be promoted.

There is usually a paralegal manager at the head of this configuration. This person can be a great source of information about the opportunities available at the firm, and because most managers are former legal assistants themselves, can also be good sources of informational interviews. (See **Chapter 7** for a description of the purpose of an "informational interview.")

> **HOT TIP:** Even if you are to be interviewed by the lawyer you will be working with, it is a good idea to contact the paralegal manager both to establish rapport and to gather information about the role of paralegals in that firm.

Some larger firms do not, as yet, have formal legal assistant programs. A legal assistant with five years of experience may have the same rank as a new person. All legal assistants are expected to report directly to attorneys, and there are no structured levels. However, experienced legal assistants at these firms have found their specific niche or specialization and enjoy status, tenure and great salaries.

Most small law firms do not have a structured paralegal program. Legal assistants are hired to work with a particular attorney who is generally overloaded. How you get along with this person is crucial to your happiness and success on the job. Be sure to talk at length with this lawyer about what is expected of you.

## CORPORATE LAW DEPARTMENT STRUCTURES

If you accept a position with a corporation, you will most likely be working in a **legal department headed by the general counsel.** You may answer directly to the assistant general counsel or a paralegal administrator. Ask about this structure and try to meet these people during the interviewing process.

In a law firm, each partner is fairly autonomous. You may answer to partner X, but have nothing to do with partner Y. In a corporate legal department, the general counsel is the boss.

19

**Corporations can offer opportunities for career growth** that are not always found in law firms. Often employees at corporations enroll in a paralegal training program—taking either a full program or just one or two courses—and then use this knowledge, coupled with their existing knowledge of the company's business, to jump into the general counsel's office. Many make this move because they believe the work will be more rewarding and interesting.

After working as a paralegal in a general counsel's office, many legal assistants have been promoted to other areas of the company where their knowledge is a specific benefit. Corporate paralegals may aspire to administrative supervisory positions, marketing management positions, or computer information management positions (sometimes referred to as MIS for manager, information systems).

---

**HOT TIP:** If you are seeking a vertical climb up the corporate ladder through the paralegal position, be sure to find out how many vice-presidents in the corporation came from the legal department. If that department has been ignored, then this may not be the place for you.

---

## ORGANIZATIONAL CHARTS TELL YOU WHERE YOU FIT

What follows are **typical organizational charts** of various-sized law firms and legal departments of corporations. As you contemplate working at a specific firm or company, try to gain an understanding of its organizational structure so you will understand how you would fit in. In a typical small firm, for example, you may be working with an associate you like very much, but have to report to an office manager who puts you off. Think twice before taking a job with that kind of structure, because you may be headed for friction you could avoid.

TYPICAL SMALL FIRM
ORGANIZATIONAL CHART

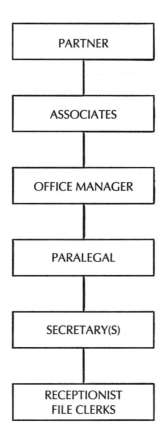

Illustration 2.1

## Typical Midsized Firm Organizational Chart

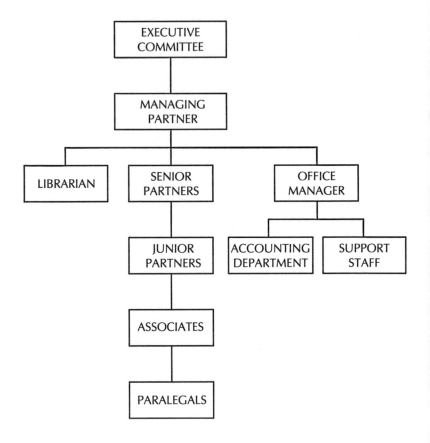

Illustration 2.2

TYPICAL MID SIZED-TO-LARGE FIRM
ORGANIZATIONAL CHART

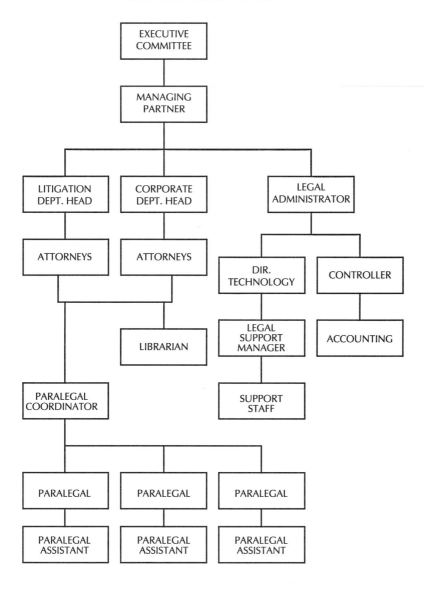

Illustration 2.3

TYPICAL ORGANIZATIONAL CHART FOR
LEGAL DEPARTMENTS OF CORPORATIONS

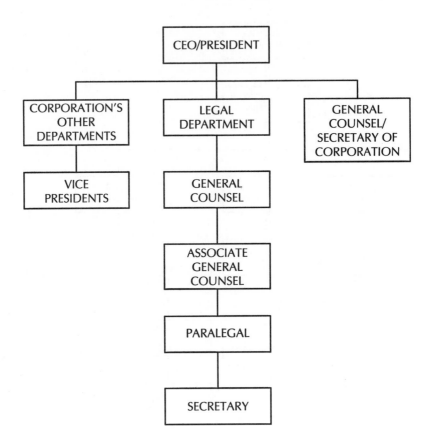

Illustration 2.4

## WHERE CAN YOU FIND JOBS?

### In Private Law Firms

Wherever there's an attorney, there will usually be a need for a paralegal. The **greatest employers of paralegals are large law firms** (50 or more attorneys), but many small (1 to 15 attorneys) and mid-size firms (15 to 50 attorneys), are realizing the benefits of paralegals and are hiring more people to fill these positions. (See **Chapter 8**, " Beginning Your Job Search," for a listing of the largest firms, along with finding aids for locating others.)

### With Corporate Legal Departments

An increasing number of corporations are using paralegals whether or not they have in-house legal departments. An in-house legal department is usually a separate department made up of attorneys and requisite staff within the company. They handle the corporation's legal work and coordinate with outside counsel. If a corporation does not have an in-house legal department, a paralegal may be hired to act as the liaison between the corporation and outside counsel.

Virtually **every industry that uses corporate counsel employs paralegals** today. Among them are companies specializing in health care, oil and gas, entertainment, financial services, accountancy services, computer technology, print and electronic media, utilities, transportation, manufacturing, publishing, food production and food services, software development, and construction, just to mention a few. Many state and local bar associations and nonprofit organizations—including The United Way, American Red Cross, Planned Parenthood, Catholic Charities, and American Civil Liberties Union—use paralegals as well. There are many other nontraditional organizations utilizing paralegals.

If you want to work as a paralegal in the corporate world, it is a good idea to seek a position in an industry that interests you as well. This is important because the work will certainly interest you more, and because you could use your paralegal job as a stepping stone into other aspects of the business.

### In Federal, State & Local Government Agencies

Government agencies employ paralegals in many different areas. Federal positions may be found in the Immigration and Naturalization Service, the Justice Department, and other government agencies listed elsewhere in this handbook. (See **Chapter 9**, "How to Land a Federal Job.") At the state level, positions can be found with the courts or the state's Attorney General's office, or within the legislature, either as a state employee or a member of a legislator's staff. Lobbying groups also employ paralegals in large numbers.

Local governments usually employ significant numbers of legal assistants. For paralegals interested in a criminal law specialty, district attorneys' and public defenders' offices offer good chances for employment. City governmental agencies like the city attorney's office, frequently hire paralegals, especially for areas like housing and job discrimination.

# 3

# Straight Talk About Paralegal Schools

**How to Make the Right Choice**

## DO YOU HAVE TO GO TO PARALEGAL SCHOOL?

No, you **don't** have to go to paralegal school to land your first paralegal job. It's a good idea; strategically, you're in a stronger position. But **it's not absolutely necessary.** That is particularly true for many law firms that hire people who are on their way to law school or graduate school to work as paralegals. These firms believe that paralegals are **transitional** and are primarily using the position to sample the legal field as a future work place. In other firms, paralegals are viewed more with an eye to **longevity with the firm.** In these firms, it is quite difficult to land a paralegal job without training—difficult, but **not** impossible. Often, you can **find both trends—transitional and career positions**—working at the same firm, at the same time.

People in other careers—teachers, nurses and legal secretaries, for instance— can **move laterally into the field without training.** The crucial determinant in such lateral moves seems to be that the candidate possess skills that ensure success as a paralegal. Teachers are skilled at digesting, organizing and articulating vast amounts of information; nurses can be invaluable in medical malpractice litigation; legal secretaries have often learned so much about a particular legal specialty that they can make the jump to paralegal in that specialty with no trouble whatsoever.

If you have already proven yourself as a valuable employee working in a corporation, but seek more interesting work, you **may be able to transfer into the general counsel's office** as a paralegal. Your knowledge of the business makes you an instantly valuable paralegal even if you have to be trained in certain paralegal functions. I know of a woman who worked for an oil company, gathering very technical information on oil well production for government-required reports. When she sought a transfer to the general counsel's office, they jumped to get her because she already had great technical knowledge and had proved herself very responsible in handling important, detailed information.

Still, I cannot minimize the importance of paralegal training. The **legal world is complex and difficult**; to function properly as a paralegal you must learn a great deal. While on-the-job training sounds like a fine way to learn, it can also be harrowing and at times debilitating. If you are the kind of person who enjoys being thrown into situations and having to learn quickly on your own, the on-the-job-training approach may be for you. On the other hand, if you are the sort who likes to feel confident that you know how to perform a task before you undertake it, the basic training of paralegal schools can put you in a much stronger position, both as an applicant and employee.

## CHOOSING THE RIGHT PARALEGAL PROGRAM FOR YOU

Paralegal training is a booming field. As chair of the Schools Committee for the Los Angeles Paralegal Association, I compile an annual list of schools in California. Each year the list grows. It is **important that you research many schools** to make sure you are getting the best education.

You will be working in a field in which your employers—lawyers—are highly educated; they want to attract employees with good academic backgrounds. Even though many paralegals are hired without a degree or paralegal certificate, or are trained in-house by attorneys, in a competitive job market, **the more education you have, the easier time you should have** in getting a position.

## Types of Programs

There are many kinds of paralegal programs, which **range in length from a few months to two years**. There are degree programs within universities. Other programs are associated with colleges as "extension" courses of study. Still others are structured more like general trade schools. Refer to **Appendix B** for a listing of legal assistant and paralegal schools.

- ▶ **Junior colleges** usually offer a two-year program. Some offer an associate of arts or sciences degree which incorporates a paralegal certificate.
- ▶ Many **four-year colleges and universities** are now offering a B.A. in paralegal studies, which are four-year degree programs.
- ▶ **Graduate and extension programs** offer a shorter schedule for those who already possess bachelor's degrees. These programs can last anywhere from four to six months.
- ▶ Private **business or trade schools** also offer programs that vary in length.

All these programs have **varying admission standards**. Some require only a high school diploma (or its equivalent) for admission. Others have much more stringent standards, requiring a bachelor's degree with a minimum 3.0 grade point average. Some programs also require **entrance examinations**, covering writing and reasoning skills. These examinations are sometimes quite demanding.

## Criteria for Choosing a School

While cost is definitely a major consideration for almost everyone, if that is your only criterion, beware! **Cost is only a fraction of the total picture**. Put on your sleuthing hat and do some investigating. You should look at a number of issues before selecting which school to attend. Some general **guidelines for choosing a school** are outlined below.

### Reputation in the Field
- ▶ What do law firms and legal departments think of this school?
- ▶ Who teaches at the school?
- ▶ Who is on the school's advisory board?

▶ What do other educators, employers, attorneys and paralegals think of the school?

*Instructors' Qualifications and Backgrounds*
▶ Have the instructors ever taught before?
▶ Are they working in the legal community?
▶ Do they use paralegals themselves?
▶ Do the instructors generally know about paralegal job descriptions?
▶ Are the instructors teaching their legal specialty?

*Enrollment Requirements*
▶ How lax or stringent are the requirements for admission?
▶ Do you need any specific educational background?

*Placement Capabilities*
▶ Do the law firms and legal departments you are interested in accept this school's graduates?
▶ How many of the school's graduates are placed in positions?
▶ Does placement of the school's students normally occur immediately after graduation?
▶ Where do the school's graduates find jobs?
▶ How long does it take for them to find positions?
▶ Does placement take a longer or shorter period of time than at comparable schools?
▶ Ask to talk directly to graduates. Get their feedback.
▶ Conduct a telephone survey of firms and corporations to find out their opinions of the school.

*Relevant Curriculum*
▶ Does the school offer a curriculum that is relevant to the paralegal practice in your region?
▶ Does the curriculum adapt to and reflect the current changes in the law?
▶ Does the school teach practical procedures as well as substantive law?

*Financial Stability*
- ▶ Is the school on a solid financial footing?
- ▶ Ask for an annual report.
- ▶ Check with the Better Business Bureau or local Chamber of Commerce to find out if there have been any complaints.
- ▶ How long has the school existed?

*Student Services Available*
- ▶ Is specialized tutoring available?
- ▶ What kind of financial aid is offered?
- ▶ Is there an active alumni association?
- ▶ What services do the student organizations provide?

*Usefulness of the Library*
- ▶ Does the school have relevant materials and books for your use?
- ▶ Does it look as though the school has made an investment in proper training materials for its students?

*Cost of Tuition and Course Materials*
- ▶ Find out whether scholarships (or assistance with tuition) are offered.
- ▶ If you are choosing a private school or graduate course, shop around to find out whether the school is competitively priced.
- ▶ The school's tuition and fee charges should fall within 10 to 20 percent of those at comparable schools. If they are higher, try to find out why.
- ▶ Junior colleges usually are the least expensive.

*Accessibility*
- ▶ Is the school a reasonable distance from your home?
- ▶ Will you be hampered because you have a great distance to commute every day?

### Importance of a Comprehensive Curriculum

Of course, the paralegal curriculum varies from school to school. However, the **following courses should be included** in order to give you a well-rounded legal education:

31

▶ introduction course to provide an overview of the law and the paralegal field

▶ legal research and writing, including training on the use of either Lexis or Westlaw legal research databases

▶ legal ethics—the obligations owed to the client and how to avoid appearances of impropriety

▶ substantive courses—those that teach the "whys" of various areas of law, such as contracts, torts and property, in which the student is required to read legal opinions and "brief" cases

▶ procedural courses—those that teach the "how to" of law and specific rules governing the lawyer's activities

Course content should include the **way things are done**, so that the student will gain an understanding of areas such as the litigation process, corporate maintenance, real estate closings and/or administration of probate.

The school should also offer **specialty certificates** and courses. The most common specialty certificates are for litigation and corporate practices. Additional courses in other specialty areas can include:

▶ bankruptcy

▶ family law

▶ entertainment law

▶ workers' compensation

▶ wills and trusts—probate

▶ commercial law

▶ taxation

▶ computerized litigation support

▶ real estate and property law

▶ ERISA and pension planning

▶ international trade law

Some paralegal candidates prefer programs offering a specialty certificate rather than a general one. For paralegals wishing to work in smaller law firms—where paralegals are usually required to know several areas of law—several schools offer a **generalization program**. It's certainly true that many experienced paralegals find job satisfaction through specialization. On the other hand, specialization certificates are less available.

---

**HOT TIP:**   If typing and clerical courses are offered, BEWARE!  As a general rule, paralegals at a professional level are **not required to perform secretarial duties**.  If a school offers such courses, it is probably **not** a professionally oriented paralegal program.  Don't, however, confuse a computer training course for paralegals with secretarial training.  While both require use of a keyboard, there's a world of difference between the two!

---

What path you choose all depends on your own unique wishes and desires concerning the type of firm or corporation you wish to join. I know of a number of legal assistants who obtained litigation specialty certificates because they thought they would enjoy working for large firms in litigation departments. More than just a few have now moved into other practice areas, and to smaller firms. **Investigate the legal field thoroughly** before you decide.

### ABA Approval

As of February 1990, approximately 140 schools nationwide have received ABA approval. The American Bar Association's Standing Committee on Legal Assistants originally decided to use an **approval system** for paralegal schools **to help standardize the curriculum**. The approval process is voluntary on the part of the school. Many schools that have fine programs have not sought ABA approval. Check with the law firms and legal departments you may wish to work for to find out ahead of time whether they require their entry-level paralegals to have a certificate from an ABA-approved school.

To be approved by the ABA, paralegal schools must adhere to the following guidelines, which are contained in the booklet, "How to Choose a Paralegal Program." This booklet is published by the American Association for Paralegal Education, in conjunction with other national paralegal associations.

The guidelines for approval require a college-level program which:
- ▶ is part of an accredited education institution;
- ▶ offers **at least sixty** semester or ninety quarter units (or the equivalent) of classroom work. These units must include general education and at least eighteen semester (or 27 quarter) units of legal specialty courses;
- ▶ has qualified, experienced instructors;
- ▶ has adequate financial support from the institution in which it is situated;
- ▶ is accredited by, or eligible for accreditation by, an accrediting agency recognized by the Council on Post-Secondary Accreditation;
- ▶ has adequate student services including counseling and placement;
- ▶ has an adequate library available;
- ▶ has appropriate facilities and equipment.

After thoroughly evaluating and investigating the legal assistant programs available in your area, choose one that meets your own personal criteria for cost, location, etc., but most importantly, **where you feel you will get the best education**. If you are about to begin your paralegal training, you will want to consult the **listing of legal assistant schools and paralegal programs** found in **Appendix B**.

# 4

# How To Stand Out From The Crowd

**Crafting the Winning Resumé, Reference List & Writing Sample**

A partner in a big-city law firm told me of a problem that most prospective employers face when hiring an entry-level paralegal. When he ran a help-wanted ad to fill the position, he was **confronted with screening over 200 resumés**. From among these, he had to select four to six candidates to interview—a few shining needles in the haystack. Although he was looking first for competence in the legal field, he was also looking for an individual with quality work standards, an ability to work well under pressure, and a personality that would mesh with those of other members of the firm.

"I realized that I was expecting a whale of a lot from a resumé," the partner recalled. "I knew some of the things I was looking for would not show up except in the interview."

The **purpose of every resumé is to get you to step two—the interview**. It cannot win you a job, but it must win attention during the screening process. Employers typically spend thirty seconds or less reading a resumé. Unless your resumé gets attention, you will sit at home!

## SELLING YOURSELF TO THE LEGAL INDUSTRY

Job hunting is **selling yourself**. A resumé is an advertisement about you. It is an example of your work product, and the prospective employer will scrutinize it carefully. Among the hundreds of paralegal resumés I have screened, I have been amazed to find many with spelling and typographical errors. One sloppy mistake can end the job hunt. Legal work is based on accuracy. You will be judged by the appearance of your resumé and cover letters. **Mistakes are not tolerated** in a law firm! A careless mistake translates in the attorney's mind as "a person who produces poor work product."

Your resumé is a brief summary of your educational and professional background. Its goal is to present your qualifications to the employer in the most favorable light. As an advertisement, it should be geared toward your target market—the legal field. The resumé can be further tailored for a specific area of law, job opening or law firm. Word processing allows you to **customize your resumé for each application**. Within one to two pages, your resumé must emphasize those skills and abilities that most interest lawyers. The rest is superfluous.

There are many styles of resumés. Regardless of the format, the **resumé must be concise, accurate, and attractive**. Laser printers can produce resumés that look typeset, but don't get carried away with design. Try to avoid very large or extremely boldfaced headings, logos, etc. Remember, this resumé is going to the legal community—a very conservative and exacting audience.


## UNDERSTAND YOURSELF BEFORE SELLING YOURSELF TO OTHERS

Whatever your background, you probably possess **skills transferable to the paralegal field**. Carpenters have become paralegals in the field of construction litigation; persons with medical backgrounds are needed in the areas of medical malpractice and personal injury; environmental experience can be applied to real estate development and environmental litigation; insurance claims handlers make great insurance defense paralegals; persons with manufacturing experience do well in products liability firms; counselors and social workers fit into family law practices; those with import and export backgrounds become international trade law paralegals; entertainers and writers understand entertainment law; real estate agents have gone to work as real estate paralegals; and escrow and trust officers gravitate toward probate. I know of a firm that is very high on hiring former teachers because the firm's management believes teachers know how to handle difficult attorneys (sometimes viewed in the same light as difficult children)!

A **self-study** is helpful before you begin your resumé and job search. You cannot sell anything that you know little about. Awareness of your strengths and weaknesses can help you decide upon realistic and appropriate job expectations. It will also make you more aware of yourself as a "product." Take time to **think through the following questions**. Take the time to **write out your answers to each question**. This process provokes thought and can be used for rehearsing interviews.

- ▶ What am I doing in my present (or past) position that brings me the most satisfaction?
- ▶ What do I most enjoy doing?
- ▶ What are my most significant accomplishments?
- ▶ Would I rather work with paper or people problems?
- ▶ Do I like to give great attention to detail or am I a "free spirit?"
- ▶ Would I rather work 9 to 5 or make my own hours?
- ▶ What are my best and worst personal qualities?
- ▶ What makes me different or special from everyone else?
- ▶ Do I enjoy taking responsibility for my actions or would I rather let someone else take the risk?
- ▶ What are my long-term and short-term career goals?

When you have thoughtfully evaluated yourself, you should have a good idea of the kinds of jobs where you will be most comfortable. As a result, you can create a stronger resumé and have more confidence when interviewing. For more examples of self-evaluation techniques and other helpful job-hunting hints, see *What Color Is Your Parachute?*, by Richard Bowles (1991 edition).

Only a small part of your self-evaluation will ultimately appear in your resumé. More emphasis on your skills and personality can take place during the interview. At that time, you will be able to accent your accomplishments.

## RESUME APPEARANCES COUNT

The appearance of your resumé is **critical**. The visual impression it makes at first glance must persuade the employer to read further. Resumés with items scratched out and corrected in handwriting and with sloppy white out go right into the circular file. Type your resumé on a word processor so you can make corrections and print new copies. Many resumés I have received had informal handwritten cover letters. Some were even torn out of spiral notebooks! These make a lasting impression—the wrong kind.    Always use easy-to-read, 10-pitch typeface (pica). If you are typing, make sure that the ribbon is dark and the keys are clean. If you use a word processor, it is best to use a laser printer or a letter-quality printer. **Consider having your resumé professionally printed** unless you want to customize it for each application.

---

**HOT TIP:** Purchase a ream of high-quality paper (such as classic linen), with matching envelopes. By buying a large quantity, you can use the same paper for your cover letter and list of references and for your follow-up thank you notes. Paper and envelopes that match look better and show the employer that you have a sense of style.

---

Your resumé should be printed in an 8 1/2" x 11" format and reproduced on high-quality paper in white, off white or pale gray on one side only. Do **not** use any brightly colored paper in blue, yellow, pink or green.

Be very careful not to mar your resumé with fingerprints or careless folding. Mail the resumé and cover letter in a large envelope or carefully fold them into a standard-size envelope. Type rather than handwrite the address. **Neatness is mandatory**.

When preparing the resumé, be aware of margins. Too much white space makes the resumé sparse. Not enough makes it appear cramped. Employers prefer a **one-page resumé for entry-level paralegals**. Two pages are acceptable only if you have been working as a paralegal for a long time. **Never** go over two pages.

Law firms are very fussy about what constitutes a good-looking resumé. Think in terms of the law firm: most prefer traditional appearance and content.

> **HOT TIP:** Typographical errors have a way of breeding when you're not looking. **Don't** trust that you will find them yourself. Ask an objective colleague to review your resumé for typographical and grammatical errors. It should be proofread at least three or four times before the final print.

Remember, the job you are seeking is **detail-oriented**. A law firm will predict your work product by the quality of your resumé. If your resumé is not perfect, it reflects poorly on you and will usually prevent you from getting an interview.

## RESUMÉ DOS AND DON'TS CHECKLIST

In article in *U.S. News and World Report* (October 12, 1987), Harold R. Kennedy presented the results of a survey of personnel officers at one hundred of the nation's largest corporations. Employers in this survey emphasized that resumés should not be more than one page for staff level employees. The most **common mistakes** are resumés that are too long, distortions about accomplishments, typographical errors and misspellings, insufficient detail, irrelevant material and failure to cite job accomplishments.

*Do:*
- ► Place your name at top of the resumé in capital letters.
- ► Make sure that your phone number is on the resumé. If you don't have an answering machine, invest in one.
- ► Include paralegal information toward beginning of your resumé.
- ► List your education in reverse chronological order. Include your degree or certificate and the date earned. If you have little job experience, include a description of the courses you have taken.
- ► In your work experience section, start with your most recent position and work backwards.

▶ Illustrate your career/job accomplishments (for example, "Reorganized law firm's entire filing system"). For a chronological resumé, describe what you did in five lines or less.

▶ Send your resumé personally to the hiring authority.

▶ Be organized and concise.

▶ List computer skills, including software packages you've used.

▶ List any foreign languages you speak or read.

▶ Follow up by phone or letter—you may be the only person who does.

*Do Not:*

▶ Write a resumé longer than two pages. One page is preferable if you are an entry-level candidate.

▶ Put "resumé" on your resumé. It's like writing "book" on a book.

▶ Use abbreviations.

▶ Include personal information like height, weight, age, health, religion, marital status or number of children.

▶ List religious, political or fraternal organizations.

▶ Include salaries, past, present, or desired, even if the advertisement you may be responding to requests this information. This subject should be reserved for later interviews.

▶ Include a photograph with your resumé.

▶ List the names of your references on your resumé. References should be on a separate sheet to be given to the employer at the time of the interview.

▶ List the names of your present or past supervisors. They can be included separately in your reference list.

▶ Include your reasons for leaving a previous job.

▶ Use the word "I" anywhere.

▶ Send out a resumé with typing, grammatical or spelling errors.

▶ Send out a resumé that is smudged or poorly reproduced.

▶ Include typing skills unless you really want to type.

▶ List high school activities or honors.

▶ Use brightly colored paper. It is best to use white, off-white or light gray.

▶ Use computer paper that is perforated or "torn off" from sides or at the top.

## MAKE SURE YOUR REFERENCES HELP YOU

It is considered unprofessional to include your references on or with your resumé. "References available upon request" should be the last line of your resumé. This statement is the conclusion and tells the employer that you know what is expected of you.

At some point during your job search, you may have to present your references. Make sure that you have a **neatly typed list of at least three people**, along with their addresses and phone numbers. Take this with you to interviews, but don't present it unless you are asked.

Your references should be **people with whom you have worked**, including supervisors, colleagues and/or paralegal instructors. Do **not** include friends, relatives, ministers or rabbis. Employers want to know how you work, not just what a great personality you have.

**Ask for permission** before you include a person as a reference. When asked, that person's reaction will give you some indication of the reference you will receive. As a placement counselor, I have contacted references who did serious damage to a prospective employee. These references were given to me cheerfully by the candidate, who assumed that the reference would be positive. Ask your reference what he or she intends to say about you, or at least **whether the opinion offered will be positive**.

Make sure your reference **knows you well enough** to verify the information on your resumé. You do not want Professor Snob to say, "Who?" Send each of your references a copy of your resumé to avoid this problem. Obtaining letters of recommendation can avoid the nuisance of telephone calls for both your references and your prospective employer.

---

**HOT TIP:** Provide your references with a copy of your resumé to refresh their memory regarding your dates of employment and job duties.

---

List references on a **separate sheet of paper**. It is a good idea to use the same paper for your references as you used for your resumé. Use the same identifying information as you did on your resumé: your name, address and telephone number. Also make sure that you list a current telephone number at which your references can be reached **during business hours**.

*Reference Examples*

John Doe, Esq.
Doe, Smith & Doe
2049 Century Park East, Suite 1250
Los Angeles, CA 90067
(213) 555-1111 (direct line; voice mail available)

Jane Smith, Litigation Instructor
University of Paralegal Studies
12201 Washington Place
San Francisco, CA 95491
(415) 555-1111

## IMPECCABLE WRITING SAMPLES CAN BE YOUR SECRET WEAPON

Writing samples are an **excellent** way to show your prospective employer the **quality of your work product** and your ability to express yourself clearly on paper. People in law firms frequently groan about the "paper trail" they must leave and the paperwork in which they are buried. However, drafting documents, letters and interoffice memos is an important part of virtually every paralegal job. Offering a **writing sample differentiates you** from other candidates and shows that you are confident about your work. Let your prospective employer know that writing samples are available by stating "References and writing samples are available upon request."

Writing samples can include writing assignments completed as a paralegal student. Documents or business letters drafted for class make good samples. Summaries of depositions, on the other hand, do not allow for much individual expression and are thus difficult to evaluate as a writing sample. Articles or short papers you wrote in college can also suffice, although they may not be as relevant as an evaluation tool, especially if they are several years old. Any original research paper is good. If these items are school assignments, it is a good idea to delete any comments, although leave in the grade if it is an "A" or the equivalent. You may also draft a sample memo, letter or short document without using real names, dates or places. Be sure you mark it "Sample." If necessary, retype your writing sample on a word processor to eliminate messy white-out or to correct any errors that may have occurred in the original.

Legal memos, complaints or other documents with points and authorities attached sometimes make good samples. However, some firms prefer to see nonlegal documents (such as detailed memos), because many legal documents (especially pleadings) contain primarily "boilerplate"—not original—language. If you are going to submit a sample from work on an actual legal matter, **all the confidential information must be removed**. This includes all references to places and products as well as names. Failure to hold legal information confidential will immediately eliminate you as a candidate under consideration. A candidate of mine was not offered a terrific job because he forgot to block out confidential information on his writing samples. Mark out or white out all confidential information, then copy the document to be sure none of the identifying language can be seen.

Your writing sample should demonstrate your **grasp of English** (sentence structure, grammar, punctuation), as well as your ability to **reason and write persuasively**. (See Strunk & White's *The Elements of Style* (3rd edition), for assistance in developing a correct and effective writing style.) Have someone proofread your writing sample, and retype it if necessary. A fresh eye is more likely to see errors you have missed. Your writing sample should ordinarily be no more than two to three pages.

Make several copies so you can distribute the samples to your various interviewers. Do **not** send writing samples or list of references when you send your resumé and cover letter. They are reserved for interviews only.

# 5

# Formats For Power Resumés

**Sample Resumés for Every Situation**

There are many formats from which to choose when writing your resumé. The most common in the legal community is the **chronological format,** which lists your educational background and work experience in reverse chronological order. This style is excellent for someone with a solid work history.

Another frequently used format is the **functional style**. This style is best for someone who has great skills but a not-so-strong employment history. The functional resumé emphasizes abilities and experience rather than consistency or longevity in job history. Functional resumés are not popular because they can be confusing. However, if you've been a "job hopper" but now want to make a long-term commitment, the functional style presents you in the best light.

## CHRONOLOGICAL STYLE RESUMÉS

### Personal Identification Data

Personal identification data is the introduction to your resumé. Therefore, you do not need to use "resumé" or "curriculum vitae" as a title. Your resumé must include the following information, usually in the center, at the top of the page:

- ▶ name (in capital letters)
- ▶ address (street, apartment number, city, state and zip code)
- ▶ home telephone number, including area code
- ▶ optional business or message telephone, including area code

Limit telephone numbers listed to two. If you do not have an **answering machine**, now is the time to buy one. Busy employers become frustrated if they are unable to reach you. In this competitive job market, **a missed call is a lost opportunity**.

### Career Title

Listing a career title tells the employer that you want the job being offered. This **optional** part of your resumé appears below your personal identification data. A career title, such as Litigation Paralegal, Corporate Legal Assistant or Litigation Support Specialist, to name just a few, should be CAPITALIZED or in listed in **bold face** type. It should be positioned two lines below the personal data.

A career title is an excellent way for entry-level paralegals to **indicate their specialty area**. It may also be used in place of a career or professional objective as described in the next section.

### Career or Professional Objective

Your career objective tells the employer what kind of position you are seeking and what your interests and short-term goals are. It must be clear, concise and no longer than three lines. This section is **optional**, because it doesn't really add much to your resumé. A career title is sufficient. Most recruiters do not bother to read the objective, and if it is poorly written, it will detract from your resumé.

Here are a few **suggested career objectives**. Be sure to write your own objective, using these suggestions as references.

- ▶ To secure a litigation paralegal position where my abilities in communication, research and writing are used.
- ▶ To obtain a position as a corporate legal assistant that offers the opportunity for increased responsibilities and use of my organizational and communication skills.
- ▶ To obtain a probate paralegal position that uses my organizational, analytical and communication skills.

▶ To secure a challenging legal assistant position that fully incorporates my litigation experience and provides continued growth and greater responsibility.

Do **not** use vague objectives like, "I am looking for a position that will use my education."

## *Summary of Experience*

If you've had a **long or established career in another field**, it might be worthwhile to summarize your experience at this point. Place the summary— which should be no more than five lines—just after your career or professional objective. The summary should be **concise** and to the point, using language not repeated elsewhere. Include your strengths, skills, years of experience and areas of expertise. For example: "Six years of supervisory experience with a major electronics firm specializing in the production of widgets."

## *Educational Background*

Attorneys place **great emphasis on education**. That is why, as an entry-level paralegal with no experience, you must **list your educational background first on your resumé**. Attorneys relate well to good educational backgrounds. They will not react as well to a field unrelated to legal, and are likely to dismiss your resumé. An entry-level paralegal's resumé with a B.A. and certificate listed first will be more favorably viewed than the very same candidate whose resumé shows experience as a receptionist first, and then lists a B.A. and certificate.

Include all post-high school education in reverse chronological order. Do **not** include information about high school. Begin with your most recent degree or certificate. If you are still attending school, list that information first. For each entry, include:

▶ the name of the institution
▶ the location, if it not reflected in the name of the school
▶ the dates you attended, your date of graduation or expected graduation in **years only**, not months (i.e., 1991 to 1994, **not** January 1991 to May 1994)
▶ the degree and/or certificate awarded
▶ your major and/or minor areas of study

▶ your grade point average **if** it is above a B+

▶ any honors or distinctions you have been awarded

Include postgraduate and continuing education courses that reflect your preparation for the kind of work you are seeking. If you are looking for your first paralegal job, you may want to include the paralegal curricula.

You can divide your education into **categories**, such as those found in the following example.

*Sample Educational Background*
> Graduate Studies
>> University of Paralegal Studies, Denver, ABA-approved
>> Certificate, Honors, 1989
>> [list specific courses here]
> Undergraduate Studies
>> University of California at Los Angeles, 1990
>> Bachelor of Arts in English, cum laude
> Continuing Education
>> Continuing Legal Education, Texas Bar Association, 1991
>> Fast Track Litigation, Practising Law Institute, Houston, 1988-1991
>> Various seminars on the litigation process, 1989-1991

---

**HOT TIP**: The **exception** to the "education first" rule applies only to those career changers who are seeking a paralegal position in a specialty directly related to their work history. For example, a pharmacist seeking a position as a medical malpractice paralegal, or a savings and loan director seeking a position in banking litigation, should definitely list their **experience first**.

---

### Skills, Abilities and Qualifications

Describe the paralegal skills you have gained through your experience or schooling, along with other relevant qualifications. If you have not attended a paralegal program, list seminars and courses you have taken that emphasize paralegal skills. For example, former real estate sales people can list their training and licenses.

Be sure to **list management, supervisory and leadership skills** as well as other personal qualities. Busy law firms look for legal assistants who can work independently, those who have great attention to detail, and people who can work well under pressure. If these qualities describe you, **you should advertise them!**

Refer to your personal skills assessment for additional abilities. **Be sure to include computer experience or skills.** Do **not** mention secretarial skills such as typing, filing, and answering phones, unless you want to use them in your work. Don't confuse typing with "keyboarding," which refers to the use of a computer keyboard. Computer experience is a very important asset for new legal assistants. You can highlight this asset by creating a separate section on your resumé to list your computer skills:

*Examples of Computer Background Listings*

▶ **Computer skills:** Programming ability, dBase IV experience, knowledge of WordPerfect 5.1, Microsoft Word, and Lotus 1-2-3.

▶ **Special skills:** Macintosh, NBI, data input, experience with search and retrieval databases.

If you've lived in another country, it would be appropriate to include such information. Don't forget to add any foreign language abilities.

*Examples of Skills and Abilities Listings*

▶ **Background skills** include supervision, administration and organization; verbal and written communication; decision making and problem solving; evaluation, interviewing, analysis and organization of data; editing and proofreading.

▶ **Personal attributes** include maturity, stability and assertiveness.

▶ **Experience** includes knowledge of basic legal concepts, procedures and sources of legal research.

▶ **Abilities** include the analyzing and drafting of documents and pleadings including complaints, answers, demurrers, motions legal briefs; managing files, indexing documents and records; summarizing documents and depositions; Shepardizing and cite-checking cases, compiling and verifying citations; and identifying and reviewing decisions for relevance to the issue at hand.

▶ **Other abilities** include handling the paperwork and procedures to form and dissolve corporations; preparing minutes; drafting agreements relating to incorporations; analyzing profit and loss statements; drafting wills and lifetime trusts; and computing federal income taxes.

You should also include skills or experience in accounting, bookkeeping, real estate or journalism. Include attendance at any courses like business law. Mention all skills you've acquired that relate to the legal profession. Be creative, and be careful not to repeat yourself.

### Professional Experience or Employment

Begin with your **most recent job and work backwards**—reverse chronological order. If you have limited work experience, emphasize the skills and abilities you have gained through your education. However, you should include some work history even if it's just a volunteer position or part-time employment while you were in college. If possible, show the relevance of your previous jobs to legal work. Detail only the last four or five positions you've had in the last ten years.

For each entry, include:

▶ dates (years only) of employment
▶ job title
▶ name of employer
▶ location (if this is not reflected in the name of the employer)
▶ a concise and pertinent job description

Use the **present tense for current jobs** and action verbs ending in "ing" to describe your current experience. These verbs add dynamism to your resumé. Your description must be to the point—usually no longer than five lines.

*Writing Compelling Job Descriptions*

Below is a list of questions that may help you in composing your job descriptions.

▶ Have you ever been a supervisor or manager?

▶ Can you give any examples of having helped your company or firm grow?

▶ Can you give any examples of how you saved money for the company?

▶ Can you show that you were promoted rapidly?

▶ Did you receive any other form of recognition that would show your ability? For example, did your salary increase substantially within a year or two? Express this in percentages, if possible.

▶ What have you done that you will be doing as a paralegal? This can include writing reports, performing research, dealing directly with clients and organizing documents.

In describing previous jobs, try to **avoid repeating duties** that you've mentioned previously. An employer is likely to favor applicants who have had some diversity of experience. To make this section of your resumé more compelling, use a variety of action verbs to describe your jobs. An **Action Word List** is included in this section for your assistance.

*No Legal Experience—No Problem*

If you have no legal experience, you may want to **gain some experience by doing volunteer work**. Contact the local legal aid society or other nonprofit law offices in your area. You will also find a list of organizations that always appreciate volunteers in **Chapter 2**, "Where Can You Find Jobs?" See also **Chapter 7**, where a variety of resource materials are listed in the section titled "Where to Find the Strategic Information You Need."

If your present or past employers are not law firms and the company names are not well known, you should include a description of about the size and scope of each company's business. For example:

▶ Retail firm with $3.8 million in annual sales.

▶ Largest real estate development company in Riverside County.

▶ National nonprofit organization founded in 1975; based in Santa Fe, New Mexico.

### *Other Activities and Interests*

This section should include legal professional organizations (such as your local paralegal association), volunteer activities (if not already listed), relevant hobbies, professional licenses or credentials (such as real estate or teaching). **Never** include religious, fraternal or political organizations.

Paralegal managers will sometimes look at your **outside interests** to see how those interests parallel the firm's needs or personality, particularly if your work history does not provide this match. A number of legal assistant managers have told me that these activities and outside interests can be helpful in determining if a candidate will be a **good match with the firm**. Dana L. Graves, former legal assistant manager for a firm in Los Angeles, liked people who had eclectic interests and showed a sense of humor in the descriptions of their outside interests. Dianna Musciannisi, paralegal administrator for Crowe & Day, looks for people who demonstrate leadership abilities through organizations such as the PTA or other volunteer groups. Debra Greenberg, paralegal administrator at Boston's prestigious Hale & Dorr, searches for legal assistants with an interest in writing, especially people who have been published or have written for college journals.

## Chronological Resumé

JANE DOE
1234 North Maple Street
Anytown, USA 90000
Home: (213) 555-1111
Work: (213) 555-1212

LITIGATION PARALEGAL

**Education:**

1991   UNIVERSITY OF PARALEGAL STUDIES, Fremont, CA.
Approved by the American Bar Association. Paralegal Specialist Certificate in Litigation
Graduated with Honors (GPA 90.15)
Course of study: Legal Theory and Practice, Directed Research and Writing, Contracts, Tort, and Litigation Specialization.

1985   CALIFORNIA STATE UNIVERSITY, HAYWARD
Standard Secondary Teaching Credential

1984   UNIVERSITY OF CALIFORNIA AT BERKELEY
Bachelor of Arts, Psychology Major
Graduated Cum Laude (GPA 3.56)

**Skills and Abilities:**

- ability to analyze documents, digest depositions, draft discovery and prepare cases for trial
- knowledge of tort and contract law, legal research techniques and basic civil procedure
- fluent in French, written and spoken
- knowledge of WordPerfect 5.1 and Lotus 1-2-3

**Work Experience:**

1985-1990   LOS ANGELES UNIFIED SCHOOL DISTRICT
Secondary School Teacher
Duties included organizing classroom materials, supervising student teachers. English department chairperson; responsibilities included creating curriculum for advanced students.

**Professional Organizations:**

Los Angeles Paralegal Association
University of Paralegal Studies Alumni Association

**References and writing samples available upon request.**

Illustration 5.1

53

## Chronological Resumé

MARY PARALEGAL
663 Hanley Avenue
Anytown, Texas 77419
(209) 111-1111

**EDUCATION:**

    1989    University of Paralegal Studies (ABA approved); Houston, TX
                Paralegal Specialist Certificate in Litigation

    1980    Stanford University, Master of Arts, School of Education;
                Palo Alto, CA
                Life Standard Secondary Teaching Credential

    1976    University of California at Los Angeles, Bachelor of Arts;
                Los Angeles, CA
                Major, History; Minor, English, Political Science and Sociology

**WORK EXPERIENCE:**

1989-1990  Privilege Private School, Beverly Hills, CA
            Substitute Teacher—all grades and subjects

1986-1987  Music Center Unified Fund, Los Angeles, CA
            Manager—responsible for development and implementation of retail operation. Executed data management systems for inventory control and financial statements. Instructed volunteer sales staff in retail sales.

Previous    Culver City High School, Culver City, CA; 6 years Experience Teacher of History, Director of Student Government, and State of California Advisor for Student Councils—wrote curriculum and trained student teachers.

**VOLUNTEER/COMMUNITY SERVICE EXPERIENCE:**

1973-1990  Junior League, Finance Coordinator
            Stanford Alumni Board, Director
            Privilege Private School, Public Relations Committee

Illustration 5.2

## Chronological Resumé

S. DONNA REED
465 N. Avenue 51
Anytown, CA 90042
Home: (209) 555-1234

ACADEMIC DEGREES AND DIPLOMAS
**General Legal Assistant Certificate**
University of Wisconsin, 1989
**Master of Arts, French**
University of Michigan, Department of Romance Languages
**Diploma of the Cours Superieur, French**
Universite de Strasbourg, France
**Bachelor of Arts, Music**
Indiana University

RELEVANT PROFESSIONAL EXPERIENCE
1990-Present    **Summarizer**
DEPOQUICK, Los Angeles, CA
Summarize depositions (part-time)
1986-Present    **Administrative Assistant/Grants Coordinator**
Skid Row Development Corporation, Los Angeles, CA
Write grants, track donations, manage office, administer benefits
**Administrative Secretary/Office Manager**
Initiated and implemented computer use in office
1985-1986    **Temporary Secretary**, Boston, MA

ADDITIONAL INFORMATION
**Languages:**    French, German, reading knowledge of Spanish
**Computer**
**Programs:**    Versed in several major word processing systems and accounting
programs including Displaywrite, WordStar 2000, WordPerfect 5.1,
MacWrite, Lotus 1-2-3 and Echo Development.

Illustration 5.3

## Chronological Resumé

**JOEL SCHNEIDER**
1234 Main Street, #105, Chicago, IL 60601
(312) 555-1212

**Education**
Roosevelt University, Extension Campus, Chicago IL
Attorney Assistant Training Program; 1990

Metropolitan State College of Denver
Bachelor of Arts in Political Science; Minor in Criminal Justice; 1990
Student Senator June 1988 to May 1990

**Employment History**

Fall 1990   **Pratt & Fall**; Chicago, IL
Paralegal intern—in charge of deposition summaries and research projects. Utilized WordPerfect 5.1.

Summers
1988 to 1990 **Kelly Services, Incorporated**; Denver, CO
Various temporary assignments: mailroom clerk—sorted mail for large publishing firm; photocopier technician—made and sorted copies for a large document processing outfit; prepared inventory for a large retail store.

April 1989   **Metropolitan State College of Denver**
Member, Student Advisory Council to the Board. Poll watcher—monitored election and counted ballots.

1987 to 1988 **Jewish Community Center of Phoenix**
Supervised the Sportscenter desk and assisted in the physical education department.

Summer
1987   **Arizona Market Research Services, Inc.**
Telemarketer for public opinion polls.

Summer
1986   **Citizens for Romer**
Volunteer campaign worker for candidate for governor of the State of Colorado—answered phones, stuffed envelopes, and organized mailings.

**Skills**
Excellent communication & interpersonal skills.
Experienced in legal research.
Experience with Macintosh SE.

Illustration 5.4

## Chronological Resumé

**SARAH MARKS**
1234 Market Way
Brooklyn, NY 11224
(718) 555-0099

**EDUCATION**

**Reading College**, Brooklyn, New York—1990
Paralegal major—ABA-approved Program
Associate of Sciences; GPA 3.5
Dean's List; Vice President of the Honor Society

**Midwest Beauty College**, Indianapolis, Indiana—1964

**California Barber College**, San Diego, California—1973

**EMPLOYMENT**

**Paralegal Field Work**, Brooklyn, New York—1989-1990
Small Claims Court—Advisor
Brooklyn Department of Consumer Affairs—Advisor

**Reading College**, Reading, Pennsylvania—1990-1991
Registration and Admissions Clerk

**Cosmetologist and Barber**, Brooklyn, New York—1964-1991
Self-employed—handled all phases of business, including purchasing, bookkeeping and payroll.

**SPECIAL SKILLS**

WordPerfect. Excellent ability to communicate with general public.

**PROFESSIONAL AFFILIATIONS**

Manhattan Paralegal Association, Associate Member

**Excellent references available upon request.**

Illustration 5.5

## Chronological Resumé

BRIGHT STARR
1234 Main Court
Mill Valley, CA 94519

Home (415) 555-1111
Work (415) 555-2222

**EDUCATION:**
**Bachelor of Arts, Anthropology; Smith College, 1988**
Convened and presided over academic hearings with faculty and the dean of the college as the head of the college's judiciary committee.

**EMPLOYMENT EXPERIENCE:**
**1990 - 1991 United States Peace Corps, Uganda**
Provincial Representative
- Managed $2000 imprest fund as a U.S. government sub-cashier, and a $4000 grant from Peace Corps, Washington.
- Coordinated U.S. Embassy staff, Ugandan government officials and Peace Corps administrators for visits to project sites.
- Mediated conflicts between volunteers and their supervisors.
- Arranged transportation, protocol and adjustment of new volunteers to post.
- Researched and analyzed prospective project sites.

**1989 - 1991 Uganda Ministry of Livestock, Fisheries & Animal Husbandry;**
Fisheries Technician/Extension Agent
- Organized logistics and protocol and helped teach a three-day seminar for 40 participants.
- Conducted 60 information sessions to promote fish culture in Uganda.
- Selected and trained five project fish farmers in pond construction, management and marketing of their project.

**1984 - 1988 Smith College**
Archaeology Field Worker/Laboratory Assistant, Department of Anthropology. Dispatcher/Secretary, Office of Safety and Security.

**SKILLS:**
- Fluent in written and conversational French.
- Knowledge of IBM WordPerfect and Macintosh Microsoft Word.

Illustration 5.6

58

## Chronological Resumé

RONALD McDONNAUGH
4567 Main Avenue
Phoenix, Arizona 85073
(602) 555-9837

**EMPLOYMENT
EXPERIENCE:**

1984 to Present **Registered Nurse, Phoenix, AZ**
Varied experience working for professional registries, hospitals
and clinics in medical-surgical, emergency room and
hemodialysis settings.

1979 to 1983 **Orderly and General Laborer, Albany, NY**

1976 to 1979 **United States Navy**
Hospital Corpsman, Honorable Discharge

**EDUCATION:**

**Phoenix College**
Legal Assistant Certificate, 1991

**University of the State of New York, Albany, NY**
Regents External Degree in Nursing, 1983

**ASSOCIATIONS:**

Phoenix Paralegal Association

**References and writing sample available upon request.**

Illustration 5.7

## Chronological Resumé

**ANDREA L. DORIAN**
1234 Bilsberg Street; Tacoma, Washington 90819
(206) 555-6833

## EDUCATION

Graduate Education
Edmonds Community College, Lynnwood, WA
> Legal Assistant Training Program, approved by the American Bar Association. Certificate in Litigation, 1990.

Undergraduate Education
Southwest College, Tacoma, WA
> Associate of Arts, Law Enforcement, 1977.

## EMPLOYMENT HISTORY

1974 - 1989 **School Police Officer, Seattle Unified School District**
> Responsible for patrolling school property, apprehending suspects, investigating crimes and making recommendations for the disposition of criminals and related matters involving the security of district facilities, personnel or pupils.

1978 - 1986 **Campus Police Officer, Edmonds Community College District**
> Duties included patrolling campus and grounds, protecting employees and school property, composing and filing investigation reports.

**REFERENCES** Furnished upon request.

Illustration 5.8

## Chronological Resumé

**JOE S. ONTE**
6789 California Street
Los Angeles, CA 90006
(213) 555-9445

### Educational History:

1991      **UNIVERSITY OF PARALEGAL STUDIES, Los Angeles, CA**
ABA-approved. Paralegal Specialist Certificate in Litigation with honors. Co-recipient of the 1990 Leslie Ridley-Tree Scholarship.

1991      **WESTLAW Training Certificate of Achievement**

1986 to 1990    **STATE UNIVERSITY, Los Angeles, CA**
Forty graduate level units completed toward State Multiple Subject Teaching Credential, with special emphasis on computer-aided instruction.

1979      **OKLAHOMA UNIVERSITY, Norman, OK**
Bachelor of Arts in Philosophy; GPA 3.2/4.0.

### Employment History:

1986 to 1990    **BEVERLY HILLS UNIFIED SCHOOL DISTRICT**, Beverly Hills, CA
Multiple Subject Elementary School Teacher, Grades K-6. Responsible for instruction in English, Mathematics, Language Arts, and Science in multi-cultural, multi-ethnic classrooms.

1984 to 1986    **PATHWAYS CHILDREN'S VILLAGE**, Sunnyvale, CA
Child Care Worker. Duties included substitute-parental care, counseling, and behavior modification program implementation, with severely emotionally disturbed children, in a residential psychiatric treatment center.

1981 to 1983    **RANDOM COMPUTER CORPORATION**, Palo Alto, CA
Quality Control Supervisor I. Responsible for hiring, training, and evaluating Quality Assurance Inspectors for printed circuit board assembly and floppy disk drive production lines.

### Additional Skills:

Ten years' experience with several personal computer systems, including word processing and DOS. Excellent oral and written communication skills.

**References furnished upon request.**

Illustration 5.9

## Chronological Resumé

WALTER C. LEE
1912 North Glendon Avenue, #5
New York, New York 10010
(212) 555-1374

**Objective:** A litigation paralegal position utilizing proven research, analytical, and communication skills.

**Education:**

**Dartmouth University, Bachelor of Science in Electrical Engineering**, 1986
Financed 100% of education through ROTC scholarship.

**Honors:** **Navy Achievement Medal**, two-time recipient of award for outstanding professional achievement. Only officer out of thirty on ship to receive this commendation.

**National Defense Medal**, for service during Persian Gulf War.

**Experience: USS Lewis**, Long Beach, California/Tokyo, Japan, 1989-1991.
**Legal Officer.** Conducted research on legal matters for Navy lawyers and the Commanding Officer. Managed the preparation of wills for the entire crew prior to the ship's six month deployment. Prepared limited powers of attorney for review by Navy lawyers. Advised Commanding Officer on interpretation of Uniform Code of Military Justice, legal procedures, and the extent to which he could impose Non-Judicial Punishment. Managed all administrative aspects of Courts Martial and personnel discharges. Coordinated depositions for trial and defense counsels with Lewis crew members. Supervised and trained the ship's Legal Yeomen in their administrative duties. Worked extensively with word processors including Microsoft Word and WordPerfect.

**Administrative Officer.** Managed personnel assigned to administrative offices. Tracked ship-wide personnel requirements. Wrote all official correspondence from the Commanding Officer.

**Strike Warfare Officer.** Managed personnel in operation of the Tomahawk Missile System.

**USS Clark, Roanoke, Virginia,** 1987-1989.

**Interests:** Tennis, Japanese history and culture, traveling.

Illustration 5.10

## Chronological Resumé

DAN MEASLEY
4567 Saddleback Road; Montgomery, Alabama 36191
(313) 555-7669

Education
Auburn University, Montgomery, Alabama.
Legal Assistant Training Program. Specialty, litigation; Certificate 1990.

Faulkner University, Montgomery, Alabama.
Bachelor of Arts (cum laude), Anthropology, 1971.

Continuing Education
Society of Real Estate Appraisers.
Residential valuation, 1987, 1989.

Huntington College, Huntington, Alabama.
Courses in Real Estate Appraisal, Finances, Law, Practices and Construction Estimating.

Employment Experience
**Paralegal internship**, Montgomery County Counsel, Real Estate Section.
Assisting with research, valuation, document organization, and other assorted duties, 1991-present.

**Real Estate Appraisal**, Freelance Contractor.
In connection with FNMA appraisals, handled research, telephone contacts, field inspections, and completion of final reports. Clients included First Federal Savings Bank of Montgomery, and Alabama Federal Savings, as well as many mortgage brokers. Position required maintenance and analysis of detailed records. Working conditions often involved high volume and high pressure. 1981-1988.

**Montgomery County Assessor's Office**
Appraised properties and assisted taxpayers with problems and complaints, responsible for map- and record-keeping of governmental assessment data. 1974-1978.

Skills
Training and experience in the use of WordPerfect 5.0 and 5.1, as well as several other systems.

Drafting abilities include complaints, answers, motions, and memos of points and authorities; document preparation and organization, as well as digesting of legal documents (interrogatories, depositions, medical reports, etc.).

Research experience with a multitude of legal resources, including LEXIS and WESTLAW on-line systems.

Illustration 5.11

## FUNCTIONAL STYLE RESUMÉS

Two **important reasons** why you should consider the functional resumé format rather than the chronological are: **gaps in employment** and **"job hopping."**

▶ If you have unexplained discrepancies or gaps in employment, this format will not emphasize your job history.

▶ If you have changed jobs every year or even more often, using the functional resumé will not highlight this fault.

A **pattern of gaps in employment** (or "job hopping"), will land your resumé in the pile of "also rans" very quickly. For this reason, as a new paralegal, you should consider staying with a new job a minimum of one year unless you have another (and **better**) job offer. Firms **prefer to see two to three years on a job**. They do not want to invest in training someone only to have that person leave. On the other hand, changing jobs every two to five years **can indicate an enterprising individual on the move**, and this pattern of change is considered normal in today's job market.

### Personal Information Data

The functional style uses the same personal information format as the chronological style.

### Career Title or Professional Objective

The career title or professional objective on a functional style resumé is the same as that used in the chronological style.

### Educational Background

The educational portion of the functional resumé is also the same as is used in the chronological style.

### Skills and Abilities

This section is the **focus of your functional resumé**. It must outshine your weak job history, so **prepare it carefully**. Condense all of your experience into three or four pertinent categories that are related to the legal field. A list of possible subjects appears below. Use action verbs to describe your experience, but do not repeat yourself. Think of law-related topics you have studied and apply them to your current skills, such as writing, supervising or managing experience. This is also the section where you should **detail your computer background**.

The format must be **brief and easy to read**. Each part of the resumé should have no more than three sentences. Remember, the resumé will be read in about thirty seconds or less, so you need to **highlight your accomplishments**.

*Skills and Abilities Category Paragraph Ideas*

Writing abilities:
▶ What documents have you drafted or prepared?
▶ Have you written any brochures, booklets or pamphlets?
▶ Have you corresponded with clients or customers?

Supervision experience:
▶ Have you hired or fired employees?
▶ Have you supervised or trained employees in projects?
▶ Have you taught?

Management experience:
▶ Have you supervised a group or division of a company?
▶ Have you been given particular projects or suggestions upon which you must act?
▶ Have you organized or coordinated activities?

Administrative skills:
▶ Have you delegated responsibilities?
▶ Have you had responsibility for company funds?
▶ Do you work with attention to detail?

Organizational abilities:
- ▶ Have you ever founded a group?
- ▶ Are you in charge of a particular division in your company?
- ▶ Have you designed or modified office systems?

When drafting this section, you should **use dynamic, action verbs** rather than dull verbs like "work" and "do." Action verbs will add a sense of vitality to your resumé. For example, instead of listing "research skills," write "researching and analyzing data." Remember to use the present tense for your current position and past tense for prior positions.

The additional **skills and abilities categories listed below** will add "zip" to your functional resumé:

- ▶ analyses
- ▶ coordination
- ▶ drafting
- ▶ instruction
- ▶ investigation
- ▶ negotiation
- ▶ operation
- ▶ programming
- ▶ research

### Professional Experience

The professional experience section of your resumé should contain—in **reverse chronological order**—all the positions you have held for the past ten years. Include the following information:

- ▶ the name of the company
- ▶ its location
- ▶ your title
- ▶ dates of employment using years rather than months

Set forth below is an **example of the professional experience** information that should be reflected on your resumé.

| 1989-1991 | XYG Corporation, Philadelphia, PA |
| | Accounting Supervisor |
| 1986-1987 | ABC Incorporated, Washington, D.C. |
| | Accounting Clerk |
| 1981-1984 | The Old School, Minneapolis, MN |
| | English Teacher |

*Other Activities and Interests*

The functional resumé style does not differ from the chronological format in this area. See "Other Activities and Interests" in the chronological resumé section.

## Functional Resumé

**NAME**
Address
Phone Number

### LITIGATION PARALEGAL

**EDUCATION**
University of Paralegal Studies, ABA-approved
      Corporate Paralegal Certificate, 1991
Harvard University
      Bachelor of Arts in English, 1984

**PROFESSIONAL ACCOMPLISHMENTS**
Writing
- Prepared extensive lesson plans.
- Drafted handbook for high school English department.
- Researched and wrote honors thesis on Edgar Allen Poe's *The Raven*.
- Drafted bylaws and articles of incorporation for nonprofit corporation.

Organizational Skills
- Founded nonprofit corporation for food distribution for the homeless.
- Organized monthly distribution sites.
- Created a variety of lesson plans for high-school English classes.

Supervision
- Recruited volunteers for homeless project.
- Developed plan for more efficient yard supervision.
- Oversaw implementation of idea from inception to completion.

Computer Skills
- IBM PC WordPerfect 5.1, Lotus 1-2-3
- Westlaw trained

**WORK EXPERIENCE**

Substitute teacher, various school districts in the Boston area; 1984 to present

**OTHER ACTIVITIES**

Founder and member, Board of Directors, The Homeless Project, Boston, MA; 1988 to present

**REFERENCES AND WRITING SAMPLES AVAILABLE ON REQUEST**

Illustration 5.12

## Functional Resumé

**GEORGE BRAIN**
P.O. Box 9978
St. Paul, MN 22222

Home phone  (612) 555-9122
Messages  (612) 555-0125

### EDUCATION

**University of Paralegal Studies**, approved by the American Bar Association.  Certificate in Litigation.  Graduation with Honors, 1990.

**New York University**, Doctor of Philosophy, Experimental Atomic and Plasma—Physics, 1976.

**Carnegie Institute of Technology**, Master of Science, Experimental High-Energy Nuclear Physics, 1974.

**Harvard University**, Bachelor of Science in Physics, 1972.

### PROFESSIONAL EXPERIENCE

Administrative
Eighteen years' experience in research and development of aerospace defense systems and associated technologies, including project and proposal management and writing, business development, strategic business planning  and market analysis.

Publications
Author of over 100 major reports in the areas of military satellite systems and strategic offensive and defensive missiles.

Technical Knowledge
Working knowledge of electrical and mechanical engineering and software development disciplines entailed in designing satellites, missiles, aircraft and ground support systems.

AEROSPACE CORPORATION, Los Angeles, CA
    Senior Systems Engineer

LARGE SYSTEMS, Los Angeles, CA
    Senior Scientist

ABC SPACE & TECHNOLOGY GROUP, Hermosa Beach, CA
    Senior Systems Manager

MAJOR RESEARCH CORPORATION, El Segundo, CA
    Member, Technical Staff

### REFERENCES AVAILABLE UPON REQUEST.

Illustration 5.13

## ACTION WORDS FOR WINNING RESUMÉS

### *Management*

| | | | |
|---|---|---|---|
| planned | operated | governed | administered |
| revised | directed | contracted | coordinated |
| executed | conducted | organized | established |
| retained | managed | supervised | took charge of |
| exceeded | undertook | obtained | controlled |
| unified | enacted | produced | implemented |
| headed | set up | responsible for | maintained |

### *Methods and Controls*

| | | | |
|---|---|---|---|
| installed | correlated | detailed | simplified |
| clarified | analyzed | examined | systematized |
| indexed | catalogued | enlarged | distributed |
| completed | scheduled | arranged | synthesized |
| budgeted | increased | decreased | accelerated |
| compiled | computed | expanded | reorganized |
| prepared | reviewed | reduced | restructured |
| compared | revised | verified | redesigned |
| focused | formulated | extracted | programmed |

### *Public Relations/Human Relations*

| | | | |
|---|---|---|---|
| hired | grouped | delegated | integrated |
| guided | counseled | advised | trained |
| harmonized | fostered | handled | motivated |
| monitored | sponsored | employed | mentored |
| wrought | led | interviewed | rewarded |

## Creativity

| | | | |
|---|---|---|---|
| inspired | effected | skilled | transformed |
| innovated | created | converted | performed |
| designed | reshaped | invented | constructed |
| devised | conceived | developed | structured |
| resolved | enabled | refined | originated |
| formed | solved | founded | formulated |
| excelled | affected | abstracted | summarized |

## Advertisement/Promotion

| | | | |
|---|---|---|---|
| sparked | influenced | promoted | actively engaged |
| marketed | recruited | convinced | accounted for |
| represented | secured | persuaded | was instrumental |
| generated | improved | recommended | played a key role |
| provided | tailored | honored | cultivated |

## Communications

| | | | |
|---|---|---|---|
| moderated | presented | straightened | participated in |
| facilitated | wrote | presided | reunited |
| served as | instructed | approved | interviewed |
| edited | demonstrated | consulted | disseminated |
| counseled | advocated | championed | exemplified |
| conveyed | linked | substantiated | instilled |

## Negotiations

| | | | |
|---|---|---|---|
| investigated | sorted | mediated | engineered |
| justified | assured | negotiated | determined |
| proposed | evaluated | bargained | compromised |

## Resourcefulness

| | | | |
|---|---|---|---|
| succeeded | initiated | trebled | researched |
| rectified | awarded | halved | strengthened |
| overcame | won | trimmed | explored |
| eliminated | identified | pioneered | accomplished |
| achieved | undertook | diverted | advanced |
| doubled | earned | expedited | surpassed |
| digested | fulfilled | perfected | supplanted |
| executed | realized | gained | engineered |
| inaugurated | launched | attained | cultivated |

# 6

# Writing A Strong Cover Letter

**Honest Clarity Required**

A "headhunter" (placement counselor) friend recently told me about a promising resumé that she'd received without a cover letter. The candidate's entire experience was in the printing business. Since there was no cover letter explaining the candidate's job search goals, the headhunter simply filed the resumé away, because she didn't know if the candidate wanted to stay in printing or make a change.

## PURPOSE OF A COVER LETTER

**Always** send a cover letter with your resumé. The letter should **focus on the position** you are seeking; **summarize your qualifications** and **request an interview**. Be sure to tell the employer that you want the job! Since the resumé is the focal point of your correspondence, your cover letter should be brief. Like a resumé, the cover letter should **reflect the personality of its sender**.

Find out the **full name of the person responsible for hiring** paralegals, and **direct your letter to that person by name**. "Dear Sir or Madam" or "To whom it may concern" never impressed anyone. Make you're spelling the person's name correctly and that you have the right job title. Your resumé will then be sent directly to that person's attention. If you bypass this step, your resumé may take longer to reach the correct person, and it may not make it there at all.

> **HOT TIP:** Call the law firm and ask the receptionist to whom paralegal resumés should be directed. Be extremely friendly to the receptionist and all other support staff. They may become invaluable sources of information for you and help you get through the door!

Develop **different cover letters to fit various situations**. For example, if someone has referred you to the job, you're answering a want ad, or are sending out a mass mailing of resumés to firms in the *Martindale-Hubbell Law Directory*, you **must** address these different situations with customized cover letters. (See **Chapter 7**, for a discussion of *Martindale-Hubbell*.) In the case of a referral, mention the name of the person who referred you in the cover letter. Naming a person the employer may know and respect, not only differentiates your resumé from the rest of the pack, it also builds your credibility.

> **HOT TIP:** Look for attorneys in *Martindale-Hubbell* (available at your local library) who are alumni of your college or law school division of your paralegal school. In the opening sentence of your cover letter state, "As a graduate of _____, I wanted to contact you about possibilities of employment as a paralegal." Your resumé should receive special attention.

Use the cover letter to expand on **how your background relates to the job opening**. Put thought into the wording of your cover letter. The first few words are important and should attract the reader's attention. Make yourself sound interesting. **Use simple, direct language** and correct grammar and punctuation. Keep it short. Introduce yourself, sum up what you have to offer, emphasize your strongest qualifications, and request an interview.

Be sure not to use cliches or vulgar language. Yes, it does happen! The cover letter is not the time to experiment with humor. Your tone should be confident, but not pushy or boastful. An **honest assessment of your qualifications** is enough.

> **HOT TIP:** Many hiring authorities will judge your writing skills by your cover and thank you letters. Work hard on whatever written communications you send out. Read them aloud to yourself and others. You need to sound strong and impressive because the quality of your writing provides a test of your abilities without your even knowing it.

On more than a few occasions, I've received letters that assured me the applicant was a highly qualified paralegal because she handled her own divorce or he oversaw the probate of his father's estate. A colleague of mine received a similar letter from a candidate who claimed to be qualified because he'd represented himself in his own murder trial! This experience does **not** necessarily present you as a qualified paralegal in the eyes of the hiring authority.

## PROFESSIONAL LETTER FORMATS

The cover letter should use the same type face as your resumé, and be printed on the same paper. **Don't** use a newspaper ad taped to your resumé as a substitute cover letter. This is only one step up from handwriting a cover letter or attaching a post-it to the resumé. When I received resumés treated this way, I didn't even bother to read them.

What follows are sample cover letters that can be used in particular situations, like answering a blind job advertisement. The first sample format is the basic format you should use for all your letters, customized for specific situations.

## Basic Cover Letter Format

Your address
City, State, Zip Code

Date

Person's name (spelled correctly)
Title
Firm or company name
Address
City, State, Zip Code

Dear (Mr. or Ms.):

### Body of Letter

**First paragraph**: Explain that you are seeking a paralegal position and have enclosed a resumé for the addressee's review. Also explain how you learned about the position.

**Second paragraph**: Describe your qualifications. Add a comment about the firm such as, "I have followed the ACME case with interest," or, "I read in _____ magazine about your lobbying efforts on behalf of _____."

**Third paragraph**: Indicate that **you will call** about an interview. In the case of a blind ad, say that you would appreciate receiving a phone call.

Sincerely,
**Your Signature Here**
Typed Name
Telephone number with area code

Enclosure

### Illustration 6.1

## Reply to Blind Newspaper Advertisement

123 Anywhere
Anytown, IL  11111

May 27, 199_

New York Times
P.O. Box 123
New York, New York  11223

Dear Sir or Madam:

I am very interested in the Legal Research Assistant position advertised in *The New York Times*. My resumé is enclosed for your consideration.

I am a recent graduate of the University of Paralegal Studies, a highly respected institution, and I have an undergraduate degree in business law.  Since you are seeking a person to analyze business agreements, you may find my familiarity with business procedures and contracts of particular interest.

I look forward to meeting with you and would be pleased to provide you with my references and writing samples during an interview.  I look forward to hearing from you soon.

Sincerely,

Susie Paralegal
(212) 555-1212

Enclosure

Illustration 6.2

## Martindale-Hubbell Mass Mail Letter

111 Main Street, Apartment 3
Schooltown, MA 22222

June 23, 1993

Ms. Roberta Law, Esq.
Law, Law & Lawyer
555 West Lincoln Street, 43rd Floor
Maytown, MA 22222

Dear Ms. Law:

My Litigation Specialist Certificate from the University of West Los Angeles School of Paralegal Studies can be a definite asset to your firm. This program, which is ABA-approved, has given me a comprehensive overview of the litigation process. I read about your firm in *Martindale-Hubbell*, and noted that you deal extensively with business litigation. Your practice offers the type of challenge for which I am looking.

As you can see from my resumé, my experience has been in real estate and business. I believe that my knowledge in these areas will make an important contribution to your law firm.

Please feel free to contact me at my business on week days (213-123-4567). At other times, you can reach me at my home telephone number listed below. I will contact you in a few days to arrange for an interview.

Sincerely,

Paul Legal Assistant
(313) 111-2222

Enclosure

Illustration 6.3

**Reply to Newspaper Ad with Name of Company**

111 Main Street
Anytown, OH 33333

June 13, 199___

John Smith, Paralegal Manager
The Organization
555 Elm Street
Anytown, OH 33313

Dear Mr. Smith:

I would like to explore the possibility of joining your company as a legal assistant. The enclosed resumé will give you information about my employment background and capabilities.

I have a paralegal certificate from the University of Paralegal Studies, an ABA-approved program. I also have a bachelor of science degree in chemistry from Ohio University. I believe that my background in chemistry can be of particular value in the patent litigation area.

If you have a position for a person with my qualifications or are anticipating one, I hope that we can meet. I would like to discuss how my background and experience may be of value to you. I will contact you soon to set up an interview.

Sincerely,

Robert Paralegal
(312) 222-2222

Enclosure

Illustration 6.4

## Mass Mail Letter—Already Employed

567 Harvard Street
Maintown, FL 44444

October 4, 199_

Janice Smith, Esq.
Acme, Acme & Smith
334 Rose Boulevard
Orlando, FL 44444

Dear Ms. Smith:

I am a graduate of the University of Paralegal Studies, an ABA-approved program, and am currently employed by a large downtown law firm as a litigation legal assistant.

I have followed the *Acme* case with great interest and feel my training in commercial law, personal injury litigation and workers' compensation, could be of great value to your firm. I have an extensive background in computerized litigation support systems.

I also have experience in legal and factual research, drafting interrogatories, preparing deposition questions, digesting depositions and drafting simple pleadings.

I believe that my education and experience are appropriate for your firm. My resumé is enclosed. I will call you within the week to set up an interview.

Sincerely,

Rose Litigation Manager
(525) 444-4444

Enclosure

Illustration 6.5

## Referred by Another

321 South Street
Dallas, TX 66666

November 23, 199_

Sarah Colleague
Smith, Smith & Smith
546 North Street
Dallas, TX 66666

Dear Ms. Colleague:

Ann Roberts, the paralegal recruiter at Jones & Jones, suggested that I write to you. I recently graduated with honors from Johnson Paralegal School with a certificate in corporate law. I am very interested in working with your firm.

My enclosed resumé will demonstrate my interest in your firm's specialty area, environmental law. With my bachelor's degree in biology, I believe that I will be a definite asset to your firm.

I look forward to meeting with you soon, at which time I will be pleased to provide you with references and writing samples. I will call you within the week to set up an interview.

Sincerely,

Joseph Jones
(646) 777-7777

Enclosure

Illustration 6.6

## College Graduate—No Experience

8989 Flowering Street
Boomtown, CA 99999

July 4, 199___

Ms. Libby Del Monte
Carrington & Company
1234 Maintown Boulevard
Anytown, CA 98888

Dear Ms. Del Monte:

Today I came across your job advertisement in the *Boomtown Daily Journal* and immediately thought that I may be the person you are looking for. As you will see on the enclosed resumé, I received my bachelor's degree from Yale in March. I possess extensive research and writing experience.

I'm sure the nature of the position, coupled with the detailed job description, has made this position difficult to fill. I too have an unusual employment desire. I have been accepted to Georgetown University Law school and will be moving to Virginia to establish residency sometime around August.

I have deferred my first year of law school for a few years in order to work in Washington, D.C., preferably with legislation or with a legal lobbyist firm. My current position has served its purpose in terms of educating and informing me about the realities of private practice. For this reason, I would love to do something different and use my research and writing skills until I make the move to Virginia.

If this position has not been filled and you believe we would work well together, I would enjoy meeting with you at your convenience. I will call you within the week to schedule an interview.

Thank You,

Betty Bates
(213) 555-6666

Enclosure

Illustration 6.7

### Response to Entry-Level Paralegal Advertisement

ADVERTISEMENT:

High-profile Downtown law firm, AV rated, is seeking an **entry-level paralegal**, with an ABA-approved paralegal certificate and a bachelor's degree, for fast-paced, fast-track litigation project. Good benefits and competitive salary.

# 2422, The Local Law Journal
123 MAIN STREET
ANYTOWN, MA  99999

COVER LETTER:

Dear Paralegal Director:

In response to your advertisement in the local law journal, I have enclosed my resumé for your review.

I have recently graduated from Paralegal University, an ABA-approved program with a certificate in litigation.  I also hold a bachelor's degree in English from Any University.  I am diligent and a quick learner with great attention to detail.

I would very much like to interview with your firm.  I can be reached during the day at (111) 111-1111 or at my home number below.  I look forward to hearing from you soon.

Illustration 6.8

## Response to Corporate Paralegal Advertisement

ADVERTISEMENT:

Downtown firm seeks corporate paralegal. Requirements: bachelor's degree or substantial equivalent experience; information/maintenance of closely held corporations and transactional due diligence; excellent writing skills. Qualities sought include: independent judgment, attention to detail, practical focus, sense of humor, professional commitment. Competitive salary and benefits commensurate with experience. **Send resumé to**: George Ball at Law and Law, P.O. Box 1028, Anytown, CA 90001

COVER LETTER:

Dear Mr. Ball:

In response to your advertisement in the local newspaper for a corporate paralegal, I have enclosed my resumé for your information.

I have recently received my corporate paralegal certificate from Paralegal School. I also have a bachelor's degree from State University. My experience with Law Firm as an intern added to my corporate knowledge. I was in charge of all corporate maintenance and UCC searches.

I hope that my skill level meets your needs. I will be speaking with you soon to set up an interview.

Illustration 6.9

**Response to Probate Paralegal Advertisement**

ADVERTISEMENT:

PARALEGAL-ESTATE
Probate and estate planning paralegal for prestigious law firm in
Smalltown.  Preparation of probate and 706 documents, along
with planning experience required. WordPerfect a plus.  Send
resumé to:

#4444, The Law Journal
111 East 1st Street, Anytown, MA  11111

COVER LETTER:

Dear Paralegal Coordinator:

I am responding to your advertisement in the Law Journal for the probate/estate
planning paralegal position.  I have enclosed my resumé for your review.

Although I have just received my paralegal certificate in probate from Legal
Assistant School, I have several years of experience as a trust officer with Big Bank
where I gained the requisite experience in probate and trust work.  I am also
proficient in WordPerfect.

I would very much like to interview with your firm.  I can be reached during the
day at (111) 111-1111, or at my home number which appears below.  I look forward
to hearing from you soon.

Illustration 6.10

85

### Alternative to Cover Letters

If you have a good relationship with a current employer who is an attorney, you should ask that person to write you a **letter of introduction**. Sent with your resumé, this letter can substitute for a cover letter. It will differentiate your resumé from the rest of the letters that the hiring authority may have received. It may also be the **one spark that will catch the interest** of a potential employer. If the recipient of the letter knows the lawyer writing the letter, it is more likely to be remembered. Be sure to follow up with a telephone call one week later.

## DOS AND DON'TS COVER LETTER CHECKLIST

### Do:

- ▶ Write a separate letter for each position you are seeking, tailoring it to the specific job description.
- ▶ Use the same paper as your resumé with matching envelopes.
- ▶ Direct your letter to the hiring authority. Ask the law firm to whom you should send your resumé. Be sure to get the correct job title and name spelling.
- ▶ Make sure the letter is grammatically correct with no typos. It should be direct, concise, and meaningful.
- ▶ State that you are enclosing your resumé.
- ▶ Remember that the first lines in the letter are vital and should appeal to the potential employer's interest.
- ▶ Briefly state one or two key contributions you can make or emphasize one or two specific qualifications that fit the employer's major requisites.
- ▶ Request a personal interview.
- ▶ Type your phone number under the signature line even though it also appears on your resumé.
- ▶ Mention that you are currently employed if this is the case. This will give you a boost with the potential employer. Remember the old saying that "It's easier to get a job when you've got a job." It's generally true!

*Do Not:*

▶ Cut out the ad and attach it to the letter.

▶ Use cliches, hackneyed or silly phrases. Do not boast or use vulgar language. These mistakes will get you the wrong kind of attention.

▶ Refer to yourself in the third person (as "he" or "she").

▶ Try to give employers the impression that they cannot live without you.

▶ Be too aggressive, use pressure or hard-sell techniques.

▶ Use your present employer's stationery.

▶ Sign your job title.

▶ Use "cute" techniques like writing the cover letter in the form of a pleading.

▶ Discuss salary.

▶ Say you are "certified" if you are "certificated." (See **Chapter 1** for a discussion on the differences between the two.)

# 7

# Beginning Your Job Search

## Organizational Systems, Research Sources & Informational Interviews

Now that you've completed your power resumé, you can begin your job search. You should expect to spend about one month of job hunting for each $10,000 in salary generally paid for the types of positions you are seeking. For example, if the positions you want ordinarily pay $30,000, generally you will spend about three months finding the right one. The job search can sometimes take longer—depending in large part on the economy in your area—so don't get discouraged.

I suggest that new legal assistant graduates **consider taking entry-level positions as paralegal aides or document clerks** to get a foot in the door. Many law firms require this career track so they can get to know you before committing to a legal assistant position. One woman I placed in a firm as a document clerk five years ago is now the Litigation Support Manager of a San Francisco law firm!

Before beginning your search, **make a list of the law firms and corporations you want to target**. Some of these may not have openings, but an informational interview can help you get to know the firm. (See "Informational Interview" in this chapter, for a discussion of its purpose.) When an opening comes up, you will have the advantage of being familiar with that organization.

**YOUR PLACEMENT FILE**

When your search starts, create a **placement file and notebook** in which you keep all **copies of correspondence** with potential employers, together with a **checklist of target firms, corporations and government agencies you have contacted**. Include contact names at each firm or corporation, along with some specific information about each individual you contact (i.e., personnel director at Smith, Jones & Johnson is a former paralegal). Place all the **business cards** you've collected in the file. If you've completed **employment applications** for a government agency or other organization, be sure to keep a copy for your records.

The information stored in your placement notebook will help you with your correspondence. You can refer to the previous letters and/or meetings, and mention the specific dates of those occurrences. This will help refresh the recipient's memory of you. Also include in your notebook and file information from any **employment agencies** with whom you have spoken, their literature and business cards. There are numerous legal assistant placement services in most large cities. You need to research which ones are considered the most reputable and effective; a good source for this information is your local paralegal association.

You should continue to update and use your placement notebook after you land a job. It is an **excellent reference book for professional contacts** if you need a referral or find yourself in the job market again. This is an excellent time to start your Rolodex system.

*Potential Employer Contact Tracking System*

Remember that **your job search must be organized**. I recommend that you use the following **Contact Tracking System** form to keep track of all advertisements you respond to, all informational interviews you set up, all networking contacts you make regarding particular employers, and all resumés you send out. These forms should be **kept in your placement notebook**. Because you will most likely be contacting several law firms or corporations, you need to know who you've talked to and when, so when you start getting those "call backs," you'll have all the information you need right at hand.

## FIRM CONTACT TRACKING SYSTEM

Firm/Corporation: _____

Address: _____

Phone Number: _____

FAX Number: _____


Contact & Position: _____


Interviewed With: _____

_____

_____


Position Sought: _____

Salary Information: _____


Referral Source: _____


Networking Comments: _____

_____

_____


|  | COMMENTS | Date of Event |
|---|---|---|

1.  Initial contact with: _____


2.  Sent resumé to: _____

3.  Follow up phone call with: _____

4. First interview with:      _____

    _____

    _____

5. Sent writing samples to:      _____

6. Thank you letter sent to:      _____

    _____

7. Follow-up phone call to:      _____

8. Second interview with:      _____

    _____

    _____

9. Third interview with:      _____

    _____

CONGRATULATIONS! If you've made it this far, you'll probably receive a job offer.

## WHERE TO FIND THE STRATEGIC INFORMATION YOU NEED

As I've mentioned earlier, your job search requires an organized and businesslike approach. Although it takes substantial effort, doing your homework up front will save you time in the long run. You will be able to identify additional job opportunities and perhaps people who can help you in your search. Talk to people in the field. They'll give you additional contacts.

### *Law Firms vs. Corporate Law Departments*

Expand your search beyond law firms to corporate legal departments. These departments vary in size from one attorney to over 75. Turnover for paralegals in corporations is generally not as high as in law firms. Paralegals often stay at corporations for their entire careers because corporations frequently offer more opportunities for promotion than law firms. The average term of employment in a law firm seems to be about two to three years.

You will encounter many issues during your search. You should consider all the items listed below in comparing different job opportunities.

▶ **Salary**—how much do you expect to be paid, how often do you expect raises or bonuses?

▶ **Benefits**—what level of benefits are you interested in, are you willing to take less benefits if the salary is right?

▶ **Duties**—what level of duties do you want, what kind of variety, do you want experience that will help you advance?

▶ **Advancement**—what level of advancement do you want to achieve, how important is it to advance?

▶ **Amount of responsibility**—how much responsibility do you want, how important it is that responsibility increases?

▶ **Firm culture**—what would be a good match with your personality, would you prefer to work in a small firm of large firm?

▶ **Attorney attitudes toward paralegal utilization**—are you looking for firms with strong utilization of paralegals or do you want to be the trailblazer?

▶ **Work categories**—what practice areas interest to you, do you plan to specialize?

▶ **Location**—how important is the physical location, paid parking availability?

▶ **Job setting**—are you looking for a traditional, conservative setting or something more modern, is it important to you to have a private office?

You should **analyze how you feel about each of these issues before looking for a job**, and decide which are the most important to you. This will help you focus your search in the right places and make the right choices. Your classmates, professional associates and personal friends in the legal field are usually the best sources of information on the issues outlined above. (See Chapter 8, "Networking—Your Most Powerful Placement Weapon.")

---

**HOT TIP:** Very few paralegal positions are openly advertised. Law firms and corporations frequently use legal search firms or rely on "blind" resumés in their files. Therefore, it is to your advantage to send out your resumé as often as possible. You should also network with other paralegals and law firm personnel. People already employed in law firms may let you know about potential openings and act as a reference for you.

---

### Paralegal Employer Reference Books

Before you begin your search, you will need to **compile a list of employers** in your area that use legal assistants. Remember that these employers are **not** limited to law firms; be sure to consider corporations and government agencies. **Include names of the people to contact** for each organization. A list of reference sources containing this information is included in this section.

If the name of the contact person is not available from these sources, **call the organization and ask who hires legal assistants**. Be sure to get the correct, full spelling of the person's name and title. Don't be put off by curt receptionists. You can get around them by calling at another time or calling another person in the firm (see the discussion of the *Martindale-Hubbell* and *Standard & Poor's* directories below).

If no name is available, send your resumé to a younger attorney in the firm who specializes in your area. You can also frequently find an attorney listed who is an alumnus of your college or university. Estimate the age of the attorney by the date he or she graduated from law school. The date of admittance to the bar, or the fact that the attorney is listed as an associate, not a partner, of the firm, are also good clues.

*Where to Look for Law Firms*

The *Martindale-Hubbell Law Directory* lists law firms and lawyers throughout the country. Law firms pay a fee to be listed, and nearly all major law firms are included. A few hours browsing through a copy of *Martindale-Hubbell* at your local library is time well spent. Each volume is organized alphabetically by state and then by city. Individual law firm listings include information about the following topics.

- ▶ firm name
- ▶ address, telephone number, and fax number for the law firm office located in the state/city in which you are looking
- ▶ all branch offices, both in the U.S. and world-wide
- ▶ all practice areas, in order of importance
- ▶ representative clients
- ▶ all lawyers in the firm, organized by partner or associate status, stating each attorney's:
  - name
  - birthplace
  - date admitted to the bar (and in which states)
  - education
  - honors
  - local bar memberships
  - legal publications

You should also periodically review all **state and local bar association journals**, which are usually published monthly, and **local legal newspapers**, most of which are published daily. These newspapers almost always carry classified advertising for various positions, including ads for paralegal openings.

---

**HOT TIP:** *Martindale-Hubbell* plans to add legal assistant information to its 1992 edition. Once this information becomes available, you'll have an easy reference source to find direct contacts with legal assistants who attended your paralegal school or university, and those who work for firms you're interested in yourself.

---

## The Top 50 Law Firms in the Country

A list of the Top 50 Law Firms appeared in the May 6, 1991 edition of *OF COUNSEL* (volume 10, number 9). The firms listed below would be **ideal places to arrange informational interviews**. The cities listed in parentheses are the locations of the home offices (or headquarters) for these firms. Many—if not most—of these firms have several branch offices in other cities. **Be sure to do your research**. To help you get started, see discussion of the law firm directory, *Martindale-Hubbell*, below.

Baker & McKenzie (Chicago)
Jones, Day, Reavis & Pogue (Cleveland)
Skadden, Arps, Slate, Meagher & Flom (New York)
Gibson, Dunn & Crutcher (Los Angeles)
Sidley and Austin (Chicago)
Fulbright & Jaworski (Houston)
Pillsbury, Madison & Sutro (San Francisco)
Morgan, Lewis & Bockius (Philadelphia)
Latham & Watkins (Los Angeles)
Shearman & Sterling (New York)
Morrison & Foerster (San Francisco)
O'Melveny & Myers (Los Angeles)
Weil, Gotshal & Manges (New York)
Mayer, Brown & Platt (Chicago)
Vinson & Elkins (Houston)
McDermott, Will & Emery (Chicago)
Winston & Strawn (Chicago)
Baker & Hostetler (Cleveland)
Milbank, Tweed, Hadley & McCloy (New York)

Akin, Gump, Strauss, Hauer & Feld (Dallas)

Hunton & Williams (Richmond, VA)

Simpson Thacher & Bartlett (New York)

White & Case (New York)

Paul, Weiss, Rifkind, Wharton & Garrison (New York)

Davis Polk & Wardwell (New York)

Cleary, Gottlieb, Steen & Hamilton (New York)

Kirkland & Ellis (Chicago)

LeBoeuf, Lamb, Leiby & MacRae (New York)

Foley and Lardner (Milwaukee)

Brobeck, Phleger & Harrison (San Francisco)

Paul, Hastings, Janofsky & Walker (Los Angeles)

Baker & Botts (Houston)

Kelly Drye & Warren (New York)

Squire, Sanders & Dempsey (Cleveland)

Dechert Price & Rhoads (Philadelphia)

Fried, Frank, Harris, Shriver & Jacobson (New York)

Graham & James (San Francisco)

Proskauer Rose Goetz & Mendelsohn (New York)

Coudert Brothers (New York)

Kaye, Scholer, Fierman, Hays & Handler (New York)

Dewey, Ballantine, Bushby, Palmer & Wood (New York)

Sullivan & Cromwell (New York)

Heller, Ehrman, White & McAuliffe (San Francisco)

Bryan, Cave, McPheeters & McRoberts (St. Louis)

Debevoise & Plimpton (New York)

Arnold & Porter (Washington, D.C.)

Reed, Smith, Shaw & McClay (Pittsburgh)

Thompson, Hine & Flory (Cleveland)

Wilson, Elser, Moskowitz, Edelman & Dicker (New York)

Pepper, Hamilton & Sheetz (Philadelphia)

*Where to Look for Corporate Law Departments*

If you would like a position in a corporation, *Martindale-Hubbell* also contains a corporate legal department section. These listings are organized alphabetically by company name.

You can also use the *Standard & Poor's Register of Corporations, Directors and Executives*, which is a listing of over 37,000 U.S. corporations, listed alphabetically by company. It includes a description of the company as well as a listing of the names of its corporate officers and general counsel. The lead attorney in the corporation could be either the General Counsel or the Secretary of the Corporation. You may address your letter to this person.

Check your local business directory for corporations in the area and make a "hit" list of companies for whom you want to work, **before** you tackle *Standard & Poor's*.

---

**HOT TIP:** Smaller law firms often do **not** list themselves in *Martindale-Hubbell*. To find them, use the yellow pages. It will usually have a section listing the attorneys by specialty.

---

## OTHER EMPLOYER REFERENCE SOURCES

### Law Firm Directories

The books listed below are some of the more common books and reference sources for finding out about law firms. In my experience, most law librarians are happy go assist you in finding more local reference sources. There may be a state-wide directory published by your state's bar association. There are also many private publishers of law firm directories; sometimes these are compiled and distributed by the same company that publishes your local legal newspaper.

▶ *American Bar Reference Handbook*

▶ *Attorneys and Agents Registered to Practice Before the United States Patent and Trademark Office*
  Listed alphabetically by state.

▶ *Best Lawyers in America*
  by Steven Haifer and Gregory White-Smith.

▶ *Best's Directory of Recommended Insurance Attorneys*
*Lawyer's Register by Specialty and Fields of Law*
National directory; good reference for those who know in what field of
law they want to practice.

▶ *Martindale-Hubbell Law Directory*
Described in "Where to Look for Law Firms" above.

▶ *Who's Who in American Law*

▶ *The American Lawyer*
Monthly magazine with features such as "Big Suits" and "Big Deals,"
which list the law firms and companies involved in major litigation or
transactions. Also a good source for articles up-and-coming law firms
and corporate law departments, and "hot" practice areas.

▶ *The National Law Journal*
Weekly legal newspaper with national outlook and national distribution.
Provides profiles of law firms primarily, although also highlights
changes in corporate law departments.

▶ *Legal Times*
Subtitled "Law & Lobbying in the Nation's Capitol," this is a weekly
legal newspaper with a national circulation. Recommended reading for
those desiring paralegal jobs with the federal government.

▶ *Yellow Pages (Local editions)*
Look for "Attorney" listings. Lawyers are usually listed by areas of
specialty at the end of the main, alphabetical section. Telephone
directories are especially helpful in locating smaller firms in specific
geographic areas.

### Legal Aid Organizations

If you interest lies with nonprofit organizations instead of private law firms, the sources listed below should give you a good start. I also recommend checking with your city library to determine which nonprofit organization can be found in your area.

▶ *National Directory of Non-Profit Corporations*

▶ *Public Interest Law Groups*
   by Karen O'Connor and Lee Epstein. Lists major public interest legal groups in the U.S. and provides institutional profiles.

### Corporate Directories

In addition the *Standard & Poor's Register*, mentioned in "Where to Find Corporate Law Departments," above, the following directories should provide you with a comprehensive listing from which to start gathering target company information.

▶ *Directory of American Firms Operating in Foreign Countries*
   New York Trade Academy Press. Volume 1 is in alphabetical order by corporate name. Volumes 2 and 3 are in alphabetical order by country

▶ *Directory of Corporate Counsel*
   Dun's Marketing Service Books

▶ *Business Rankings*

▶ *Directory of Service Companies*
   Listed alphabetically, geographically and by industry.

▶ *Million Dollar Directory*
   Similar to *Standard & Poor's Register* but not as extensive.

▶ *Reference of Corporate Management*
   National directory of management personnel.

▶ *Regional Business Directory*
Lists businesses by location in regional areas of the U.S.

▶ *500—The Directory of U.S. Corporations*
Trenton, New Jersey

▶ *Hoover's Handbook*
Profile of over five hundred major corporations.

▶ *Martindale-Hubbell Law Directory*
As mentioned above, the last volume in the set contains a biographical section on corporate legal departments.

▶ *Moody's Directories*
*Bank and Financial Manual*—Lists over 10,000 banks and financial institutions. Ideal for paralegals interested in the banking field.

▶ *Guide to Business*
*Industrial Manual*—Information on companies listed on the New York and American Stock Exchanges. General counsel is often listed.

▶ *McMillan Directory of Leading Private Companies*
First listed by state, then alphabetically. Includes officers, managers and general counsel.

▶ *Reader's Guide to Periodical Literature*
Current articles on different companies, organized by subject matter, proper name and periodical of publication.

▶ *Standard & Poor's Register of Corporations, Directors and Executives*
Lists over 37,000 U.S.-based corporations and corporate officers, as well as general counsel. Discussed in more detail in "Where You Can Find Corporate Law Departments," above.

▶ *Walker's Manual of Western Corporations*
    Lists all corporations in the Western United States in alphabetical order,
    by regions. Also names corporate officers.

▶ *Ward's Business Directory of U.S. Public and Private Companies*
    Companies are listed both geographically and alphabetically. Includes
    corporate officers.

## THE INFORMATIONAL INTERVIEW

Talking with attorneys, practicing paralegals, law firm managers and other people employed in a law firm is a good way to research information. You should try to set up **informational interviews** with people on your list of target firms and corporations. Simply call the appropriate person and ask if you could schedule an appointment to discuss paralegal careers in that organization. Most people will be flattered that you chose to consult them for their expertise. Be sure to say that you want an informational interview. That way, even if there are no immediate openings, you can still schedule the interview. For a "script" of a conversation to set up such interviews, see **Chapter 10**, "Effective Job Search Strategies" (in the section captioned Telephone Solicitations).

Dana L. Graves tells the story of how she ended up hiring a paralegal who had obtained Dana's name while attending "Legal Tech." (This is a conference held several times a year around the country to explore new applications of technology to law firms.)

> He set up an appointment with me to discuss the use of computers in the legal field. He had no real legal experience, but he had just received his M.A. degree and appeared to be quite talented with the use of database programs. A month after our meeting, I realized that I had a need for just such a person. I called him up, hired him, and the rest is history.

**Prepare your list of questions** before the interview. You are conducting the interview and can structure it your way. Be professional and polite, and try not to take much time. Fifteen to twenty minutes should suffice. Extend the interview **only** if the interviewee seems interested. Always ask for the names of additional people in the field with whom you may speak. Also ask your contact to keep you in mind for future openings. Follow up by writing a thank you note.

Appropriate questions to ask during an informational interview include:

▶ How many paralegals are employed in the firm and what do they do?

▶ What are the salaries and benefits?

▶ Who does the interviewing and hiring?

▶ What type of on-the-job training is available?

▶ Can you refer me to anyone else or suggest an additional source of information, either in this firm or another?

▶ Does the firm have a paralegal program? (See Appendix A, "Buzzwords," for an explanation of this term.)

▶ Is there room for advancement?

▶ What are the duties expected of an entry-level paralegal?

▶ What opportunities and demand do you see for paralegals in the future?

▶ What do you look for in an entry-level paralegal?

▶ Do you think the demand for legal assistants will continue?

With all this information you should be able to pinpoint the type of work you want in the right setting with good benefits and salary.

# 8

# Networking
**Your Most Powerful Weapon**

Networking is the single most powerful placement tool in the legal world. It consists of developing a system of contacts and resources to help you achieve your professional goals. Networking is all about people and word-of-mouth. Good networks are avenues to good jobs.

## TYPES OF NETWORKING SYSTEMS

**Formal networks** include professional organizations such as your local paralegal associations or alumni groups. You can usually join both as a student. Paralegal schools in the area can give students a contact person in these various organizations to call about membership. Be on the lookout for mention in the your local legal newspapers about meetings of these associations, and attend as many as you can. An **informal network** includes people with whom you work, classmates, friends and acquaintances. To begin your own network, **list all possible contacts** who can help you gain information about the job you want. Note if your contact has access to the people who will make the hiring decision. Even if that person doesn't, he or she might know someone who does.

Often the best and easiest way to get a job is through personal contacts. Over and over again, I tell new paralegals that you will get a job by using your friends. This is how I have gotten all of my jobs! Just consider all the people you know personally:

- ▶ friends and acquaintances
- ▶ fellow students
- ▶ relatives

▶ co-workers
▶ customers
▶ fellow professional association members

**Be all inclusive**. Anyone, regardless of profession or position, has the potential to provide you with a job contact. I have found that professional networking with friends while sailing and skiing has produced invaluable contacts.

Sue, now a corporate paralegal for a major Atlanta firm, tells how she once took her first skiing trip to Aspen. She somehow managed to sit next to two attorneys on the flight to Aspen. After engaging in the usual chitchat, Sue found out that not only were the two attorneys from Atlanta, but also that their paralegal had recently left to go to law school and they hadn't found anyone to replace her. Sue asked for and got their business cards and followed up immediately upon her return home. Sue's follow-up call, together with an informal setting and opportune moment, helped her to land her first paralegal job.

Additional networking leads can be obtained from all the people you know through your own personal business dealings. Be sure to ask the following people if they know any attorneys or people working in law firms or corporate legal departments.

▶ bankers
▶ brokers
▶ insurance agents
▶ doctors
▶ dentists
▶ travel agents

You should include **any other professional acquaintances** whose businesses involve attorneys and legal professionals as clients. All these contacts can tell you about job openings or give you leads to people hiring paralegals.

You must **be straightforward and let them know that you are job hunting.** Discuss the type of position you are seeking. **Send everyone a copy of your**

**resumé** so they can see your qualifications. They might even pass it on to a potential employer! Even if you don't end up with an interview, you may get leads to positions, information on prospective employers, or contacts for future job openings.

---

**HOT TIP:** Always **carry extra copies of your resumé** with you. You never know when a social chat could develop into an important networking relationship or even turn into an informal job interview. You should also **carry printed business cards** with your name, address and phone number.

---

It is wise to keep in touch with other paralegals who are looking for or have jobs. **Other paralegals are the best source of information** regarding job openings, and they can also give much needed moral support while you are hunting. Exchanging information about leads and sources is very valuable.

Once you have your job, **keep up your paralegal contacts**. Such groups share important information on salaries, benefits and working conditions. If you decide to change jobs, you will be one step ahead by knowing the best places to work.

## APPROACHES TO DEVELOPING A NETWORK

### Membership in Professional Groups or Organizations

There are many national, state and local paralegal associations which operate free-of-charge **job banks** that **are rich sources of job leads**. As a paralegal student, you are entitled to join almost any of the paralegal association chapters. If you are thinking about entering the field, but are not enrolled in a paralegal school, you still may be eligible for associate membership. This is crucial for your job search because the association members are in the best position to be of assistance to you in making contacts in the legal field.

Access to job banks is one of the services provided with your association membership fee. Many associations also publish newsletters, and frequently these **newsletters contain job listings**. Local law firms and corporations know that paralegal professional association job banks provide excellent candidates, especially for entry-level positions. Because the associations do not charge a search fee, major law firms in your area will usually list job openings with your association.

A **list of national, state, and city professional paralegal organizations** appears in **Appendix C**. Another excellent way to locate the groups in your area is to ask the placement office at local legal assistant schools. You can also call the National Federation of Paralegal Associations (NFPA) or the National Association of Legal Assistants (NALA). The addresses for these two organizations are also found in Appendix C.

Because many of the associations change officers every one or two years, some of the listings in Appendix C may have changed. Contact the your state association, NALA or NFPA for the most up-to-date information.

Of course, participation in the events sponsored by your local legal assistant association is a **great way to start networking**. You can have fun, tap into the local grapevine, and job hunt at the same time!

Over the past five years, there has been a movement in a number of attorneys' professional associations to **grant legal assistants formal recognition through membership**. Both the American Bar Association (ABA) and the American Trial Lawyers Association (ATLA) have associate membership status for paralegals. Many local, state and county bar organizations have followed suit.

Although you'll need to research whether associate membership is possible for associations in your region, if it is, I recommend that you join. You will not only make great contacts, but you will also receive each group's publications. Most attorney association publications are an **excellent source of information** and timely professional articles.

### Attend Seminars & Workshops

In addition to becoming active in your area's legal assistant professional group, there are always a number of **continuing legal education (CLE) opportunities**. Area bar associations, law schools and paralegal associations offer educational seminars each year, and will frequently sponsor training workshops. These are excellent places to meet people in your legal community in a professional setting, obtain information on job opportunities, and make valuable contacts.

When you are a new paralegal looking for your first job, you will have to pay for the seminars and workshops yourself. That's the bad news. The good news is that most organizations offer **special reduced rates** for students and associate members of the organizations. However, once you are working in the legal field, most employers will pay for both your association dues and frequently for seminars or workshops in your legal specialty.

*Workshops and Seminars*

- ▶ Continuing Education of the Bar (CEB)
- ▶ The Rutter Group (in California, Rutter sponsors numerous seminars for paralegal training)
- ▶ Philadelphia Institute—Seminars for Paralegals
- ▶ American Bar Association, Division for Professional Education
- ▶ American Bar Association Section of Antitrust Law
- ▶ American Bar Association Section of Business Law
- ▶ Andrews Conferences, Inc.
- ▶ The Bureau of National Affairs
- ▶ Cavalcade of Law Office Technology, Inc.
- ▶ Dickinson School of Law
- ▶ Federal Publications, Inc.
- ▶ The Institute for International Research
- ▶ John Marshall Law School
- ▶ Law Journal Seminars-Press
- ▶ National Association of Criminal Defense Lawyers
- ▶ National College of Advocacy/Association of Trial Lawyers of America
- ▶ National Institute for Trial Advocacy
- ▶ New Jersey Environmental Exposition
- ▶ Norton Institutes on Bankruptcy Law
- ▶ Practicing Law Institute (PLI)
- ▶ Professional Programs Group
- ▶ Southern Methodist University School of Law
- ▶ Southwestern Legal Foundation
- ▶ The University of Texas at Austin School of Law
- ▶ University of Wyoming Western Trial Advocacy Institute

### Attend Legal Conferences & Conventions

Below is only a **partial list of conventions and conferences that paralegals may attend.** Announcements for these—and other—events can be found in paralegal association newsletters and legal publications such as your state bar journal or local legal newspaper. Remember, conferences and conventions are also excellent places to meet people in your legal community, obtain information on job opportunities, and make valuable contacts.

*Conventions and Conferences*

▶ American Bar Association (ABA)
▶ National Federation of Paralegal Associations (NFPA)
▶ Legal Assistant Managers Association (LAMA)
▶ National Association of Legal Assistants (NALA)
▶ Legal Tech (sponsored by Price Waterhouse, and held at several locations in the U.S. yearly)
▶ American Association for Paralegal Education (AAfPE)
▶ Association of Legal Administrators
▶ Local and State Bar Associations
▶ Local and State Paralegal Conventions

### Maintain Relationships with Classmates & Former Employers

One of the best sources of information for jobs are your peers and former employers. Because of their past association with you, they more than likely will to want to help you find your perfect paralegal job. Today's classmate or co-worker may be tomorrow's reference.

Over my years as a paralegal recruiter, I have seen many examples of **peers helping peers.** Ben and Sam went to George Washington University together. Ben went on to become a teacher, while Sam went to law school. When Ben decided to change careers to become a paralegal, he looked up Sam, even though he hadn't seen him in twenty years. Sam gave Ben plenty of leads among his lawyer friends. Ben was able to use the introduction to several law firms by saying "Sam suggested that I give you a ring." Sam's referrals led to a great job for Ben in a prestigious D.C. firm. Staying in touch with your peers and

110

colleagues helps you grow, not just through contacts, but through the **benefit of accumulated group experience**.

**Make time for a periodic telephone call and an occasional lunch.** Even if you are totally buried in work, believe me, your career is better served by taking an hour to network rather than working that sixtieth hour at your firm. If you keep your contacts in mind, they are more likely to remember you for pivotal career opportunities.

### *Join Civic Organizations*

You've come so far—don't stop now! Networking includes putting yourself right in the thick of **activities where attorneys search for business**, and that includes civic organizations. Arts organizations in many cities have a high representation of legal professionals and company leaders. So do nonprofit sports organizations, such as the Special Olympics. Sometimes large religious organizations are another source. The Jewish Federation has a Lawyer's division with thousands of members. These groups help to raise funds for a good cause.

You should also contact the Chamber of Commerce, local business associations, real estate boards and city councils, to name just a few. Pick your cause or activity based on what you enjoy and believe in. Get active. Who knows what "people perks" along the way may open new career opportunities for you.

### *Volunteer in Legal Clinics or Government Agencies*

Volunteering to work for legal aid clinics, government agencies and nonprofit programs is another good way to meet lawyers and paralegals. Most major cities have **legal aid clinics** that are funded by a combination of government money and support from the private sector. These clinics serve low-income citizens and are always in need of additional help.

The **court system** in your state may provide excellent volunteer opportunities as well. For example, the State of Minnesota has a Guardian Ad Litem program staffed by volunteers who represent the interests of minors in family court. This program is open to non-attorneys, and is an invaluable source for future job contacts.

Volunteering to work in **nonprofit legal programs** keeps you abreast of new developments and active in the legal community. If you have no paralegal experience at all, this is a **great way to gain credible credentials**. Check with the following organizations or in the yellow pages for other legal clinics and other volunteer opportunities in your city.

► American Civil Liberties Union (ACLU); most states have chapters
► Legal Aid Society
► Local feminist and civil rights organizations, such as National Organization for Women and the NAACP
► Law in the Public Interest
► Local Poverty Law Agencies, such as Women's Shelters
► County and State Legal Offices, such as Public Defender, District Attorney and County Counsel

---

**HOT TIP:** Volunteering for **Law Day**—a day set aside in many communities to assist those persons seeking attorney referrals and free legal advice—is invaluable for making contacts. (Law Day is usually scheduled for May 1st each year in most areas.) Find out if and when your community holds this type of event and sign up to answer phones and assist with questionnaires. A kind of "bonding" with your fellow volunteers will have happened by the end of the day, and most likely you'll have made very good contacts you can call upon for a long time. "Volunteer, Law Day," is also a valuable addition to your resumé, particularly if you have no prior legal experience.

---

## SEARCH ORGANIZATIONS CAN HELP

If you are graduating from a paralegal program, your school may have a **job placement service**. Many of the best firms in the nation place requests at the top schools for entry-level legal assistants. They know that they will get high-quality candidates without paying an expensive search fee. These placement services, along with paralegal association job banks, are the **best sources of outside aid to the beginning paralegal**, and they cost you nothing.

A **paralegal search company** may be another excellent source of outside help with your search. Most large urban areas have one or more search firms that work primarily with legal assistant placements. Some of these are national in scope. If you live in Houston but want to move to Denver, a national search firm from Los Angeles may be able to place you. In this example, you would, of course, also check with Denver paralegal associations for job banks, as well as with Denver area placement companies.

Search firms are able to offer excellent job placement possibilities because they build **strong, trusting relationships with law firms and corporate clientele.** Many law firms place exclusive job orders that "never hit the papers" because the search firm eliminates the law firm's having to screen hundreds of resumés and conduct time-consuming interviews. The law firm really only wants to see the top two to three candidates.

To find placement companies, look in the telephone book under "Employment." You can also call your local legal assistant school for referrals. Most associations can recommend well-connected placement companies to you.

When you are scheduling interviews with paralegal placement companies, **be sure to distinguish between "search" firms, "employer-retained" agencies, and "applicant fee-paid" agencies.** The "search" firm and "employer-retained" agency is fully fee-paid by the employer and costs you nothing. On the other hand, **you must pay** the "applicant fee-paid" agency's fee—a cost which few starting paralegals can afford.

When you call an agency, ask what type of positions they have available. **If you're asked to take a typing test, you are in the wrong place.** Paralegals should **not** perform secretarial duties. They may use a computer to input their own documents, but they do not type! Use your network to find out which are the best placement agencies.

Some agencies are reluctant to represent entry-level paralegals because the law firms will not pay a fee for "baby" legal assistants. Many law firms feel that they can get qualified recent graduates from good paralegal schools for free. Some agencies do offer **temporary assignments** for entry-level legal assistants. If you are able to work on a temporary basis, then you should apply. Temporary paralegal services often look for paralegal help in handling some of the **"paying your dues" work.** The types of tasks at this level include coding, organizing, photocopying, and/or digesting documents, which can at least give you some legal experience and a foot in the door. Temporary positions will often lead to permanent jobs.

## NETWORKING WORKS BUT IT TAKES TIME

Even though you have cast out all your nets to the various placement services and job banks, **do not** depend on them to haul in a job. **Start your own job search as soon as you finish writing your resumé**. The process is not difficult, but it is time-consuming. If you are unemployed, treat your job search as a full-time job. The more time you spend out in the world looking, the more contacts you'll make, and the quicker you'll find that elusive first position. Plan on spending four to six hours each day for your search.

If you are employed but wish to change positions, you may not have that kind of time. If you can, budget at least one to two hours per day, either at the beginning of the day, during the lunch hour, or at the end of the day.

Your job search is the **time to lean on your classmates and friends for moral support**. Ongoing emotional support is important throughout your job search. Turn to your paralegal association for networking, advice and support. You'll feel a part of the legal assistant profession more quickly if you do.

Above all else, during your job search **be patient and persistent**. Your first job is the most difficult position to find.

# 9

# How To Land A Federal Job

Federal paralegal jobs can be great. I know of an Army paralegal who travels around the world working on interesting cases. **Paralegals working in the Justice Department are involved in some of the most important litigation of our time.** But there are drawbacks. The federal government tends to be highly structured. Rising up through the ranks may be painstaking and time consuming. You may be tested to achieve promotions rather than relying on your past performance. Still, the pay is usually comparable to private industry, and the **benefits are fantastic.** Moreover, there are **job protection guarantees** that should insulate you from the business fluctuations of private practice.

## WHERE TO FIND FEDERAL JOBS

Many agencies of the federal government hire paralegals. Although most people will think of the courts or the Department of Justice for paralegal jobs first, there are many other places within the federal government utilizing legal assistants. **Remember, not all federal jobs are located in Washington, D.C.** Most federal agencies and departments have offices in major cities throughout the U.S. Be sure to check the list of Resource Publications at the end of this chapter for additional information.

What follows is a partial list of federal agencies, departments and commissions employing paralegals.

- ▶ Administrative Office of the U.S. Courts
- ▶ Agency for International Development (AID)

- ▶ Army, Department of (Defense Dept.)
- ▶ Bureau of Land Management (BLM) (Interior Dept.)
- ▶ Commission on Civil Rights
- ▶ Commodity Futures Trading Commission
- ▶ Corps of Engineers
- ▶ Defense, Department of (DOD)
- ▶ Drug Enforcement Administration (DEA) (Justice Dept.)
- ▶ Energy, Department of
- ▶ Equal Employment Opportunity Commission (EEOC)
- ▶ Executive Office of the President
- ▶ Federal Aviation Administration (FAA) (Transportation Dept.)
- ▶ Federal Communications Commission (FCC)
- ▶ Federal Deposit Insurance Corporation (FDIC)
- ▶ Federal Emergency Management Agency (FEMA)
- ▶ Federal Maritime Commission
- ▶ Federal Railroad Administration (Transportation Dept.)
- ▶ Federal Reserve System, Board of Governors of the
- ▶ Federal Retirement Thrift Investment Board
- ▶ Federal Trade Commission (FTC) (Commerce Dept.)
- ▶ General Services Administration (GSA)
- ▶ Interior, Department of
- ▶ International Trade Commission
- ▶ Labor, Department of
- ▶ Library of Congress
- ▶ Merit Systems Protection Board
- ▶ National Highway Traffic Safety Administration (Transportation Dept.)
- ▶ National Labor Relations Board (NLRB)
- ▶ Navy, Department of (Defense Dept.)
- ▶ Office of Attorney Personnel Management (Justice Dept.)
- ▶ Offices of the Secretary (Commerce Dept., Health & Human Services Dept.)
- ▶ Office of the Solicitor (Labor Dept.)
- ▶ Office of the Solicitor General (Justice Dept.)
- ▶ Office of Thrift Supervision (Treasury Dept.)
- ▶ Patent and Trademark Office (Commerce Dept.)

▶ Resolution Trust Corporation (RTC)
▶ Securities and Exchange Commission (SEC)
▶ Small Business Administration (SBA)
▶ State, Department of
▶ Transportation, Department of
▶ U.S. Postal Service
▶ Veteran Affairs, Department of

### *Paralegal Job Titles*

Job titles for paralegals vary from one agency to another. This difference is primarily a function of the employing agency's attempt to define the purpose of the job in the title. Whatever the exact title, however, **all the positions listed below require a legal assistant background**. When scanning job listings, be on the lookout for job titles with "analyst" and "specialist" terms. Before you apply for a particular job, of course, you should check the **Qualifications Information Statement** (see the discussion below for more on the QIS).

▶ Environmental Protection Specialist
▶ Security Specialist
▶ Foreign Service Diplomatic Security Officer
▶ Foreign Law Specialist
▶ Civil Rights Analyst
▶ Employee Relations Specialist
▶ Labor Management Relations Examiner
▶ Mediator
▶ Freedom of Information Act Specialist

### *Paralegal Salary Schedules*

Paralegals are usually paid according to the Federal Employer's Pay Schedule. Each general rating schedule under that system has ten levels of pay, termed "GS levels." (GS stands for general schedule.) Entry-level paralegals typically begin their careers with the federal government at a pay scale classified as "GS 5" or above. In 1991, GS-5 salaries ranged between $16,973 and $22,067, depending on which rating schedule was assigned to particular positions.

## HOW TO APPLY FOR FEDERAL JOBS

To apply for employment with the federal government, you must first find out which jobs are available. Refer to the **Qualifications Information Statement (QIS)** which is available from any **Federal Job Information Center (FJIC)**, at any of the 39 **Offices of Personnel Management (OPM)** around the country.

FJICs are listed under "U.S. Government" in most metropolitan telephone directories. You can also call the college federal job hotline at (900) 990-9200, for job openings and information. There will be a nominal charge for these calls.

The **OPM is the central federal personnel office** responsible for providing each agency with hiring guidelines. It conducts testing for selected positions, and also delegates other testing responsibilities to certain agencies. **OPM is responsible for examining entry-level paralegals** through the "Administrative Careers with America" program. You should check with the OPM to find out whether you can apply for open positions directly to the specific agency.

As an entry-level legal assistant, you must submit **OPM 5000-B**, a three-part form, to take the appropriate **written test for participation** in this program. You can pick up a form at the FJIC office, or request that one be sent to you. A few weeks after submission of the form, you will receive one copy back with the location and date of the test. Make sure that the number "5" appears under the "Title of Examination." You will also receive a basic application form, a geographic code list, and a practice test.

For **positions at GS-9 and above**, you must contact the OPM area office covering the location where you want to be considered for employment. Positions may be filled through **OPM registers**, through **OPM-issued recruiting bulletins**, or by **applying directly to the specific government agency**.

### How Positions are Filled

If you pass the examination, your name will be placed on a competitor inventory and **certified to agencies as vacancies occur**. In addition, you **may apply directly to agencies** if you meet the Outstanding Scholar Provisions listed in the Qualifications Information Statement. When you are contacted by a federal agency for employment consideration, you will be asked to provide **more detailed information about your background and qualifications**. This normally will involve submitting **SF 171**—a Personal Qualifications Statement—

which is an **application for federal employment**. (SF stands for Standard Form.) You may also submit a resumé. Another government form, **OPM Form 1170/17**—a listing of college courses taken—or a transcript of your college course work, must also be submitted.

### How to Fill Out SF 171

When applying for a federal government position, SF 171 the **Personal Qualifications Statement is usually used in place of a resumé**. Applications must be complete—**every** space filled in—and descriptive, so the reviewer will be able to rate your application in accordance with your education and experience.

Your application is reviewed for completeness by an agency recruiter. If the application is incomplete, it will be returned to you. Returned applications cause delay in the process and, if not received by the agency in a timely manner, may cause you to miss being considered for upcoming hirings.

---

**HOT TIP:** A **separate application** must be completed for **each** position for which you apply. I recommend that when you are completing the form, leave blank the sections for job title, announcement number, options for which you wish to be considered, primary places you wish to be employed, the date and signature. Photocopy as many copies as needed, then **go back and fill in the blanks**. This will save you time, because it takes a minimum of two hours to complete this particular form. Remember, photocopied applications are accepted by the government, but **each must be signed individually**.

---

If the announcement, QIS, or recruitment bulletin is **missing pieces of information** required for the application, contact the agency personnel department or Post-of-Duty Recruitment Coordinator for specific data. **Be very precise about the position, grade level and announcement for which you are referring**. Each agency has many positions, and within each agency, some of the position titles are quite similar.

Follow each instruction in the announcement or recruitment bulletin on how and where to apply. The application form—like a resumé—is the employer's first impression of you. **Professionally prepared applications will set you apart from the other applicants**. Neatly typed applications which include thorough descriptions of your education and work experience will assist the Personnel Staffing Specialist in the rating process. Try to tailor your application to the job you want. **Handbook X118** contains **hiring standards for paralegals**. It should be reviewed **before** you start filling out SF 171.

Always retain a complete set of copies of all forms you've submitted, in the event that your application is not received. If this happens, simply resubmit the copies of your application, along with a cover letter informing the agency about the situation.

### Eligibility

If you are **classified as not eligible** for the position, you will be notified before other applicants. If the position for which you applied is **not open**, you will be informed when the position does become open. A determination of your availability will be made at that time. If you are applying for a position which **is open**, you should contact the agency to determine if your application has been received, after you've allowed two weeks for processing.

Four to six weeks should be allowed for processing if your application is submitted to a Special Examining Unit. A "Notice of Rating" will be issued to you within this period.

If the application is sent directly to the agency that is hiring, the agency will contact the best qualified candidates for an interview immediately. At least two to three weeks after the selection date, "not-selected" letters are issued.

### The Interview

After successfully passing the examination and the completing the application procedure, you will be contacted for an interview. Review the **interviewing tips found in Chapters 12 and 13 in this book**, and be prepared. Each agency publishes an annual report and each legal office has published a "mission statement," both of which will be sent to you upon request. The more equipped you are for the interview, the more promising your chances are to be placed at the top of the list and chosen for the position you want.

## ADDITIONAL RESOURCE MATERIALS

You can obtain more detailed information regarding federal careers by writing to:

Office of Personnel Management
Room 5L45
1900 E Street, NW
Washington, D.C. 20415

OPM publishes a variety of materials. I recommend that you ask for:

▶ "Definitions of Groups and Series Relative to Paralegal Specialists" from the *Handbook of Occupational Groups and Series*
▶ List of government agencies with legal departments
▶ Pay rate schedule for the grade series GS-5 through GS-12
▶ Copy of the government's Paralegal Hiring Standard from *Handbook X118*

More information can be obtained from your local OPM. Another good source of information is an article titled "Challenges of Government Jobs: Opportunities for Paralegals," by Terry Howard, published in *Legal Assistant Today* (volume 8, number 5, May/June 1991). Of particular interest in this article is the discussion found on pages 84-91.

Finally, you can gain more valuable information by reviewing the following publications concerning federal government employment. Write to the addresses listed to obtain each particular publication. The publication cost information is **current as of 1991.**

▶ *The Paralegal's Guide to U.S. Government Jobs: How to Land a Job in 70 Law-Related Fields.*
Federal Reports                                    (202) 313-3311
1010 Vermont Avenue NW, Suite 408
Washington, D.C. 20005                    **Cost: $12.00**
   This booklet describes paralegal hiring standards for the U.S. Government and procedures on how to get a federal paralegal job.

▶ *Federal Personnel Office Director*
Same address as above                    **Cost: $20.00**
   A listing of over 1500 U.S. Government hiring offices.

▶ *Federal Career Opportunities*
Federal Research Service, Inc.                    (703) 281-0100
P.O. Box 1059
Vienna, Virginia 22183
         **Cost: $36.00 + $1.00 shipping for 6 biweekly issues**.
   Practical, current newsletters on how to find and land a federal job.

▶ *U.S. Government Manual*
Superintendent of Documents
Government Printing Office
Washington, D.C. 20402-9325                    **Cost: $21.00**
   Official Handbook of the U.S. Government, listing agencies, departments, commissions and officials.

▶ *Federal Executive Directory Annual*

▶ *State Executive Directory Annual*

▶ *Municipal/County Executive Directory Annual*
Carroll Publishing Co.
1058 Thomas Jefferson St., NW
Washington, D.C. 20077                    **Cost: $117.00 each**
An excellent source for local government officials, listing appointed and
elected officials in all levels of government.

# 10

# Effective Job Search Strategies

In addition to networking, there are many other effective methods for landing a job. Some of the tools utilized in these methods are similar to those you've developed for networking. As I've mentioned before, however, **no one method** will prove to be the magic one. You should try a variety, to see what you're comfortable with, and find out what works best for you.

## MASS MAILINGS

A mass mailing is an effective way of **getting your resumé into the hands of as many employers as possible**. Include your resumé and an effective cover letter, both printed or neatly typed on the same kind of paper, and placed in a matching envelope. Be sure that your letter and envelope are addressed to the name of the hiring authority, not just to the personnel department or office manager. **Send out at least ten resumés per week**. It really can pay off!

Gary Maxwell, Director of Administration of Irell & Manella, a major Los Angeles firm, tells the story of receiving a cover letter and resumé from an aspiring legal assistant who was so confident of her abilities, she stated in her letter that she would make herself available to work for the firm in a temporary capacity for one week, just so the firm could see that her claims were justified. Gary was so impressed by her undaunted assurance that he forwarded her resumé to the firm's Legal Assistant Manager for special attention.

It is not unheard of to send out over two hundred resumés each time you look for a job, so be prepared! This is definitely when you need to **start keeping copious notes in your placement file**. Nothing is worse than bombarding a prospective employer with five or six resumés.

You do **not** want your resumé to end up in resumé heaven, so **follow up your letter with a telephone call**. (See "scripts" of effective telephone calls in the next section, "Telephone Solicitations.") Now is the time to overcome any telephone phobias you may have. **Be businesslike and direct**. You will probably have to go through a secretary to speak to the hiring authority. The secretary may put you off. **Be friendly, but persistent**. Ask when is a good time to call, and be sure to ask that your message be conveyed. Even those pink telephone call reminder slips have marketing value!

---

**HOT TIP: Always** be friendly to the secretary. If the secretary becomes your ally, you will have easier access to the boss.

---

Once you have reached the hiring authority, ask if your resumé was received. (The secretary may also answer these questions.) If it was, then ask if you would be able to come in for an interview. If there are no openings, ask if you could call again next month to check in. Law firms will usually keep your resumé on file for a length of time, most often six months. It is wise to resubmit your resumé, if necessary, every four to six months.

Occasionally, you will receive a **rejection letter**. This can be viewed as an invitation to keep the lines of communication open, because most firms do not feel obligated to respond to every resumé they receive. Of course, you should be guided by the language of this letter. If the letter is noncommittal in tone, call the firm the following month to see if any positions have become available.

## TELEPHONE SOLICITATIONS

While gathering the information about your target employers, the receptionist may offer to put you directly through to the hiring authority. This is an excellent opportunity to preface the mailing of your resumé. Remember, **each exposure to your name will make you more memorable**. Be direct when

126

talking with the person. Get straight to the point and don't waste his or her time. A good example of how you should handle this type of call follows.

> Hello, my name is _____. I am very interested in working for your firm. I just graduated from Paralegal University, an ABA-approved program, and I would like to set up an interview if possible. . . . Oh, you don't have any openings.
>
> Well, in that case, I would like to send you my resumé for your files in the event a position opens up. I'll call you sometime next week to see if you have received it. Thank you for your time.

---

**HOT TIP:** If you have trouble getting past the secretary, **try calling early in the morning or after office hours**. Frequently, the hiring authorities and attorneys are in the office before and after the support staff. You may get right through to the proper person if you call at these times.

---

Even if the firms you reach by telephone do not wish to see you, **send them your resumé for future reference**. The fact that you spoke to someone will trigger recognition when your resumé and cover letter are received. As a result, the firm will be more apt to remember you when a job opens up. Make sure that you mention in your cover letter the name of the person to whom you originally spoke.

### Setting Up an Information Gathering Interview

As discussed earlier in **Chapter 7**, talking with attorneys, practicing paralegals, law firm managers and other people employed in a law firm is a good way to research information. When you gain access to the appropriate person, ask if you could schedule an appointment to discuss paralegal careers in that organization. Be sure to say that you want an informational interview. That way, even if there are no immediate openings, you can still schedule the interview. Outlined below is a good way to handle this request.

| | |
|---|---|
| **Paralegal:** | "Hello, could you please tell me the name of the person who is responsible for hiring paralegals?" |
| **Receptionist:** | "That would be Ann Roberts." |
| | |
| **Paralegal:** | "What is Ms. Roberts' title?" |
| **Receptionist:** | "She is our Paralegal Manager." |
| **Paralegal:** | "Could you please connect me with her office?" |
| | |
| **Secretary:** | "Ms. Roberts' office." |
| **Paralegal:** | "Is Ms. Roberts in, please?" |
| | |
| **Secretary:** | "May I tell her who is calling?" |
| **Paralegal:** | "Yes. This is Bob Jones" |

Do **not**, at this point, tell the secretary **why** you are calling. The secretary may put you right through.

| | |
|---|---|
| **Secretary:** | "May I tell Ms. Roberts the nature of your call?" |
| **Paralegal:** | "Yes. I am conducting research for a project for my paralegal class." |
| **Secretary:** | "One moment, please." |
| | |
| **Manager:** | "This is Ms. Roberts." |
| **Paralegal:** | "Hello, Ms. Roberts. My name is Bob Jones. I am a student at Paralegal University and I am hoping you can help me. I am trying to obtain information to take back to my paralegal class about job searching techniques . . . how to get a job, what top employers look for and what constitutes a great candidate. Is it possible to take 12 minutes of your time next Tuesday afternoon?" |

---

**HOT TIP:** By stating you only want 12 minutes of the interviewee's time, you will get his or her attention. Saying you only want "five or ten minutes" is meaningless because you haven't, in fact, set a firm time limit for your conversation.

---

**Manager:**     "Why, yes, Bob. I would be happy to help."

*Following Up on Mailed Resumé*

You should **always** follow up on resumés you've mailed by telephoning the person to whom the resumé was sent. Remember to review your placement file and information tracking chart before calling. You may need to refer to exact dates, job titles of the persons you sent your resumé to, or something specific about the firm's practice.

**Paralegal:**     "Good morning, Ms. Roberts. My name is Jackie Thomas. I'm following up on the resumé I sent you last week. Have you had a chance to review it?"

**Manager:**     "Yes, Jackie. However, we are really looking for someone with more experience."

**Paralegal:**     "I can appreciate that. Training entry-level paralegals does take time. I'd really appreciate it though if I could take only 12 minutes of your time to meet with you to find out what top firms such as yours look for in candidates. I also may be able to share with you my expertise and how it relates to this particular position.

I believe my medical background, while not in the legal field, is particularly relevant to the personal injury cases your firm handles. I noticed in *Martindale-Hubbell* that you also represent hospitals. My history as a physical therapist can probably be of some use to you."

**Manager:**     "You know, you may have something there. How about meeting next Tuesday at 1:00?"

Even if don't get past the hiring authority's secretary, you **can still make an impression**, and perhaps even an ally in your job search.

| | |
|---|---|
| **Secretary:** | "Ms. Roberts' office." |
| **Paralegal:** | "Hello, this is Nancy Martin calling for Ms. Roberts." |
| | |
| **Secretary:** | "May I tell Ms. Roberts the nature of your call?" |
| **Paralegal:** | "Yes, I am following up on a resumé I sent to her last week." |
| | |
| **Secretary:** | "Nancy, she'll have get back to you. Ms. Roberts is not taking any calls at this time regarding positions." |
| **Paralegal:** | "I can appreciate that. Can you tell me your name, please?" |
| **Secretary:** | "I'm Viola Johnson, Ms. Roberts' secretary." |
| | |
| **Paralegal:** | "Viola, I was curious to know if there are any particular qualities that this firm looks for in a paralegal position. I am new to the field and need all the information I can gather. Can you help me out for just a moment?" |

---

**HOT TIP:** Avoid using the phrase, "I was wondering if . . . ." This is too tentative and sounds as though you didn't have anything better to do that day. Use a more positive approach such as, "I am seeking a position with your firm and would like to set up an interview with you."

---

| | |
|---|---|
| **Secretary:** | "Well, Nancy, this firm always wants people who can write well. That's the first thing they look for." |
| | |
| **Paralegal:** | "Great, Viola. If I send Ms. Roberts a writing sample, even though I generally give this to the interviewer at the interview, could you see that she gets it?" |
| **Secretary:** | "Sure, Nancy, I'll be happy to help you out." |

Sometimes you will be granted an interview even if no position is open. Use this opportunity as an informational interview to **meet the person in charge of hiring** and gather more data about the firm. It will also give you **interviewing experience**, putting you more at ease in the future.

## TRACKING LAWSUITS

Many firms hire additional paralegals for **large litigation cases**. Entry-level paralegals interested in litigation have a number of options for tracking such cases. Remember, cases like antitrust or bankruptcy are usually **very document-intensive**, and those are the types of cases for which firms might hire several additional paralegals or document clerks.

---

**HOT TIP:**    While you're studying local law journals and legal newspapers, **look for firms hiring associates**. Check out the "Attorneys Wanted" classified advertisements. If the organization appears to be expanding, more than likely they will also need paralegals. Suggest this in your cover letter.

---

Look for **articles in local legal newspapers** or the *National Law Journal* about law firms and attorneys working on any large litigation matter. (See also the publications listed below.) If you find a case which interests you, contact the attorneys (or hiring authority) at that firm to ask about employment opportunities for paralegals. Be sure to check the "Big Suits" feature of the *American Lawyer*, for significant litigation matters. For those of you interested in a transactional practice, you should also check "Big Deals," a listing of major corporate or real estate acquisitions, takeovers and/or mergers.

Review **recent federal and state case law reporter** advance sheets (the most recent published court opinions), for the courts located in your part of the country. At the beginning of each opinion, there is a **list of attorneys who represented the parties** in that case. If the opinion is in an area of law in which you have an interest, call or send your resume to the attorney. Talk about and ask questions regarding the case. Then inquire about employment opportunities for paralegals in that area of law. (Review the informational interview techniques discussed above.)

## TRACKING OTHER AREAS OF LAW

Start reviewing the **articles in your local bar journal or magazine**. These can ordinarily be found in a law library. The articles and comments are usually written by local attorneys and will cover most practice areas. These articles are then indexed by subject matter in that publication's reference guide. If an area interests you, call or write the author. (You can obtain the telephone number and address from your state's attorney directory *Martindale-Hubbell* or the phone book). Ask a question or two about the topic of the article and the area of law involved. Then ask about employment opportunities for paralegals in that area of law.

Your **state bar association** is another excellent source of information for specific practice areas. These associations typically establish specialty committees for each practice area. As an associate member, you can attend the committee meetings of your choice and get to know people working in that area of law. Frequently, the activities of these committees are also reported in the bar association journals. Call the attorneys who are mentioned to see if you can arrange informational interviews.

### Legal Publications to Review for Law Firm Information

The following is a **partial list of legal publications** which should be quite helpful to you in gathering information about the activities of law firms and corporate law departments. While most of these publications do **not** contain specific job listings for paralegals, some do, and you can gain tremendous insight and knowledge of current events in the legal field by reviewing them periodically. You may find mention of some exciting litigation matter being handled by a major firm in your area, and, as a result, will know that **now** is the time to send in that resumé!

- ▶ *ABA Journal* (American Bar Association magazine)
- ▶ *ALA News* (Association of Legal Administrators magazine)
- ▶ *American Lawyer* (national magazine mentioned above)
- ▶ *California Lawyer* (California Bar Association magazine—other states publish similarly titled magazines)
- ▶ *Computer Law Strategist*

- *Daily Journal* (Los Angeles local legal newspaper containing classified job listings for attorneys and legal assistants—check the library to find the legal newspaper in your area)
- *L.A. Lawyer* (Los Angeles Bar Association magazine)
- *Law Journal Information Systems*
- *Law Office Computing* (national magazine specializing in the use of computers in the law office)
- *Legal Management* (magazine published by the Association of Legal Administrators)
- *Legal Assistant Today* (national paralegal magazine)
- *Law Practice Management*
- *Legal Exchange* (newsletter concentrating on attorney job listings with some paralegal openings listed)
- *Legal Tech Newsletter*
- *Legal Times* (weekly legal newspaper with national circulation
- *Litigation* (publication of the ABA Section on Litigation)
- *Managing Attorneys*
- *Marketing for Lawyers*
- *National Law Journal* (weekly national legal newspaper)
- *National Paralegal Reporter* (magazine published by the National Federation of Paralegal Associations)
- *Of Counsel*
- *The Recorder* (San Francisco daily legal newspaper)
- *Texas Lawyer* (Texas Bar Association magazine)
- *Trial Magazine*

In addition to the publications listed above, there are many newsletters published by local paralegal associations, local city legal newspapers, and local and state bar journals. Call the particular legal assistant or attorney associations to find out which ones are in your region.

## DOOR-TO-DOOR CONTACTS

Going door-to-door is another way to contact employers. This method is **not** popular in some cities, but is thought to be more effective in smaller towns. Find out what your city's firms think of this technique **before** you try it.

Law firms are frequently clustered in the skyscraper section of town. Visit these buildings and make a list of all the firms. Then call each firm to ask who hires paralegals. When you return to the buildings—in your "dressed for success" clothes (see Chapter 12)—go to each office and ask to see this person.

**Always** indicate a willingness to return at a later time if it would be more convenient. If you are asked to return, leave a copy of your resumé with a note stating why you would like to speak to person who hires paralegals. If you are able to get an interview on the spot, you should **be prepared to state why you requested it and what you want**. Since you have initiated the meeting, you must be ready to get the ball rolling.

Keep in mind that most prospective employers will be unable to see you without an appointment. The strategy of the door-to-door approach is to get your name in front of the firm. By all means follow up by sending your resumé.

## SELF ADVERTISING

Advertising yourself in local legal journals is an unorthodox, but sometimes effective way to find a job. Place a **brief advertisement** in the classified "services available" section of your local legal newspaper. Your ad should simply state that you are an entry-level paralegal (with a specialty, if applicable), and that you are available to work in a particular area of town. Be sure to state where you went to school, and that your **salary is negotiable**.

Believe it or not, **this method has worked for several new paralegals**. It is one more idea to use in a competitive job market. You may be offered a temporary or part-time position from a firm that does not use formal hiring channels. The following ad copy is an appropriate approach.

Entry-level paralegal is seeking a litigation position with a respected downtown law firm. I have a B.A. degree in History from State University, as well as a paralegal certificate from Paralegal School, which is ABA-approved. I am well organized and understand the litigation process. My salary is negotiable, and I am available immediately. Please call Jane Hoskins at (323) 341-3349, for an interview.

## A MENTOR CAN BE YOUR BEST ALLY

Many successful people have started their careers by finding a **mentor**—someone who has expertise in the field you wish to enter and takes a personal interest in your career. **A mentor can ease your way into the job market.** This individual must care about your success and be in a position to give you good advice.

You may meet your mentor at paralegal functions, alumni meetings or at formal interviews. A mentor could be a teacher you had in paralegal school or a recruiter you met during your job search. One of the best mentors to have is an experienced paralegal who is willing to commit the time necessary to help you with your career development. Likewise, someone who has been a paralegal but has moved into other arenas of the legal field like management, recruiting or education, can provide that much needed support and guidance.

Nurture such relationships, and value them highly. Be careful, however, to avoid taking undue advantage of your mentor's time and contacts.

Once you've been hired, try to find a person in your law firm (or corporation) who will **help you through the maze of office politics and personalities**. Sometimes if you just have a little inside knowledge, you can avoid certain difficulties. Unfortunately, not everyone is lucky enough to find such a person, but if you do, you'll find that having an experienced guide is of enormous value to your career at that firm.

# 11

# Moving Up From Legal Secretary To Paralegal

You have been a legal secretary for years, and the next step you want to make in your career plan is to become a paralegal. How do you make the transition? It's not as difficult as you may think if you use a little initiative and planning.

## MAKING THE MOVE AT YOUR CURRENT FIRM

### Getting Experience

Some law firms allow legal secretaries to handle paralegal responsibilities. If you are working for such a firm, you have a **great advantage** over paralegals coming into the field from outside the law firm environment. You have the **opportunity to gain experience**. A legal assistant on the job market with as little as one year of legal secretarial experience can find a job far more easily than someone with no legal experience at all.

A former legal secretary I know, Sherry, tells a great story about her **successful transition to a paralegal position.**

> I once took a temporary secretary position with a top litigation attorney. He obviously had no clue as to what paralegals could do. One case he was working on involved a great deal of factual investigation. I suggested a research work plan for him, implemented the plan, and wrote a memorandum outlining my results. He was so impressed that he suggested I sign on at the firm as a litigation paralegal. At that time, I wasn't interested in working anywhere as a permanent employee. I suggested that I stay on as a temporary legal assistant so we could "try each other out."
>
> One year later, the firm gave me what they thought was their last permanent offer. I told the firm, "Great. I would love to have the job as long as you appoint me the head of the paralegal department." Their response was "We don't have a formal program." I told them "That's why and how you need me." The rest is history. I've been here four years now and absolutely love it.

Ask the attorney you work for if you can take on any paralegal duties that fall into your legal area. Your goal is to **increase your skills so your resumé will look more impressive.** Some duties you should try to start handling include preparing and reviewing the following:

*Litigation*
- ▶ document organization
- ▶ document indexes
- ▶ simple pleadings
- ▶ boilerplate forms, subpoenas and court documents

*Corporate*
- ▶ routine corporate maintenance
- ▶ SEC and Blue Sky research of a straightforward nature

*Real Estate*
- ▶ leases and loan documents
- ▶ closing binders
- ▶ title insurance reports

*Probate*
- ▶ simple wills and trusts
- ▶ tax accounting
- ▶ title searches and insurance reports
- ▶ sale of estate assets.

Remember that legal assistant work includes "any substantive legal work that requires knowledge of legal concepts and is customarily, but not exclusively, performed by a lawyer." You **may have been doing paralegal work for some time without getting recognition for it**. (See **Chapter 1** for a list of typical legal assistant responsibilities.) Evaluate your past duties carefully and include any paralegal level work on your resumé. If a portion of your work has been paralegal in nature, you should **list your position as secretary/paralegal**.

### Changing Your Title

If you can't get an actual paralegal position, ask your employer about changing your job title, even just to reflect a split in responsibilities, as indicated by "secretary/paralegal" (or "legal secretary/legal assistant"). You can always take the title with you if you leave in search of a full-time paralegal position, and it's a **definite plus on your resumé**. You will be able to advance more easily because the firm has officially recognized your job duties.

### Taking Paralegal Courses

To increase your credibility and marketability, consider taking paralegal courses or beginning a legal assistant certificate program. You may already know most of the terms and legal procedures. However, many firms are now requiring the legal assistants they hire to complete an ABA-approved paralegal program. By enrolling in such a course of study, you will also **impress upon your current employer that you are serious about your career move**.

If you do decide to attend paralegal school, choose well. Check out the school's reputation through contacts in local paralegal associations. Your current law firm's personnel administrator is also likely to know paralegal school ratings. Distance and cost are important considerations, but the **quality of the education you receive is the critical factor**. (See **Chapter 3** for a thorough discussion regarding paralegal schools.)

**Continuing Legal Education (CLE) courses** are also available to enhance your knowledge. Ask the attorney with whom you work to route his or her CLE brochures to you, so you can get on the mailing lists. These programs usually offer lower paralegal rates, and your firm might have a policy of paying for the training if it is relevant to your job. (See Chapter 5 for CLE listings.)

Another strategy for legal secretaries is to take the National Association of Legal Assistants (NALA) exam to obtain the **Certified Legal Assistant designation**. This is a 2-1/2 day exam given to certify that certain paralegals have experience and knowledge of the profession. You must have completed certain requirements prior to the exam. Call NALA to obtain more information. This designation may help you advance into the paralegal profession.

### Advantages of Staying with Your Firm

There are many advantages to staying with your current firm while making your transition. First, the attorneys **know and trust you**. They are more likely to give you higher level paralegal work if you request it than lawyers in a new firm might. You can build on the foundation you've already established as a legal secretary.

Second, you **may not face a salary cut**. It is unfortunate but true that many entry-level paralegals are paid significantly less than many experienced legal secretaries. Fewer people are going into secretarial work, and the law of supply and demand governs legal secretary salaries. But don't be discouraged; senior paralegal positions offer a much higher salary range, and a ceiling for these salaries has not yet been established.

*Disadvantages of Staying with Your Firm*

If you decide to stay with your current firm once you've made the transition to a paralegal position, be aware of a **possible "caste system" that may be difficult to break.** When you were hired as a legal secretary, your position and status as a clerical assistant was set. People will still relate to you that way. Don't be surprised if someone, either innocently or maliciously, drops a typing assignment on your desk. Take the assignment back to that person and politely explain your new situation. Be gentle but firm in breaking the mold.

Sometimes you may be asked to stay late to help with typing a document that is due the next day. No one else is available. Should you pitch in as a team player or hold your ground as a legal assistant? This is a difficult judgment call. It is certainly easier to establish yourself as a paralegal in a new firm. It is **more difficult to redefine yourself in your new position if you stay where you originally worked as a legal secretary.** But you can do it if you are determined and assertive. (See more on assertiveness in **Chapter 16.**)

*Moving On*

The greatest advantage to changing firms is leaving the caste system behind. In a new firm, you will be viewed as a paralegal, **not** a glorified legal secretary. If no one knows about your secretarial skills, you won't be asked to stay late keying documents. Unless you are hired as a combination legal secretary/paralegal, you **should receive the full paralegal title** and be assigned strictly paralegal work.

I have already discussed the greatest disadvantage to moving—a possible pay cut. **Be prepared to negotiate,** pointing out your legal experience. This will make you a more valuable employee to your new firm because you can be effective immediately. It also cuts costly training time. See **Chapter 14,** "Getting Paid What You're Worth," for tips on negotiating skills.

## THE "BUILDING BLOCK" RESUMÉ

To create a resumé that builds on your legal experience, you should emphasize the paralegal skills and education that your prospective employer will value for your new job. Both the chronological and functional resumé formats work well. (Follow the guidelines in **Chapter 4,** "How to Stand Out in a Crowd," and **Chapter 5,** "Formats for Power Resumés" on writing a winning resumé.) The trick is to present your legal knowledge and level of responsibility in the best light. Be sure to **join paralegal organizations** so you can add those memberships, and **don't forget to network!**

### Educational Background

If you have earned your paralegal certificate or are currently completing a program, place **education first** on the resumé. If you do not have any formal paralegal education, then your **work experience** is the most important factor in your career and should appear first. The most critical information should appear at the top of the resumé.

### Job Experience

If you have **handled paralegal responsibilities, list those tasks first,** followed by some of your secretarial duties. Also **emphasize computer skills,** because these enhance your value as a legal assistant. This includes the use of document assembly, spreadsheet and database software. **Do not** list clerical skills that are relevant only to secretarial work such as typing speed, filing proficiency, or experience using a dictaphone or calculator.

### Resumé Introduction

Use a job title to **let the employer know that you are seeking a paralegal position.** If you want to explain what you are looking for in more detail, use the career objective.

## SAMPLE RESUMÉS

Legal secretaries who wish to move to paralegal positions should use one of the following sample resumes in making the **transition to a new position.** Of course, you should modify the resumé form to fit your particular educational and experience backgrounds.

## Chronological Resumé

HARRIET SECRETARY
600 CHERRY AVENUE, UNIT 12
NEW YORK, NEW YORK 11111
(212) 555-5515

**EDUCATION:**  LONG BEACH CITY COLLEGE—Long Beach, NY
Legal Secretary Program Certificate, June 1984

**EXPERIENCE:**

1986 to Present  INDEPENDENT CONTRACTOR, Nassau County, NY
Paralegal/Secretary positions for various law firms. Specialized in corporate law, city planning, probate, guardianship law and personal injury.

1984 to 1986  MARK DOE, ESQ., New York, NY
Legal Secretary/Receptionist in personal injury and immigration law firm. Performed duties as secretary; calendar responsibilities; prepared pleadings and performed paralegal research.

1980 to 1984  SMITH, GRAVES & DIXON, New York, NY
Legal Secretary for firm specializing in civil litigation, personal injury, worker's compensation and family law.

**COMPUTER SKILLS:**
Lexis, Westlaw and WordPerfect 5.1

**ORGANIZATIONS:**
New York Paralegal Association
National Federation of Paralegal Associations

Illustration 11.1

## Chronological Resumé

JANE DOE OLSON
1234 Main Street, #5                                        (123) 555-1212
Atlanta, GA 64810

### EDUCATION

**GRADUATE EDUCATION**
**University of California, Berkeley**, University Extension Attorney Assistant Training Program, offered in cooperation with the Boalt Hall School of Law, approved by the American Bar Association. Certificate in Litigation. Graduation with Honors, 1990.

**UNDERGRADUATE EDUCATION**
**University of California, Berkeley**, Bachelor of Arts in Political Science, 1979.

### EXPERIENCE

**LEGAL SECRETARY**
**Robert Baskin, A Law Corporation, Atlanta, GA**
Responsible for all facets of office management. Researched and prepared pleadings. Administered the complete accounts receivable cycle. Composed correspondence. Assisted with the bookkeeping for trusts. Prepared various trust documents. Maintained the computer. 1990-1991.

**EXECUTIVE SECRETARY**
**Dean of Administration and Finance, Harvard Medical School**
**Boston, MA**
Responsible for scheduling and planning meetings. Composed correspondence. Prepared the department budget. Managed records. Maintained and ordered office supplies. Interfaced with various departments of the school and the university. 1985-1990.

**ADMINISTRATIVE SECRETARY**
**Business Services Administration, Centinela Hospital Medical Center, San Francisco, CA**
Responsible for providing clerical support to seven quality assurance committees and the utilization review committee plus five members of the business services staff. Supervised the business office receptionist. Managed the accounts receivable for a small subsidiary of the hospital. Resolved patient billing problems. 1981-1985.

### SKILLS /ABILITIES
    WordPerfect 5.0
    Notary Public Commission

Illustration 11.2

## Functional Resumé

**NAME**
ADDRESS
CITY, STATE, ZIP
PHONE

### PROFESSIONAL EXPERIENCE

**Legal Procedures**:
* Prepared subpoenas, notice of depositions, settlement demands
* In charge of tickler system
* Composed simple contracts, declarations, court forms
* Filed court documents, prepared instructions
* Researched state agencies' rules and procedures

**Administrative Responsibilities**:
* Prepared office procedures manual
* Scheduled deponents and witnesses for depositions
* Designed directory systems
* Recruited clerical staff
* Calculated fee schedules

**Computer Skills**:
* Expert in WordPerfect 5.1
* Expert in use of IBM PC and WANG
* Familiar with Lexis/Westlaw

### WORK HISTORY

1988 - Present:   **Day & Knight**
Legal Secretary to Litigation Department Managing Partner

1985 - 1988:   **Polk, Samuels & Daniels**
Legal Secretary to Litigation Partner

### EDUCATION

Associate of Arts Degree, Business Administration, 1980
Smith College, Minneapolis, MN

---

Illustration 11.3

## SALARY NEGOTIATIONS

Be ready to **sharpen your negotiating skills** and bring them to the table. First, review **Chapter 14**, "Getting Paid What You're Worth," on salary negotiations. When you're getting prepared to negotiate, remember:

▶ You know how a law firm works.
▶ You are very familiar with legal procedures.
▶ You will not need as much training as an entry level paralegal.
▶ You can be profitable to the law firm **immediately**.

These facts should be mentioned during your negotiations. Make sure that you have **solid references** as well as **written work samples** to back up your claims. Remember to redraft all your writing samples to remove confidential material.

Once your salary negotiations are complete, you are on the threshold. Welcome to a new legal career!

# 12

# After You Get Through The Door

**Ensuring a Successful Interview**

Up to this point, your entire job search—research, networking, resumé, cover letter—has focused on one goal, getting an interview for the job you want. **Now you are there**. You have been pulled out of the pack, and the prospective employer wants to talk with you in person. The interviewer is looking for the answer to a single question, "Why should I hire you?"

## HOW TO APPROACH THE INTERVIEW

The interview enables you to enhance your resumé, to shine, to be the one person they want to hire. You can discuss your applicable skills and abilities in more detail, describing how you will use them in your new position. You can show your enthusiasm and desire. The prospective employer can see you as a poised professional who will be an asset to the firm.

**Getting a job is like getting married**. You will be with your colleagues for eight hours a day, so you must ask questions that will tell you if this is a place where you will be happy. The interview gives you the opportunity to learn about the firm.

Over the years, as a recruiter, I have interviewed all types—from outstanding candidates with excellent professional demeanor, to people chewing gum or wearing what seemed like a bottle of perfume. This chapter discusses the "dos" and "don'ts" for interviewing. **Two basic rules apply to all legal interviewing. First,** dress conservatively. Even if your personal style is punk or neo-hippie, if you want a job in the legal industry, you **must** dress in **traditional business attire**—no heavy makeup, outlandish hairstyles, or casual clothes. You must be neat, clean and professional in appearance.

**Second**, you must have good verbal communication skills. The resumé demonstrates your writing abilities; **the interview demonstrates your speaking talents.** This means you must prepare your questions and rehearse answers to questions that you believe will be asked. You **must also be friendly and positive.** Do not malign a previous employer or become arrogant toward the interviewer. I once actually had a woman swear at me when I told her we had no immediate openings. She had an excellent educational background, but although she may have just been having a bad day (like everyone does), her resumé was filed away permanently, never to see sunlight again.

Interviews are usually comprised of at least **two sessions**: the initial interview and a "call-back" second (or even third) interview, if the firm is considering making you an offer or is narrowing the scope of candidates. This chapter will give you an overview of the interview process, so you'll know what to expect at each stage.

Sometimes job candidates jump the gun and ask questions that are appropriate only in the second interview. An **initial interview** usually reviews the **basic information** presented in your resumé.

- ▶ background
- ▶ education
- ▶ work experience
- ▶ interests
- ▶ skills
- ▶ abilities

When you are **asked back for a second (or third) interview**, you will probably cover some of these same areas with the different people who will be involved in the hiring decision. However, you will also discuss **salary, benefits and working conditions** with the legal assistant manager (or other hiring authority). It is certainly appropriate to bring up these types of questions at this point. (See **Chapter 13**, the section headed "Questions to Ask the Interviewer.") Being asked back for further interviews means the firm or company is definitely interested in you, and is willing to now address financial concerns. (See also **Chapter 14**, "Getting Paid What You're Worth.")

## BEING PREPARED WILL BUILD YOUR CONFIDENCE

The **initial phone call** asking you to come in for an interview is most likely the first time the employer will be contacting you. Therefore, the call should actually be **considered part of the interview**. Obviously, you don't want to miss any calls, so if you don't have an **answering machine**, buy or borrow one now.

If you're not at home to receive any calls from potential employers, think about the impression the outgoing message on your answering machine will make. Your machine should **not** have a cute, clever message or loud music in the background—leave out the barking dogs, limericks, and singing children. Your **outgoing message** should be **straightforward and businesslike**, asking for the caller's name and telephone number, and assuring that the call will be returned.

> **HOT TIP:** Your answering machine may be the **very first impression** the potential employer has of you besides your resumé. Create a message that sounds as though the potential employer has called your **home office**.

When you are called for an interview by a law firm or corporation, **be sure you get all the information you need**. Write down **all** of the following:

- ▶ name of company or firm
- ▶ address
- ▶ room, suite or floor number
- ▶ city
- ▶ phone number
- ▶ name of person(s) you will be seeing (write the names phonetically to **be sure of the pronunciation**)

▶ time of the interview

▶ where to park (if applicable)

If you do not know the location of the company or firm, call the receptionist to ask for directions.  If possible, take a trip to the location of the firm or corporation **before** the scheduled interview, in order to find out how much time you need to arrive. During this trip, you can also discover the best place to park.  If you will be taking public transportation, familiarize yourself with the schedule so you arrive on time. **If you're more than just a little bit late in arriving for the interview**, it is usually all over before the interview begins.  **Do not be late!** If an unforeseen problem like car trouble stalls you, you should call the interviewer and explain the situation.

---

**HOT TIP:**  Do **not** ask the firm if they will pay for parking.  You should take along extra money, just in case they do not!

---

**Learn as much as you can** about the people and the organization with whom you are interviewing.  An interviewer will be impressed that you took time to research this information.  In your earlier research to target the firms and companies you're interested in, you should have become familiar with the *Martindale-Hubbell Law Directory* and the *Standard & Poor's Register of Corporations, Directors and Executives*. These directories are good sources of basic information.  You should also check *The Readers' Guide to Periodical Literature* for recent articles about the company or law firm.  You can also ask a corporation to send you an **annual report**. Since many law firms these days publish **quarterly newsletters** for their clients, ask for a copy.  You should also ask if the firm has a **brochure**—these typically discuss the history of the firm, representative clients and practice groups.

When you are called for your interview, **clarify the position for which you will be interviewing**.  Knowing what position is open will help you determine beforehand what the interviewer is looking for and what will be expected of you as an employee of the firm. Of course, the interview will be the appropriate time to delve into these issues in detail.  Although you will have to use your own judgment about when and how to ask them, a **list of questions to ask the interviewer** is included in **Chapter 13**.

150

**Know the information on your resumé thoroughly** and highlight it during the interview. Be prepared to discuss and describe any relevant prior work experience, both paid and volunteer work. In lieu of experience, paralegals just out of school can describe course work, research papers and projects that have some relevance to the legal field.

You should also **know how to describe yourself.** Prepare a "thumbnail sketch" which includes your education and relevant work experience. The personal aspects of your life are private and need **not** be included unless you choose to reveal them. Sometimes sharing your personal interests is good strategy because outside interests, like hobbies and sports, can make you memorable to the interviewer. However, if you do not choose to share this information, it is actually none of the employer's business!

*Sample Self Description*

> I am a recent graduate of Paralegal University, an ABA-approved program. I graduated with honors and have a litigation certificate. Some of the courses I took were: legal research, writing, and litigation procedures including the discovery process and various pleadings. I have a bachelor's degree from State College where I also received a teaching credential. I taught English, my college major, for three years at the high school level. Toward the end of my tenure, I was elected chair of the English department. One of my primary responsibilities was curriculum development.

*Checklist: What to Bring to the Interview*

- ▶ copies of your resumé (even if you have already supplied copies to the firm or company)
- ▶ list of references
- ▶ reference letters
- ▶ list of questions you need answered
- ▶ writing samples
- ▶ money for parking and/or transportation
- ▶ directions

Make enough copies of your printed materials so you can give at least **two additional sets** to the interviewer. They might be needed for that second interview!


## REHEARSALS HELP YOU GET IT RIGHT

An experienced interviewer will ordinarily make quick assessments of potential employees. Because of this, you should **prepare for the interview as much as possible.** Rehearsing the interview, using questions you believe will be asked, is a **must** if you want to appear calm and poised, and have well thought-out answers. Some questions are easy. "What was your major in college?" doesn't take too much thought. On the other hand, "What are your weak points?" is difficult to answer. You want to be honest, of course, but you need to frame your response in a positive light. For example, if you work slowly, it is because you are very thorough. How do you know what questions you will be asked? Most interviewers ask similar questions, and a list of the most common ones can be found in **Chapter 13.**

If you have left a job and are unemployed, you will invariably be asked "Why?" Do **not** just blurt out, "The company is a sweatshop" or "My job was boring." Plan your answer and **make it as positive as you can.** It is much more effective to say, "I am taking time to enhance my career." You can also frame your answer around the features you are looking for in your new career. You may be looking for a firm that offers paralegal training, a new area of law, or combines your past experience with the paralegal field. Emphasize these points if they fit your interviewer's profile.

By carefully planning what you will say, you will present yourself as an intelligent and polished candidate. Go through the questions on the list. Find the questions that are difficult for you or require a negative answer. Prepare positive answers and rehearse them.

> **HOT TIP:** Employers are **put on the alert** when they receive the following responses to their questions:
> - ▶ I am willing to take a pay cut.
> - ▶ I left for personal reasons.
> - ▶ I am looking for a greater challenge.
> - ▶ I did not see eye to eye with my employer.
> - ▶ There was a conflict with my co-workers and/or supervisor.

Consider **audio or videotaping your answers** to hear and/or see how your answers appear. In order to see your body language, practice in front of a mirror. Watch your facial expressions. Avoid frowning or looking gloomy. Look yourself directly in the eye. There is nothing more distracting or uncomfortable than an interviewee who looks everywhere but directly at the interviewer.

Through practice you will be able to develop self-confidence. You will radiate how you feel by the way you walk, sit and speak. Employers are impressed by candidates who present themselves positively.

### Interview Rehearsal Checklist

Do:

- ▶ Think about what you will wear (see next section).
- ▶ Practice positive answers about your past employer even if you were fired or forced to quit.
- ▶ Practice establishing eye contact.
- ▶ Practice a firm handshake with family members and friends.
- ▶ Time your trip to the interview location, allowing for traffic and parking.
- ▶ Review questions you will ask the employer.

*Do Not:*

▶ Decide you do not need to interview.

▶ Assume you know all about the job.

▶ Adopt a passive or indifferent attitude.

▶ Have a know-it-all attitude (even if you did attend law or graduate school).

▶ Embarrass the interviewer (even though you read about an event about the firm in the local law journal, your interviewer may not have).

Use **positive, powerful "action" words** to describe what you have done and want to do. The word list found in **Chapter 5** will give you some ideas. Choose words that will enhance your image, but with which you feel comfortable.

## "SUIT" YOURSELF—IT'S YOUR APPEARANCE

Your appearance is of the **utmost importance**. First impressions are crucial, and you do not get a second chance. The legal world is, for the most part, very conservative, and traditional professional attire is expected for the interview. It is as inappropriate for you to wear casual clothing to your interview as it would be for a lawyer to wear jeans and a T-shirt to court. The lawyer will not win the day and neither will you.

Sometimes we are unaware of the impact we make with our clothing. I'll never forget "The Lady in Black," a candidate of mine who I'd briefly coached on how to "dress for success." I unfortunately just **assumed** that she would know what I meant by "dress conservatively." Immediately after her interview, I received a call from the paralegal administrator to whom I'd referred the candidate. "I want you to know," she said, "that I just saw your candidate and I really appreciated your sense of humor." I wondered what on earth was she talking about. "Oh, you know," said the administrator, "that gag of sending her in here wearing a black suit, black blouse, black shoes, black stockings, black hat and black gloves!" Uh, oh.

---

**HOT TIP:** Dress as though you are applying for the **interviewer's** position.

---

*Appropriate Dress for Women*

The best choice for women is a business suit in conservative colors such as navy blue, gray or beige. The suit fabric should be appropriate for the season: wool for winter and linen for summer. A combination of fibers is acceptable. The suit blouse should be simple, in white or a pale color to complement the suit. Do not wear a low-cut or v-neck blouse or dress, nor one that is too bright, has too many ruffles or is see-through.

If you choose to wear a dress, it must be in a tasteful print or a color that is flattering to you, preferably in silk or a good quality fiber mix. Avoid cotton since it has a more casual look. If you need to wear a wrap over your dress, wear a blazer to complement the color. A sweater is not appropriate.

Wear skin-tone stockings, and closed-toe leather pumps with a moderate height heel (less than two inches is preferred), or flats in a color which coordinates with the outfit. Do **not** wear black leather shoes with a brown or navy suit. Likewise, do **not** wear white shoes with anything other than a white suit. If you usually wear tennis shoes when you leave your office, make sure you have pumps with you on the day of the interview.

Jewelry and perfume must be kept to a minimum. Do **not** wear jingly, noisy jewelry; long or dangling earrings; or anything that indicates a religious, fraternal or political affiliation. Makeup should be minimal, and hair should be clean and neatly groomed. Go easy on the hair spray and mousse.

Take a good quality briefcase or portfolio with you instead of a handbag. If you choose to carry a handbag, make sure it complements your outfit and is not your "every day" bag. Include the following items in your portfolio: copies of your resumé (at least five), list of references, writing samples, the questions you've prepared for the interviewer, legal pad for notes (if necessary), pens, car keys, wallet, brush and makeup.

---

**HOT TIP:** You may want to ask the advice of an image consultant, if you are at all unsure of your appearance. These consultants can usually be found at larger department stores.

---

### Appropriate Attire for Men

Think Brooks Brothers. Wear a two-piece business suit or sports jacket and slacks in a muted color—either in gray or navy blue, **never** brown or black. Do not wear a sweater except as a vest or underneath a sports coat. Your pants should be long enough so that when you sit down, no skin shows above your socks. Wear a white shirt with a conservative collar. Make sure all the buttons button when you sit. The tie should also be conservative and blend well with the ensemble. Always wear dark socks that match your pants; **never** wear white socks. Avoid the "no sock" look, no matter what fashion dictates. Shoes should be tied laces or loafer style, no boots.

Jewelry and after shave or cologne must be kept to a minimum. Hair should be neatly cut in a conservative style. If you have a beard or mustache, it should be neatly trimmed.

Carry a quality briefcase or portfolio. Include the following items in your portfolio: copies of your resumé (at least five), list of references, writing samples, the questions you've prepared for the interviewer, legal pad for notes (if necessary), pens, car keys and wallet.

### Dressing on the Job

Once you get the job, you can change the way you dress to fit your own style, **provided** it fits in with the firm's typical dress standards or culture. Observe how other members of the firm dress. However, you must **always present yourself in a businesslike manner**. Dressing appropriately on the job will help ensure that you are treated as a professional.

## THE INTERVIEWING PROCESS

### Arrival

Arrive ten minutes early for your interview. You may need the time to fill out an application. If you are earlier, drive around the block a few times or take a short walk. If you are going to be late—even by five minutes—call to let the interviewer know your approximate arrival time.

Do **not** take anyone else with you. If you are driven to the interview by someone else, have your friend wait in the car or go for a cup of coffee. Do **not** bring your children! You should have enough notice to arrange for adequate day care. If you are not able to find someone to care for your children, reschedule the interview. If you are ill, change your appointment for another time. You want to **present yourself in the best light possible**.

---

**HOT TIP:** Choose a straight-backed chair to sit in while you wait. If you sit on a cushiony, low couch or chair, chances are you will be trying to awkwardly extricate yourself just as the interviewer walks up to greet you. Bad impression!

---

### Application

Be prepared to fill out a job application. Do not get upset about this requirement or feel the firm is treating you as clerical help. In today's job market, which is governed by so many regulations, some firms even require attorneys to complete job application forms. It's just part of the game. Fill out the form as quickly as possible. For information reflected on your resumé such as education and work history, write "See Resumé." Be truthful, **especially** about dates and past salaries.

---

**HOT TIP:** Some firms actually notice how long it takes you to fill out the application, as an indication of how quickly you might complete your work product. Try to take no more than ten minutes to complete the application.

---

Your job research should have informed you about starting salaries in your region. If there's a question about salary requirements on the application form, leave it blank. Also, do not write "negotiable." If you do write a salary range, more than likely you will be offered the lower figure if a job offer is extended. See **Chapter 14**, "Getting Paid What You're Worth," for more techniques on salary negotiation.

## Getting Acquainted

Introduce yourself to the interviewer and **offer to shake hands**. First impressions are the most important. Many employers make their decisions in the first few seconds. The rest of the interview will only add to or subtract from their initial impression of you. If you have sweaty palms, be sure to discreetly wipe them off before the interviewer appears.

When you enter the interviewer's office, sit in the chair indicated to you. Once when I was interviewing, a candidate sat by accident in my chair. The applicant was very embarrassed and did not get the job, not for that reason alone of course, but it did get things off to a bad start.

Place your briefcase on the floor beside you, **not** on the desk. Sit up straight during the interview, don't slump or become too comfortable. **Never** lean over the interviewer's desk, put your elbows on the desk or grab your resumé back from the interviewer to clarify something. People can be quite territorial about their personal space. Try to sit with your feet together or crossed at the ankles.

## CREATING A STANDOUT IMPRESSION

Create a positive and professional attitude. Always **maintain eye contact** and speak clearly, **showing interest and enthusiasm**. Employers are not only trying to determine if you will "fit in," they are also trying to gauge how you will appear to others. If you are hired, **you'll be representing the firm** whenever you work with clients, other law firms or corporations, judges and juries. The firm must feel comfortable with the image that you will project to these significant people.

Use the interview to personally enhance the employer's impression of you. **Demonstrate self-confidence** about your skills, interest and achievements. Concentrate on giving clear and concise responses to questions you are asked. Responding with vague generalities shows that you have not given much thought to the interview.

Express yourself as well as possible. Use correct grammar. Listen to your rehearsal tape recording. Notice if you say "um" of "uh" frequently. **Eliminate sentence fillers** like, "you know," "like," and "I mean." These speech patterns make you appear hesitant, and as a result, will weaken your presentation.

Do **not** be afraid to stress your attributes. It is **appropriate to sell yourself** in order to get the job. It cannot hurt to emphasize those skills or qualities you possess which you feel are particularly well suited to the job. This is the information the interviewer needs. On the other hand, you need to **avoid** appearing boastful, overbearing or conceited.

Be careful about criticizing or belittling the paralegal profession. When a candidate confides to me that, "I'm only doing this until I find a real job," the interview might as well be over. I've already determined from this comment that the candidate is not willing to make real commitment to a legal assistant career.

**If you don't know the answer** to one of the interviewer's questions, **say so.** You are not expected to know everything, particularly if the subject relates to substantive law. If you are asked a question requiring experience that you do not have, be honest about it. If you **do** have related experience, point that out. This will let the interviewer know that you've made the connection between the topic of question and the experiences you do possess.

### *Winning Personality Traits*

The **successful candidate** will possess certain traits that interviewers like to see. Among these are:

*People Skills*
- ▶ enjoys working with all kinds of people and personalities
- ▶ gets along well with everyone
- ▶ has a sunny disposition—no chip on the shoulder

*Initiative and Drive*
- ▶ strong desire to succeed
- ▶ driven to fulfill that desire to succeed
- ▶ has a pattern of success in school and work
- ▶ consistently pushes and seems to be driven by an internal combustion engine
- ▶ supervisor doesn't have to worry about motivation!

*Sensitivity*
- ▶ sensitive to the needs of others
- ▶ listens well
- ▶ concerned with others, and respects co-workers ideas

*Spirit*
- ▶ project enthusiasm—the kind of spirit that comes from deep within
- ▶ self-confident
- ▶ radiates warmth through smile, eyes, body language

## INTERVIEW PREPARATION CHECKLIST

### *Getting Ready*
- ▶ Write resumé.
- ▶ Make contacts.
- ▶ Network.
- ▶ Make appointments from mass mailings, telephone solicitations and network contacts.

### *Before the Interview*
- ▶ Know your resumé.
- ▶ Be familiar with a typical application form.
- ▶ Know something about the company or firm. Check *Martindale-Hubbell* or *Standard & Poor's* directories.
- ▶ Have a list of good questions to ask the interviewer, and know **when** to ask them.
- ▶ Rehearse your answers. Then rehearse **again**.
- ▶ Plan "thumbnail" sketch of yourself. Include educational and work-related information.
- ▶ Know the location of the interview site and where to park.
- ▶ Be on time or even somewhat early.
- ▶ Go alone.
- ▶ Bring copies of your resumé, list of references and writing samples in a briefcase or portfolio.

> **HOT TIP:**  Research the law firm or corporation through your local legal newspapers or other periodicals.  If you can, find out about a recent case, merger or corporate client the firm is handling. Let the interviewer know that you have been following the case or matter with interest.  While the interviewer may not be able to discuss the matter with you, you will have demonstrated research ability and knowledge of the firm, appealing to the ego of the firm.

### The Introduction

▶ Dress the part.

▶ Do not smoke, eat, chew gum or drink coffee.

▶ Maintain good eye contact and good posture.

▶ Shake hands firmly.

▶ Establish rapport and be cordial **without** being overly familiar.

▶ Be positive—convert negatives to positives.

▶ Remember that **first impressions are lasting impressions**.

### The Interview

▶ Be sure you supply all important information about yourself.

▶ Sell yourself—no one else will.

▶ Use correct grammar.

▶ **Don't** be afraid to say, "I don't know."

▶ Schedule the next interview or contact.

▶ Try to anticipate problem areas like inexperience or gaps in your job history.

▶ Be prepared to handle difficult questions, and know how to overcome objections.

▶ Keep your answers brief, 30 to 60 seconds.

▶ Ask your questions at an appropriate time.

▶ Find out when a decision will be made.

▶ Do **not** answer questions on age, religion, marital status or children **unless** you wish to.

### After the Interview

- ▶ Immediately document interviews in your placement file.
- ▶ Send thank you letters.
- ▶ Call to follow up.

# 13

# Successfully Handling The Job Interview

## Selling Yourself & Gathering the Information You Need

Not too long ago, another placement counselor told me about one **particularly unusual job interview**. The legal assistant candidate was interviewing with a law firm partner who apparently didn't like his new phone system. During the interview, a telephone transfer to him was botched. He became so angry that he ripped the phone jack out of the wall and threw the phone across the room! He repeated this performance with his secretary's phone, and then went back to the interview. The legal assistant applicant—showing great presence of mind—carried on as though nothing had happened. She now has an **excellent** senior legal assistant position with that firm.

In this chapter, I've tried to present just about every situation you can find yourself in during a job interview. However, each interview is unique. If the interviewer surprises you, don't get flustered. **Prepare, rehearse, and expect the unexpected.**

## STRUCTURE OF A TYPICAL INTERVIEW

A fairly well established pattern for job interviews, such as the structure set forth below, is usually followed. Nearly all interviews consist of the same components.

### Small Talk and Introduction

The interview will be **warmed up with small talk** about subjects like the weather, traffic, and finding the building. Always answer positively. Tell your interviewer that, "I love the rain," or "Your directions were perfect" (even if they weren't!). Comment on the firm's lovely offices or excellent view of the city. Do not challenge or disagree with a statement the interviewer makes. You want to impress, not antagonize the interviewer. The chat at the beginning of the interview should relax you and put both you and the interviewer at ease.

### Purpose of the Interview

The interviewer should tell you a little about the job and what should be accomplished during your time together. You can ask if you will be meeting other staff members or attorneys. Also ask about the general procedures for this interview. Is this a screening interview? Will you meet the attorneys or legal assistants with whom you might be working? Will you be expected to come back for more interviews?

### Background Information

At this point, the interviewer will explore the background information presented on your resumé. You will definitely be asked questions about your education and work experience. These questions might be presented as follows:

- ▶ Why did you choose the paralegal field?
- ▶ Why did you leave your last job?
- ▶ What skills do you have that relate to the position we are offering?

There are many other possible questions on this issue. See the list of "Questions You Might Be Asked," below.

*General Information*

You will be asked questions that test your ability to reason, your philosophy and your personality. These aspects are frequently tested by asking how you would handle a hypothetical situation. Topics will include your strengths and weaknesses. You might also be asked your opinions on various subjects, perhaps about a new U.S. Supreme Court nominee, or other current events topics.

*Your Questions*

Prepare and rehearse questions about the firm and the duties of the particular position. The more pertinent questions you ask, the more **thoughtful and prepared** you will appear. Even if all of your questions have been answered, try to think of something else. A list of appropriate questions you can ask the interviewer during the initial interview are also presented below.

**Never** ask about salary or benefits in the initial interview **unless** the interviewer brings up the subject. Salary negotiations generally take place at the end of the interview or during the second interview. Information about benefits (health insurance, vacation policy, etc.), is usually provided by the interviewer toward the end of the first interview. Don't be surprised if a second—or even third—interview is required. Most law firms conduct the interviewing process in stages, usually involving the attorneys at the final interview only.

*Closing*

Before leaving the interview, be sure you understand the details of the position. Don't drag out the interview, however. If you have further questions, ask them in your follow-up letter. Clarify when you should expect to hear back from the employer. Shake hands as a final closing, and **always** thank the interviewer for his or her time.

## QUESTIONS YOU MIGHT BE ASKED

This section is divided into eight sections for ease in picking out those questions that most affect you. During your preparation for the interview, you should make an honest assessment of yourself, frame your answer, and then rehearse it. It is a good idea to role play your answer, with a friend acting as the interviewer.

165

### Experience and Skills Interview Questions
1. How soon will it be before you can make a contribution to this firm?
2. What are the most important accomplishments thus far in your career?
3. How did you get along with your last supervisor?
4. Did you enjoy working for your last employer? Explain.
5. How will your major strengths help you in this job?
6. In what way do you feel you can make the biggest contribution to this firm?
7. Why are you leaving (or why have you left) your present company?
8. Does your present company know you are planning to leave?
9. What did you like best about your last job?
10. What qualifications do you have that make you successful in this field?
11. What is your experience?
12. If you could have made improvements in your last job, what would they have been?
13. Describe some emergencies in some of your jobs for which you had to arrange your time.
14. Tell me about the time when you had to make a decision quickly.
15. Tell me about the best supervisor you ever had. The worst.
16. Can you describe a typical day?
17. If you ran into a certain situation (make one up for rehearsal), how would you handle it?
18. How could you make your company be more successful?
19. What risks did you take in your last few jobs and what were the results of those risks?
20. What are your qualifications as a paralegal?
21. What does a paralegal do?
22. Why did you specialize in this particular area of law?
23. What are your computer skills?
24. Describe your last two positions.

### Behavior and Attitude Interview Questions
1. Which is more important to you, salary or the work itself?
2. Describe the best person who ever worked for or with you.
3. What do you think determines a person's progress in any firm?

4. What do you generally find to criticize in most people?
5. If you could tailor make a job for yourself, what elements would it include?
6. Have you ever thought about becoming an independent paralegal or starting your own company?
7. Describe a time when you were able to have a positive influence on others.

## Personality Interview Questions

1. Can you tell me something about yourself?
2. What magazines do you read?
3. Who in history do you most admire?
4. Do you work well under pressure?
5. Do you consider yourself a competitive person?
6. What hobbies do you enjoy?
7. What kind of books do you read and how much time do you spend reading?
8. What kinds of people attract you?
9. What kinds of people annoy you?
10. Who or what influenced you in your career?
11. How flexible are you?
12. If you were starting all over, what career would you enter?
13. How do you spend your spare time?
14. If you could go back to a place in history, where would it be?

## Education Interview Questions

1. Tell me about your education. Which courses do you like best?
2. Why did you major in _____ ?
3. What were your extracurricular activities in school?
4. How did you spend your summers while you were in college?
5. Do you think your school grades reflect your true abilities?
6. How did you happen to get into this field?
7. Why did you decide to go to this particular college?
8. Do you plan on finishing your bachelor's degree?
9. Why did you choose this particular paralegal school?
10. What did you study in your paralegal program?
11. Are you planning to go to law school? If yes, why? If no, why not?

### Personal Philosophy Interview Questions
1. Do you prefer working alone or with others?
2. What do you think are the most serious problems facing law firms today?
3. What motivates you?
4. What are your short-term goals?
5. What are your long-term goals?
6. What is your greatest strength?
7. What is your greatest weakness?
8. Are you creative? Give an example.
9. Are you analytical? Give an example.
10. How intuitive are you?
11. How do you handle conflict?
12. What is your philosophy of life?
13. Everyone has pet peeves. What are yours?

### Management Skills Interview Questions
1. Are you a good manager? Give an example.
2. How do you feel about an employee suing for injuries sustained while working?
3. Are you a leader? Give an example.
4. How do your subordinates get along with you?
5. Do you motivate people? How?
6. Why do you feel you have management potential?
7. How would you define leadership? Success?
8. How would you define supervision?
9. Do you manage your time well?
10. What is your philosophy for managing others?
11. Tell me about your experience managing others.
12. What do you like about managing?
13. Tell me about the people you have hired. How well did they work out?
14. Have you any experience in supervising?

*Compensation Interview Questions*
1. What do you feel this position should pay?
2. What was your previous salary?
3. What is your current salary?
4. What salary are you worth?
5. How much would you like to be earning in five years?

*General Interview and Career Questions*
1. What sort of job would you really like?
2. How can you justify our hiring you?
3. Why have you changed jobs frequently?
4. Are you willing to relocate?
5. How long would you stay with us?
6. What are you looking for in a job?
7. Why do you want to work for us? This job?
8. Why did you want to interview with this firm?
9. What do you know about this firm?
10. What is the most interesting part of your career?
11. What are the disadvantages associated with the paralegal career?
12. How would you like our firm to assist you if you join us?
13. Can you take instructions without becoming upset?
14. Are you considering any other positions at this time?
15. What kind of references will your previous employer give about you?
16. Can you work overtime? Travel?
17. If you could have any position in this firm, what would it be?
18. With your background, we believe you are over/under qualified for this position.
19. Does your employer know you are planning to leave?
20. Have you ever been fired from any job?
21. Why have you been unemployed so long?
22. Why do you have gaps in your resumé?
23. Why has it taken you so long to find a job?

## HANDLING INAPPROPRIATE QUESTIONS

The interviewer may ask inappropriate questions or questions that you are **not** required to answer. In fact, asking **some types of questions violates federal and state laws** against discrimination. If you are prepared ahead of time for this possibility, you can **refuse to answer gracefully**. Such questions may deal with your age, marital status, family planning, or something else which has no relevance to your ability to work effectively.

**Most interviewers are aware that these questions are inappropriate** and will **not** ask them at all. Even if the questions are asked, the interviewer will most likely refrain from pursuing the matter if you indicate that you are not willing to answer. For example, if you are asked whether your home life will prevent you from working long hours, a good answer is: "Everything in my home life is supportive of my career efforts." **Nothing else need be said**.

### *Sensitive Areas of Preemployment Inquiry*

Title VII of the Civil Rights Act is a comprehensive, anti-discrimination federal law enacted in 1964. This law **prohibits preemployment inquiries which either directly or indirectly solicit information which may be used for discriminatory purposes**. Some states also prohibit inquiries on job application forms concerning race, color, religion, sex or national origin **unless** that employer is seeking such information in order to implement affirmative action programs.

---

**HOT TIP:** If you are asked an inappropriate question, and choose to answer (even though you are **not** required to do so), you should look beyond the question itself to **determine what the interviewer is really asking**. If you are asked a question about your age, you may respond: "If what you are asking is do I have the required energy necessary for this type of position, the answer is yes."

---

Employers may **not**, and should not, ask candidates questions about the following topics:

▶ **Age**

Any inquiry suggesting a preference for persons under forty years of age.

▶ **Arrest**

Any inquiries relating to arrests not accompanied by a conviction.

▶ **Citizenship**

Any inquiry about citizenship status must be limited to requirements for completing the Federal I-9 citizenship verification form.

▶ **Convictions**

Questions about possible convictions seeking to solicit information not related to fitness to perform a particular job. Note, however, that questions related **solely** to convictions or prison releases within seven years of the date of the job application, are **not** prohibited.

▶ **Family**

Questions tailored to specifically elicit information about your spouse, spouse's employment or salary, children or child care arrangements and whether you have any other dependents.

▶ **Handicaps**

Inquiries which are so general that they would reveal handicaps or health conditions not related directly to the applicant's fitness to perform the job.

▶ **Height/Weight**

Questions not based on actual job requirements.

▶ **Marital Status**

Anything related to an applicant's marital status. This includes checklists that ask applicants to check a category: Mr./Mrs./Miss/Ms.

▶ **Military Service**

Inquiries asking about discharge or request for discharge papers.

▶ **Name**

Questions about a name or its origin that, if answered, would divulge marital status, lineage, ancestry, national origin or religion.

▶ **Nationality**

Questions relating to lineage, ancestry, national origin, descent, birthplace, mother tongue, or any similar inquiries about your spouse.

▶ **Organizations**

Any requirement that an applicant list all memberships in organizations, clubs, societies or similar groups.

▶ **Photographs**

Any request for your photo prior to hiring.

▶ **Pregnancy**

Inquiries regarding pregnancy, medical history or family planning issues.

▶ **Race**

Questions regarding race or skin color.

▶ **Relatives**

Any inquiries about names and addresses of relatives that might reveal discriminatory information.

▶ **Religion**

Questions about religious choices including holidays.

▶ **Residence**

Any inquiry about names or relationships of persons with whom the applicant resides, or any questions about home ownership.

▶ **Sex**

Any question regarding sex or gender.

## HOW TO ANSWER DIFFICULT QUESTIONS

The following difficult questions may be asked by the interviewer. I've listed some suggested answers and hints of **what not to say**.

1. I see you haven't worked in a while. Why is that?
   a. I was continuing my education and will receive my degree/certificate in a few months/soon.
   b. I took some personal time that does not relate to my paralegal work.
   c. I have been working in another field, but I would like to get back into the legal field.
   d. I realize I have not worked in a while. However, as you can see from my resumé, I have been taking continuing education courses to hone my legal skills.
   e. **Wrong answer**: I was so stressed out from my last job, I wanted to recuperate.

2. You do not have any legal background, so tell me why should I hire you?
   a. My background lends itself nicely to this entry-level position. My organizational skills and attention to detail are excellent.
   b. You will notice that in my previous positions, I organized documents, reviewed contracts and/or did the corporate minutes (list whatever skills you possess which are applicable). All these skills, I believe, are transferrable to the paralegal field.
   c. **Wrong answer**: I do have legal background. I organized my own divorce/criminal/traffic court trial.

3. This position requires a little more experience than you have.
   a. If you will notice my years of business experience, I believe that translates to the experience level you are seeking.
   b. Because of my excellent legal education and internship, I know I can handle the position.
   c. **Wrong answer**: Can you explain, then, why you called me for an interview?

4. Why don't you have any computer skills?
   a. I am currently taking a WordPerfect course at the local college.
   b. In two weeks, my paralegal school will offer a course in litigation support. I plan to take it.
   c. I am working hard on my computer at home.
   d. **Wrong answer**: I do not and will not type.

5. Your specialty is in corporate law. This is more of a real estate position.
   a. Corporate and real estate are very similar at the entry level. I have learned about corporate acquisitions that utilize similar skills, namely UCC searches and dealing with banks and other outside associations.
   b. I am very interested the real estate field, as well as corporate.
   c. **Wrong answer**: My resumé doesn't indicate that I have real estate experience.

6. Your grades are not really good enough for this firm.
   a. If you will notice, I did exceptionally well in paralegal school.
   b. I realize that my undergraduate grades were not exceptional because I: 1) had a family crisis during my senior year, 2) worked full time while going to school, 3) supported a family while attending college. (Fill in the appropriate reason, but stick with the truth.)
   c. You are entirely correct. However, you will notice that I have excelled in my work history.
   d. **Wrong answer**: Well, my college was a party school. I goofed off my last year in college.

7. We cannot train you. Will that be a problem?
   a. Because I belong to the local paralegal organization, I have a vast resource of qualified paralegals who will be happy to answer questions I may have.
   b. I learn very quickly, and see no problems with that.
   c. **Wrong answer**: Yes, I don't know how I can be expected to learn the job without training.

8. You do not have a B.A., certificate, a paralegal certificate from an ABA-approved school, etc.

   a.  My lack of education has been made up through my work experience.

   b.  I realize that my certificate is not from an ABA-approved school, which is a hiring requirement of this firm. However, I feel I went through a very substantial program, and I learned what to do on the job. I am confident my performance will be excellent.

   c.  **Wrong answer:** I really don't feel I need the extra education. I've gotten this far.

9. This is not a legal secretarial position.

   a.  I am making the transition to paralegal and feel my extensive background in litigation qualifies me for this position.

   b.  I realize that my previous experience as a legal secretary is not necessary for this position, but my five years' work in real estate has provided me with a truly hands-on view of the practice.

   c.  **Wrong answer:** Great, I don't want to type anymore.

10. Why were you fired?

   a.  Economic conditions were not very good at the time, so unfortunately I was let go.

   b.  I did have a problem with one of the attorneys, although the remainder of the staff was great and will give me excellent references.

   c.  **Wrong answer:** It was the worst place in the world to work. It's really a revolving door over there.

11. Why have you changed jobs so often?
    a. My previous positions were problematic because:
       1) the firm/company folded/relocated/dissolved my particular division.
       2) financial constraints made it necessary to seek higher compensation.
       3) I reached the highest level I could achieve within that company/firm.
       4) I underestimated the commute time.
       5) I am now trying to increase my responsibilities.
    b. **Wrong answer:** Personality conflicts with my supervisors; I was never happy.

12. Why are your earnings so low?
    a. I was hired at a low salary so that I could gain the necessary experience to do a great job.
    b. Now that I have this experience, I am worth and expect more.
    c. **Wrong answer:** My employers were really cheap.

13. Why have you been looking for a job for so long?
    a. I am very selective. I want to stay at my next position for a very long time.
    b. I am looking for exactly the right opportunity.
    c. **Wrong answer:** I have three job offers right now. I am trying to see who offers the most.

## QUESTIONS TO ASK THE INTERVIEWER

During the interview, you should ask some of the following questions **tactfully and at the appropriate time.** Some of these questions might be omitted or reserved for the final interview, depending on the circumstances. Note that this list does **not** include questions regarding salary. This topic is covered thoroughly in **Chapter 14**, "Getting Paid What You're Worth."

### Questions About Job Duties
1. Will I be expected to travel?
2. Will I have an expense account?
3. Will I be required to perform any clerical or secretarial duties?
4. Will I be expected to travel locally on court runs or other errands? If so, will I use my own car? Will I be reimbursed for gas and/or mileage?
5. Will I be required to do any kind of investigative work?
6. Will I be expected to relocate?
7. Am I replacing a paralegal or is this a newly created position?
8. Why is this position open?
9. What characteristics do you most desire in the person who will fill this position?
10. Would you describe the job duties for me?
11. What do you consider the ideal experience for this job?
12. I have read about this firm's involvement with (fill in the appropriate information). Will I have a chance to work on that case/deal/matter?
13. What types of cases will I be working on?
14. To whom will I be reporting? Who is in charge of giving me work?
15. What are the negatives about this job? The positives?
16. Will I have my own computer?

### Questions About Firm Structure
1. Which attorneys will I be working for?
2. How often are performance reviews given?
3. Will I have my own secretary or will I share with others?
4. What type of office will I have?
5. Will I work closely with any other paralegals?
6. What opportunities for advancement does the firm offer?
7. How many paralegals does the firm or company employ?
8. Have the attorneys for whom you're hiring a legal assistant previously worked with paralegals?
9. What do you consider the largest single problem facing your staff today?
10. Could you tell me a bit about the other attorneys and paralegals with whom I would work?

11. I understand that your firm specializes in _____ law. How does this position relate to that specialty?

12. Why do you like working for this firm/company? What don't you like?

13. Could you give me a rundown of the firm's hierarchy?

## Questions About the Paralegal Program

1. Do you have a structured paralegal program?

2. Will I be expected to obtain additional education and/or training?

3. Will I be trained on the job?

4. Is there a paralegal career path? What are the perquisites accorded to a senior legal assistant?

5. Does the firm require a specific minimum number of billable hours? How many?

6. What is the average tenure of your paralegals? What is the turnover rate?

7. What exactly would I be expected to accomplish in the next two years?

8. Where can I expect to be with regard to this firm next year?

## Questions About Benefits

1. What will be my regular work hours?

2. What benefits are offered by the company?

3. What holidays does the firm provide?

4. What vacation time is available?

5. Will the firm pay for continuing education?

6. Does the firm pay for professional organizations?

7. Will paid parking be provided?

## Questions You Should NOT Ask at the FIRST Interview

1. Will I have to work much overtime?

2. What happened to the person who had this job before me? (It is **okay** to ask why is this position available.)

3. What are the office politics like here?

4. What is the salary?

5. Do you pay overtime?

6. What kind of bonuses do you offer?

## TIPS FOR THE SECOND (AND THIRD) INTERVIEW

If you are called back for a second interview, chances are that the firm is **seriously considering making you an offer,** or at least narrowing the scope of possible candidates. You should approach this next stage as not only another chance to sell yourself, but also to determine **whether,** if you are offered the job, **you want to work at this particular firm.**

### *Meeting the Lawyers*

Most lawyers for whom you will be working will want to meet and talk with you. Since paralegals usually work for more than one attorney, a third interview may also be necessary to schedule meetings with all the attorneys. **Ask to meet everyone with whom you will be working,** including the elusive senior partner.

For the second (or third) interview, **draft and rehearse additional, more substantive questions** to ask the lawyer(s). Concentrate several of these questions in your area of law. For example, you may want to ask how a certain procedure in litigation is handled at that firm. You should also put your research on the firm to work, asking questions about articles concerning the firm that you may have read.

---

**HOT TIP:** Don't take out your list of questions during the interview; memorize them instead. Also, don't start taking voluminous notes. This can appear threatening to a lawyer or other members of the firm.

---

**How the lawyer responds** to your questions is as important as the content of the responses. Believe me, **you don't want to end up working for an ogre.** How can you tell in advance if the attorney you're meeting for the first time will be tough to work for? The best advice I can give you is to **ask this person to describe his or her approach to working with legal assistants.** You'll be able to glean good clues from the answers offered. For example, descriptions such as "I give a person one chance and one chance only," "I don't like a lot of questions," or "I tell a person once what I want and expect them to get it," are dead giveaways that this person will not be easy to work with. **Don't be shy.** You are entitled to know about this person's working persona, **before you accept the job offer.**

179

## Meeting the Paralegals

Try to meet as many paralegals as possible. At your second interview, you may be questioned by the senior paralegal in the department of the firm considering your employment. Be sure to **clarify the relationship**. This person may become your immediate supervisor. The "chemistry" you establish with the senior paralegal is important to your success in first getting the offer and later on the job.

Also ask if you can meet other legal assistants in the department to **discuss what they do and how they like their jobs**. **Don't** suggest that you want to grill them about the firm. Suggest a social setting such as a lunch meeting. If the firm will not arrange a meeting with the legal assistants at the firm, try to get in touch with these people through your network. Your local paralegal association's membership book will identify the firm or company of each member. Accepting a job is a serious decision and it merits the time you take checking into it.

## Touring the Firm's Offices

Request a tour of the office. See where **your office** will be located in the firm. It may be important to you to have a window office. If the firm only provides carrels, or has legal assistants share offices, this will be a problem. If you are shown the firm's **law library**, look around to see the level of resources offered.

You should meet your **prospective secretary**, since this is crucial professional relationship. The legal team is composed of the lawyer, legal assistant and legal secretary, not necessarily in order of real importance. Also ask to meet the **word processing support staff** if it will be someone other than your secretary.

Find out what **technical tools** you will have. The firm **may have the latest computer equipment and resources or be lagging behind** in developing this area. A variety of technical support tools may be necessary, depending on your area of law. If you specialize in litigation, does the firm have in place a good document search and retrieval database system? If you'll be working in real estate or probate law, will you have document assembly software to assist with drafting? If necessary, you should review the computer courses you've taken in order to prepare pertinent questions around this issue.

### The Firm's Personality and Culture

While you're in the lobby, try to get a "feeling" about the firm. **Each law firm and company has its own personality, its own culture.** Does it meet your professional expectations? What messages do the furnishings, art and decorations send about how the firm views itself? Is the atmosphere highly formal or more approachable? Are the people you've met and seen during your visit friendly, formal or hostile with each other?

The **reception lobby of a law firm** is sometimes thought to be an indicator of the personality of the firm. For example, a dark panelled lobby with English antiques and oriental rugs could indicate that the firm is very conservative. A high-tech lobby with splashy modern art or a neo-classic look could indicate the firm has a progressive or forward-thinking attitude. However, generalizations do not always hold true. One candidate of mine talks about how she almost didn't go through with an interview when she came through the doors of one firm:

> The lobby was panelled in dark mahogany, and decorated with those English hunting prints, rich oriental carpets and antiques. While it was quite impressive, my first thought was, "Oh, no, this is going to be one of those **really stuffy** firms." For once, appearances were deceiving. The firm turned out to be very modern, open minded and liberal, with many fast-track and entertainment clients. I'm glad I took the time to find out what the firm was really like.

Pay attention to other clues. How prosperous does the firm feel? Do the phones ring often? Is there a busy hum in the office? Does this firm fit with your personality? Do you feel comfortable? **Go with your feelings**. If something feels wrong about the place, respect your intuition and think twice before you accept an offer.

## INTERVIEW EVALUATION FORM

Because there are so many issues to consider in making a decision to accept a job offer, you should make notes after each interview about all the positives and negatives of the firm and the position available. The Interview Evaluation Form which follows gives you the structure to record these notes. It also provides a checklist of questions you should consider in making your decision.

## INTERVIEW EVALUATION FORM

FIRM/COMPANY: _____

ADDRESS: _____

DATE OF INTERVIEW: _____

INTERVIEWED WITH: _____

Title:_____

_____

Title:_____

POSITION: _____

1. **My initial reaction was:**

   ___ Very excited     ___ Seems appealing     ___ Not for me
   ___ Need more info     ___ Not sure

2. **I met with the supervising attorney:**

   ___ Yes     ___ No

3. **I felt:**
   ___ Very good     ___ Intimidated
   ___ This is not the person with whom I will be working.

4. **The firm seems to have training for entry-level paralegals:**
   ___ Yes     ___ No     ___ Unclear

5. **This job has a career path that:**
   ___ Is exactly what I want          ___ May meet my goals
   ___ Will take one or two more steps
   ___ Not sure                        ___ Will not meet my needs

6. **I met with the other paralegals who:**
   ___ Seemed helpful                  ___ Seemed happy
   ___ Were not informative            ___ Did not meet with

7. **The salary is what I am seeking:**
   ___ Yes                             ___ No

8. **The salary is not within my range, however, the firm offers other advantages:**
   ___ Yes                             ___ No
   ___ Not important                   ___ Not clear

9. **The perks and benefits were explained. I am excited by what is offered:**
   ___ Yes                             ___ No
   ___ Not important                   ___ Not clear

10. **I need another interview to clarify:**
    ___ Career path                    ___ Salary
    ___ Benefits                       ___ Job responsibilities
    ___ Colleagues                     ___ Reporting structure
    ___ Environment                    ___ Continuing education
    ___ Working conditions             ___ Other: _____

11. **Areas to negotiate:**
    ___ Salary                         ___ Benefits
    ___ Title                          ___ Continuing education
    ___ Responsibilities               ___ Bonus
    ___ Office                         ___ Career path
    ___ Start date                     ___ Other: _____

12. **This position offers potential because:**

_____

_____

_____

13. **The drawbacks of this position are:**

_____

_____

_____

14. **In one year, I see myself doing:**

_____

_____

_____

15. **I have discussed this position with my network, colleagues, mentor or board of advisors:**

_____ Yes                      _____ No

16. **I would like to pursue this position:**

_____ Yes                      _____ No                      _____ Thinking about

## REVIEW OF INTERVIEW DOS AND DON'TS

*Do*:
- ▶ Dress conservatively, neatly and carefully.
- ▶ Plan to arrive at least ten minutes early.
- ▶ Announce yourself properly to the receptionist or secretary by stating your name and the name of the person you will be seeing.
- ▶ Complete application forms neatly, completely and quickly.
- ▶ Have a good, firm handshake.
- ▶ Sit up straight.
- ▶ Look the interviewer in the eye.
- ▶ Make sure the interviewer knows your name, how to pronounce it, and the job you are applying for.
- ▶ Ask if the interviewer has your resumé. If not, supply another copy.
- ▶ Use positive responses to break the ice.
- ▶ Be prepared to overcome negative responses.
- ▶ Be prepared to answer typical questions.
- ▶ Be positive and assertive.
- ▶ Conduct yourself as if you are determined to get the job.
- ▶ Ask for the next interview.

*Do Not*:
- ▶ Wear heavy makeup, exaggerated hair or clothing styles, or strong cologne.
- ▶ Be late; there is **no** excuse for this.
- ▶ Drink coffee or eat anything. Politely refuse if it is offered.
- ▶ Chew gum.
- ▶ Smoke, even if you are offered a cigarette.
- ▶ Be overly aggressive, boastful, flippant or boisterous.
- ▶ Be meek and mild.
- ▶ Be negative about your previous or present employer.
- ▶ Answer only with a "yes" or "no."
- ▶ Be a "motor mouth."
- ▶ Use incorrect English or offensive language.
- ▶ Ask about salary, vacation or retirement **until** interviewer signals it is all right to do so.

▶ Attempt to prolong the interview when the interviewer stops.
▶ Start adding new thoughts or qualifications as you are walking toward the door.

# 14

# Getting Paid What You're Worth

**Salary Negotiation Strategies**

Here's the **exciting part**—negotiating for your salary. This can be one of the most difficult segments of your job search **only if** you are unprepared. The good news about entry-level paralegal positions is that, at this writing, **starting salaries** are anywhere from $16,000 to $25,000 per year, depending on type of firm, region of the country, specialty and your work history. The bad news for career changers is that it is possible that, initially, you may have to take a cut in pay. However, remember that in this field, you are generally recognized as a "senior" at about the five-year experience level. Many **senior legal assistants make well over $40,000 per year**. Some paralegals with management responsibilities or high-level specialties **earn between $60,000 and $70,000 annually**.

Law firms are known for increasing starting salaries at a very rapid pace, particularly in the early stages of your career. This is because **the steep learning curve is recognized and rewarded**. In addition, law firms have historically compensated legal assistants well above cost of living increases. However, in recessionary times, this practice has changed. More than likely, the trend will revert to its former path, although perhaps not at the same pace.

## WHERE TO FIND OUT HOW MUCH YOU WILL EARN

Your homework for starting salaries starts with your local paralegal association which will be happy to tell you about prevailing salary levels in your area. Most state and local paralegal associations **conduct salary surveys** that are made available to members. The National Federation for Paralegal Associations (NFPA), the National Association for Legal Assistants (NALA), and *Legal Assistant Today* magazine all conduct periodic national surveys.

Bear in mind, however, that some national salary surveys **do not** break down the information gathered by **region of the country**. Looking at just national averages can give you a skewed picture of prevailing regional averages. For instance, if most of the national survey's respondents work in large cities, you will ordinarily find a higher salary average than normally prevails in smaller towns. To obtain the most accurate picture, **you should also spend time reviewing both regional and local surveys**.

Most surveys are generally broken down by **experience level** and **area of law**. That is, in some surveys, you can find information on what a corporate paralegal with two to five years' experience is ordinarily paid. In addition to salary, overtime and bonuses, other compensation issues like fringe benefits are addressed as well.

## WHEN TO DISCUSS SALARY

The discussion of salary is generally timed by an experienced interviewer to occur at the end of the first interview or sometime during the second interview. **Allow the interviewer to bring up the subject first**. Be careful not to jump the gun. Your positioning is to appear as interested in the work, level of assignments, firm or corporation as possible. Your **emphasis should be on how your skills, abilities and determination to succeed in this environment will benefit the firm**. If you appear too anxious to discuss salary or benefits, you could come across—to paraphrase John F. Kennedy—as more interested in what the firm can do for you, rather than what you can do for the firm.

## HOW TO NEGOTIATE

Law firms are populated with master negotiators. Attorneys spend years in law school learning the latest techniques. Non-attorney staff members also learn to be just as sharp simply by being part of the environment. If you haven't had previous negotiating experience, **you can still play this game skillfully** by understanding your "opponent" and knowing:

- ▶ what you want;
- ▶ what you will settle for;
- ▶ what the potential of the job is;
- ▶ the history of the firm regarding its use of paralegals;
- ▶ who you are negotiating with and what kind of power he or she has to get you what you want;
- ▶ if the firm pays a year-end bonus;
- ▶ when the next raises are scheduled;
- ▶ whether the firm pays overtime.

The overtime issue is **critical to your negotiations**. You can easily earn an extra $2,000 to $10,000 per year in overtime **alone**. On the other hand, if the firm is known for generous end-of-year bonus payments, this might outweigh getting paid overtime.

Skilled interviewers will **place the ball in your court** by asking you first, "What kind of salary are you looking for?" By conducting your pre-negotiating research, you will already have a general idea about what firms in your area are paying for entry-level paralegals. There is a natural tendency to throw the ball back in the interviewer's court by asking, "What does the position pay?" Some interviewers will respond to your question. But others will indicate that your response is required first.

Let's say that you have conducted your research and determined that a good starting salary in your region is between $22,000 and $24,00 per year. Now is the time to tap into your paralegal network, school or placement agency to gain **inside information**. You must first determine whether:

- this level of starting salary holds true for the firm/corporation with whom you are interviewing;
- you can accept this salary;
- you can be flexible in the exact amount of dollars you will accept;
- you can gain more dollars than the "norm" due to your transferable skills.

You can answer the question, "What kind of salary are you looking for?" in several ways. Some good responses are:

- I am looking to be paid at market rate.
- My salary requirements are in the mid-20's.
- My salary range is $23,000 to $26,000 per year.
- I understand the going rate for paralegals at this level of experience is $___.

If you choose to respond with a salary range **be aware that stating a range gives the interviewer permission to offer you the lower salary**. It is unlikely that an employer will offer the higher end of the range because you have already stated that the lower amount is acceptable to you. It is therefore a good idea to raise the lowest amount to the salary you really want. If you are really looking for $24,000 per year, then indicate that your salary range is $24,000 to $26,000 annually, **not** $22,000 to $24,000. **Never** set a specific dollar amount because you then leave no room for negotiation.

You may be asked about the **amount of your present salary**. If you are changing careers, your current salary may be higher than the salary an entry-level paralegal normally makes. There are several answers you may give to the "present salary" question:

- I know that I have to take a cut in salary to begin my new career. However, working for your firm is exactly what I would like. Therefore my salary range would be between $ _____ and _____.

- I realize that my current salary is higher than what an entry-level paralegal may expect but with my background in _____, I feel that I should be worth $ ___ to your firm.

If you are a career-changer whose present career ties in specifically with this paralegal position, you may say:

▶ My current salary as an R.N. is $35,000 per year. Given that the medical malpractice position you are offering utilizes most of my current skills, I would be willing to make a lateral move at that salary.

If your current salary is lower than the norm, do **not** pad it. Your interviewer can easily check on the amount. Just mention that you are being paid below market value and you expect $ _____, which is what entry-level paralegals are being paid. **Quote the most recent survey by name.** Law firms are used to documentation and should not be offended when you substantiate your information.

## IF THE OFFER IS LESS THAN YOU EXPECTED

If the offer is less than you expected **go ahead and negotiate!** Do not be intimidated. Lawyers love to argue. It's what they do best! Some **effective answers** to lower-than-expected salary offers are:

▶ I am worth more because of my education and prior experience.
▶ The current salary survey states that entry-level paralegals make $ _____.
▶ My _____ background relates to the paralegal field. It will not cost the firm as much to train me.

### Negotiate for Perquisites

You can also negotiate further benefits and perquisites (or "perks") which can translate into more dollars. In attempting to do doing so, you **must sell the interviewer on the value to the firm** of bestowing these items upon you. Some of these perks, and their selling points, include the following items.

### Continuing education

By granting you a continuing education allowance, the firm will gain a more valuable employee who can more quickly learn the position. You can even offer a cost-cutting benefit! When you return to the firm, you can educate other paralegals about what you learned, saving the firm the cost of sending everyone.

### Law or Graduate School Tuition

Some firms will grant paralegals law school or graduate school tuition if the paralegal will agree to stay on at the firm utilizing the education for an extended period of time. For example, once the paralegal has passed the bar exam, he or she will agree to stay with the firm at least two to three years as an associate. Firms that have paid for undergraduate or graduate degrees obtain similar commitments for positions such as specialty paralegals. One firm I know of paid for a portion of a paralegal's Masters of Business Administration degree and then asked that person to stay on as the Director of Administration.

### Early Salary Review

If you feel that you really want the job but the salary is just too low, you may ask for a **salary review in three to six months after date of hire**, instead of the usual one year. Of course, you must earn that raise—just having your salary reviewed at this time does **not** mean you will automatically be given a raise if your performance does not yet warrant one. But, if you "knock their socks off," you can gain a substantial increase like a litigation legal assistant I know. On my advice, she'd negotiated for an early salary review, and, at the end of her first six months with the law firm, she was given a 16% increase over her starting salary!

Be sure to ask for a **salary review and not a performance review**. A performance review may just get you a "You're doing great" pat on the back with no increase in salary. You may also request the promise of a salary review in writing keeping in mind that law firm management personnel does change. A new person may not honor your request.

### Bonuses

You can also use **exempt status** (no overtime pay) and a bonus as negotiation issues. Find out if the firm gives legal assistants bonuses at the end of the fiscal year. If the firm does not have an established paralegal policy or you will be the only paralegal, you **may be able to negotiate a bonus for yourself**. I know of a legal assistant who successfully negotiated a six-month review bonus for herself, in lieu of a salary review at that time.

### Hiring Bonus

A hiring bonus is **often used to attract associates**. This is a one-time bonus given at hiring. If you have heard the objection, "this is the maximum our budget will allow," and you are bringing an extra-special talent to this position, the firm **may** be willing to give you this one-time bonus. The benefit to the firm is that, amortized over a one year period, a hiring bonus is a minuscule amount of money. The firm can also probably pull it from a different part of the budget, thus keeping within its compensation guidelines for paralegals.

### Association Dues

Many firms do not hesitate when asked to pay the dues for their professional staff. It's worth asking for, and will indeed be a benefit for you.


## OVERCOMING OBJECTIONS

Objections to hiring you are bound to occur. **Don't let it throw you**. Objections will most likely be raised regarding your lack of legal expertise, salary expectations, or that your previous work experience does not relate to the job for which you are applying. Some effective key phrases you can use to counter these objections follow.

- ▶ "Let's look at a different perspective to that."
- ▶ "One alternate solution may be . . . ."
- ▶ "It's certainly understandable how you have reached that conclusion. A different interpretation of that data may be . . . ."
- ▶ "I am open to any suggestions you may have to overcome that problem."

Whatever phrasing you choose to use, **do not issue ultimatums**. If you do so, you will immediately be designated as an adversary. You want your approach to be that of a **team player**, a quality that law firms in particular seek for people filling paralegal positions.

## IF YOU ARE USING A PLACEMENT AGENCY TO NEGOTIATE FOR YOU

If you are using a good agency, the representative should be able to negotiate the best possible compensation package for you. Your **agency should be aware** of starting salaries, and they will know the hiring practices, benefits, times of raises, continuing education policies, and history of the firm's utilization of paralegals. However, even if the representative has explained all this to you, it is in your best interest to learn this information during your own job interviews. A skilled recruiter will relay all offers to you and let you know if he or she believes the firm will offer a higher salary. It's entirely up to you to accept or reject the offer. Recruiters can only relay your specific instructions to the prospective employer; they **cannot** decide for you.

## WHAT YOU SHOULDN'T USE AS NEGOTIATING TECHNIQUES

The **fastest way to terminate a salary negotiation session** is to appeal to the emotions of the interviewer. Anything that does not have anything to do with what you will actually do on the job is **not** relevant and **not** negotiable. Here are some sure-fire ways to make sure the salary negotiations end **unfavorably** to you.

- ▶ "I cannot live on this amount."
- ▶ "My friend got $ _____ and that is what I want."
- ▶ "I want more money because I have to travel farther to get here."
- ▶ "Whatever you give me is fine."
- ▶ "I'm a little older than most of the people here and therefore am worth more."
- ▶ "I have two children at home and need more."
- ▶ "I have a better office where I am now."
- ▶ "Parking is more here."
- ▶ "I need to buy new clothes to work here."
- ▶ "I want more because I just feel that I'll do a better job than anyone else."

Believe me, a law firm does **not** care what salary you can live on. They are more concerned with their bottom line. Citing a friend's salary is not quoting an official source of information. It's much **harder for the firm to argue your worth when you have a salary survey in hand.**

## DEADLINES FOR NEGOTIATION

According to Herb Cohen, author of *You Can Negotiate Anything*, conclusions to negotiations will occur as close to the deadline as possible. Therefore, you must **establish a date for resolution** of the issue. Ask the interviewer when the firm will be making a decision. Don't hesitate to call the firm on that date to find out how the decision-making process is proceeding. Ask if you can offer any further information about yourself or if anyone at the firm would like to see you again.

If the firm tells you that the decision is between you and one or two other candidates, let them know that you would appreciate knowing by a certain date, as you have other offers to consider. **Don't**, however, push yourself out the door by being overbearing or insisting that the firm react to your deadlines. **Be flexible and accommodating.** Many firms make decisions on a committee basis, which is not always a quick process.

## TAKE AN ACTIVE ROLE

Take an active role in the negotiations over your salary. You are entering a field whose members make their living through the negotiation process. Practice negotiating with a friend so that you sound confident and self-assured, even if in reality you are very nervous. **Stay realistic with your salary expectations** and above all, have fun with this process!

# 15

# Wrapping Things Up

**The Importance of Interview Notes & Follow-Up Letters**

## EVALUATING THE INTERVIEW

Evaluating your interviews will **assist you in making a decision** about whether or not to accept a job. It will also help you to recognize ways you can improve future interviews.

Make notes **immediately** after each interview. Your notes **should be specific**, containing information about the organization of the firm or company, description of job responsibilities, paralegal program structure, career growth opportunities, and benefits and compensation plan. List the clerical and technical support that will be available to you. Also include your impression of the firm culture, working environment and physical facilities. Refer to **Chapter 13** for the "Interview Evaluation Form." This form should help you organize your thoughts and impressions.

File your notes in your placement file for future reference. They will refresh your memory if you are participating in numerous interviews. If you receive more than one job offer, your notes will be invaluable in helping you choose a firm, because you will have already considered most of the important issues.

Once you have accepted a position, you are in! Congratulations! Your hard work and patience have paid off. **Do not throw away your placement file,** however. Your interview evaluation notes will be helpful if you decide to seek another position a few years down the road.


## THANK YOU LETTERS ARE OPPORTUNITIES FOR MARKETING

After an interview, write a thank you letter to everyone who interviewed you. This letter **reminds the employer who you are** and can serve as **another writing sample.** It can also be used to furnish references or any other information that may have been forgotten or requested during your interviews. This letter is your **last effort to sell yourself.**

> **HOT TIP:** Always try to tie in something that was discussed in the interview with how your skills fit in. This is generally accomplished in the second paragraph. (See Sample Letter 15.2, following.)

The letter should be professional in tone, and typewritten on stationery that matches your resumé. Even if you have been asked to address the person who interviewed you by his or her first name, it is wise to use full names in any correspondence. Call the receptionist for information if you are unsure of the spelling or title of anyone with whom you interviewed.

The letter lets the employer know that **you want the position** and **encourages the firm to seriously consider you.** It is also quite appropriate to make a follow-up telephone call a week or so after you've mailed your thank you letters if you are interested in a position and have not yet been contacted. Remember that law firms are somewhat slower to make hiring decisions that other organizations, so it may take some time before you hear the final results.

Several sample thank you letters follow. Be sure to spell names correctly, use the right title, and remember, this is a marketing opportunity!

## Sample Thank You Letter

123 North Main Street
Anytown, RI 33321


June 4, 199_

Larry Lawyer, Esq.
Law & Law
111 Elm Street
Anytown, RI 33321

Dear Mr. Lawyer:

Thank you for meeting with me last week. The interview and tour of your offices were most informative. I remain very interested in joining Law & Law.

I would also like to emphasize that my experience as a teacher has helped me to develop skills that transfer well to paralegal work, such as writing and supervising.

If there is anything further you need from me in order for your recruitment committee to reach a decision, please let me know. I would be more than willing to meet with you again. Please feel free to contact me at my home phone number, listed below.

Sincerely,


Sally Teacher
(232) 555-5555


Illustration 15.1

## Sample Thank You Letter

July 12, 199_

Lee Kramer, Esq.
Kramer, Cramer & Chramer
2333 Main Street
Anytown, U.S.A. 15689

Dear Ms. Kramer:

Thank you for an enlightening interview yesterday regarding the paralegal position with your firm. I was very impressed by everyone I met.

The new law regarding products liability for automobile seat belts is a hot issue in the state legislature. I understand your firm's concern regarding such cases. As we discussed, my background as a researcher fits in nicely with the new cases your firm is handling.

I look forward to hearing from you soon regarding this position. I would appreciate the opportunity to demonstrate my abilities at Kramer, Cramer & Chramer.

Sincerely,


Andrea Schwartz

Illustration 15.2

## Not Interested Sample Letter

123 Any Street
Anytown, CA 95432

June 14, 199__

Joe Lawyer, Esq.
Lawyer & Lawyer
345 Main Street
Anytown, CA  95432

Dear Mr. Lawyer:

Thank you for taking the time to meet with me on June 1st.  I thoroughly enjoyed speaking with you and your colleagues at Lawyer & Lawyer.

Your presentation of the litigation position was exciting; however, **[choose one of the following phrases that fits or make up your own]**:

1) I have decided to accept another position.
2) I am really trying to land a corporate paralegal position.
3) The hour-and-a-half hour commute to your office's location unfortunately prevents me from accepting an offer at this time.

I appreciate your time and thank you again for the opportunity to meet with you.

Sincerely,

Polly Paralegal
(444) 444-4444

## Illustration 15.3

**HOT TIP**: You may be in a situation of interviewing for a position, which for various reasons, you are not interested in at this time. Write a follow-up letter to the employer stating why you are not interested. This can **leave a favorable impression** with the interviewer, who is potentially a valuable contact for other positions in the future. (See Sample Letter 15.3.)

# 16

# Congratulations! You're Hired

It's your first day on the job and you're excited. You will probably want to start right in and go to work, but first you must learn the layout of the law firm, find out who the important players are, and about certain procedures peculiar to this firm.

## GETTING YOUR BEARINGS

During your initial orientation, find out who you should speak to for work assignments, payroll, office services and who to consult when you have problems. Find out the firm's history, office procedures, and billing requirements. It is **very important to understand how things are done**. An office manager of a large firm told me that there are two things she looks for in a good employee: solid legal skills and an **ability to follow office procedures**. The firm's legal secretaries and other members of the support staff can be your **best allies in the law firm maze**. They are a good source for learning how the office really works.

Also during your orientation, ask about attorneys with whom you will be working. Later, you should **locate their offices and take the time to introduce yourself**. Learn where to find the office supply room, copying center, and central files department. (Don't forget to find the lunch room and bathroom!) Get acquainted with the office layout so you won't get lost.

After the orientation, take your own tour of the office space. Introduce yourself to the support staff even if you have met them before. Some firms are large enough so they have staff telephone listings or maps of the offices. If you take these items with you on your tour, you can be sure to put names with the faces.

## WORKING WITH LEGAL SECRETARIES & SUPPORT STAFF

It is important, when dealing with the firm's support staff, to be **clear and concise in giving directions.** If your secretary is working on a project that requires following a certain court rule, make sure that you know the rule, and can communicate what is needed. If you're unfamiliar with the rule, **ask your secretary, who probably has more experience, to assist you.** If you're unsure, don't bluff.

Assuring the secretary that you want to make the best use of his or her time is vital for a smooth-running operation. You should structure the relationship with your secretary as a matter of teamwork. If you are smart enough to **realize how much an experienced legal secretary can help you,** you are on the right track.

Respecting the support staff is not only polite but shows that you are considerate of others' feelings. If a secretary works for you as well as other people, **cooperate with the others** to be certain everyone's priorities and deadlines can be met. You should avoid constantly requesting your secretary to do work at the last minute. Use the phrase "This is a rush," **sparingly,** and only when it is truly a "rush" project. Try to work with your secretary to make the best use of his or her time.

## ASSERTIVENESS TRAINING HELPS

As a paralegal, you will be interacting with professional and clerical personnel who, for the most part, are thorough and exacting. To be effective in communicating with these people, **you must learn to be assertive.** By this, I mean that you must learn how to handle difficult situations and how to ask for the support you need.

Attorneys **prefer to work with paralegals who are not shy** about speaking up. If you are not assertive, attorneys will lose confidence in you. You may find yourself burdened with too many or simply dull work assignments. Paralegals who do not assert themselves are often stuck with low pay, poor working conditions and boring situations.

In order to have a manageable workload, you must **learn how and when to say no tactfully but firmly**. If you grudgingly accept a new assignment because you are afraid to decline or are afraid you will offend the attorneys, you probably end up being disgruntled and resentful of the situation. But if you tell the attorney that the new assignment will conflict with your other priorities, you will **avoid overburdening yourself**. Make sure that the person understands that you are not trying to get out of doing the work.

**Paralegal:**   "I would like to do the research project for you, Mr. Jones, but I have to draft a complaint for Mr. Smith that must be filed today. I won't be able to do your research today, but I'd be happy to do it tomorrow. Will that be O.K.?"

You might even **suggest someone else who can do the project** if the attorney really does need it right away.

If you are asked to take care of an unfamiliar task, do **not** say okay and then not do it. **Ask questions about the project and write down the instructions**. It's quite all right to say that you have not completed this type of assignment before, but are willing to try it. An attorney may not be aware of exactly what you do not know. However, **don't** accept the project unless you really are willing to handle it.

Many employees are afraid to assert themselves because of irrational fears that someone will dislike them. If you constantly seek approval from others, you will find yourself intimidated and unable to do your best work. This is especially true in a law firm, where praise for a job well done is sometimes hard to find.

Learning to assert yourself takes time and practice. There's no question that attorneys **can** indeed be intimidating. Just remember, as long as you honestly have all the work you can do, you have a right to say no to additional assignments.

## KNOW WHAT IS EXPECTED

It is very important to find out **exactly what you are expected to do** on the job. For instance, if you were hired as a document clerk, you will probably be organizing documents on large litigation cases, and that is all you will be doing. If, on the other hand, you were hired as an entry-level paralegal and all you are doing is number-stamping documents, then you may be able to change your fate. **Complete the present assignment to the very best of your ability**. Then, if your next assignment is a repetition of the first, speak to your supervisor about increasing your responsibilities.

Be forewarned that your first assignment will **not** be researching a Supreme Court brief or drafting a multimillion dollar deal. You may organize boxes of documents or assemble closing binders. Do these projects well, and maintain a positive attitude. Remember, attorneys are ultimately responsible for your work. **You must first earn their trust** before the attorneys will feel comfortable delegating more significant work to you. If you consistently do well, the attorneys will realize that they **can trust you with more advanced assignments**. If you are pleasant and persistent, I guarantee that you'll get the kind of work you know how to do.

## A LAST WORD OF ADVICE

Welcome to the world of paralegals! It is a profession that is constantly growing and changing, offering new challenges and opportunities. Remember, starting at the beginning is starting at the beginning. It takes hard work and perseverance to reach the top.

I'm glad you've chosen this career. You're bound to have exciting, challenging experiences that will allow you to maximize your potential. Being a legal assistant is great career and it's getting better all the time.

From an "old" paralegal to a new paralegal, I wish you outrageous success!

# APPENDIX A

# Buzzwords

## Terms You Will Hear at the Law Firm

Have you ever been caught in a conversation where discussions about working in a law firm are flying around, and because you don't know what they all mean, you can't contribute? What follows is a listing of some of these **commonly used terms**, along with definitions.

This list is **not** meant to replace legal dictionaries and the like. Instead, it's intended to define some of the common terms used in talking about the **business** of practicing law.

- A -

**ABA**

Abbreviation for the American Bar Association.

**ABA-approved**

Designation awarded by the American Bar Association to paralegal or legal assistant schools and programs meeting stringent requirements for scholastic excellence and thorough coverage of subject matter.

**abstract**

In some practice areas, this term has a very specialized usage, such as in "abstract of title." Generally, however, it means a brief precis' or overview of a document, highlighting only the key elements.

In litigation, abstracts of documents are frequently computerized for easy retrieval. Sometimes, deposition summaries which focus only on key issues or words are called abstracts of the deposition.

## ALS

1) **Automated litigation support** or **computerized litigation support**. The terms refer to the use of computers to automate the retrieval of pertinent information from the documents involved in a case.

2) Abbreviation for **American Legal Systems,** one of the largest companies dedicated to providing litigation consulting services.

## *American Lawyer, The*

A national monthly magazine focusing primarily on the **business** of practicing law, as opposed to specific developments in the law.

## Aspen Systems Corporation

One of the larger computerized litigation support vendors.

## associate

An attorney in a firm who is not yet a partner. Associates are considered employees of the firm, and are compensated by a salary plus bonus.

Until recently, the "track" for partnership was five to seven years, meaning that an associate worked for a firm that long before he or she would be considered eligible for partnership. This has changed in the past five or so years, coinciding with the trend in law firms to think and act more like business organizations. One result has been that partnership tracks are now longer, some reaching 10 or more years.

See also **partnership track.**

## ATLIS Legal Information Systems

One of the larger computerized litigation support vendors.

**audit letters**

> Information requested from law firms representing corporations to complete statements of liabilities required in annual statements and by other Securities Exchange Commission (SEC) regulations.

**AV rated**

> Rating for law firms developed by *Martindale-Hubbell*, publishers of the most widely known directory of lawyers in the United States. An AV rating is the highest accorded by the directory.

- B -

**baby attorney**

> A **first-year associate**, one with no experience. A term most often used pejoratively. (It is not recommended to refer to a first-year associate by this term to his or her face.)

**BASIS**

> Database software program frequently used in litigation support applications.

**Bates stamping**

> A method of **numbering documents sequentially**, by utilizing a small hand-held numbering device manufactured by the **Bates Company**. The purpose is to have a unique identifier for each page of each document.

> The current trend is away from using Bates stamping toward the use of small, self-sticking labels with computer-generated sequential numbers.

**billable hours**

> A "billable hour" is a shorthand reference for any legal service performed in an hour for which a firm's clients can be charged. Most firms have minimum billable hour requirements for each timekeeper, attorneys and legal assistants alike, and compensation above base levels frequently depends heavily on whether these requirements are exceeded.

211

Billable hours requirements are set on a per-year basis, such as 1800 billable hours (or higher) per year. This number does not refer to the total hours worked, however, as billable time does not cover administrative tasks such as office organization, training, and special projects such as pro bono or bar association activities.

For legal assistants, billable hours requirements can range from 1500 to 1800 per year. In larger firms, these totals are easily reached, especially in a litigation specialization.

**blacklining**

Underlining **new** sentences in a revised document, as opposed to underlining all changes.

See also **redlining**.

**Bluebook**

The shorthand term for *A Uniform System of Citation*, a paperback, spiral bound book published by The Harvard Law Review Association. Named for its historic and distinctive blue cover, the Bluebook is a well-accepted guide for citation of all types of legal authorities.

**boilerplate**

Used to describe documents (or portions of documents) containing standard verbiage, such that very little, if any, modification is required to tailor the document to specific situations. For example, most contracts, real estate documents and some pleading forms contain "boilerplate" language that can be used over and over again.

See also **cut and paste**.

**bonus**

> A perquisite given to attorneys, paralegals, and sometimes to other staff members, usually at year end, to reward merit, tenure at the firm, billable hours or other significant performance-based criteria. Bonuses can be given more often than just at year end, but this perquisite is usually reserved for associate attorneys.

**brief**

> This term has two usages. To "brief" a case or opinion means to pick out the pertinent facts, identify the issues involved, determine the holding (or decision), and define the reasoning behind the court's decision. In most paralegal schools, students are taught to brief cases, in order to understand the legal reasoning process.

> The second usage of "brief" is as a noun. A brief that will be filed with the U.S. Supreme Court, for example, may present arguments for overturning an appellate court opinion. Attorneys file briefs in trial courts as well as appellate courts. Because briefs are the published work product of a law firm, they must usually follow strict style guidelines both internally and in accordance with court rules. Of course, any legal document containing citations to legal authorities must be **cite checked** and **Shepardized**.

### - C -

**calendar**

> Used both as a noun—in referring to a firm's calendar (or docket) of upcoming events—and a verb—the act of placing events on the firm's docket. The **act of calendaring** involves reviewing incoming and outgoing pleadings and correspondence for important dates, and recording such dates in either a manual or computerized tickler or reminder system. A firm's calendar can be specific to attorneys or departments, or apply generally to everyone in the firm.

Proper placement of items on a firm's calendar is a very important task, especially in the avoidance of legal malpractice claims. In a large firm, legal secretaries will ordinarily review all documents for pertinent dates and turn that information over to another department for checking and compiling into a calendar. Sometimes, a firm will assign the document review job to a paralegal, since statutory deadlines and local court rules frequently must be determined in order to set the reminder dates properly.

See also **tickler file.**

**case manager**

A position usually filled by an experienced litigation paralegal. Duties involve organizing a case's pleadings, overseeing the mechanics of producing documents and maintaining the resulting document library. This job is either very hands-on or quite managerial, depending on the size, complexity and expected duration of the case.

On large matters, the person selected as a case manager will have gone to trial on at least a few cases, have supervised the work of other paralegals and document clerks, and worked with litigation support applications. In a small case, organizational skills are the primary requirement.

**case management**

Approaching the management of a litigation matter as a project needing input from many people, and various support departments of a firm, in addition to outside vendors.

**CEB**

California's Continuing Education of the Bar program, which sponsors numerous seminars and publishes associated materials. Attendance at most CEB seminars applies to the attorney's required hours of continuing legal education.

See also **CLE.**

**cedar file**

An expandable file folder. See also **Redwell**.

**Centrex**

A phone system operated by an outside vendor, frequently the local phone company. The system is comprised of the switching equipment, telephone instruments, voice mail and the software to make it all operate together.

**certificated**

A paralegal or legal assistant possessing a certificate from a paralegal institution of higher learning. NOT to be confused with the term "certified."

**certified**

A state-recognized or organization-recognized designation usually given upon successful completion of a complex examination. NALA offers the "CLA" designation, which refers to Certified Legal Assistant.

**Chinese wall**

See **conflict of interest**.

**cite checking**

Cite checking involves, at a very basic level, checking all citations to legal authority that might be found in a legal memorandum or brief to confirm that they are still "good law." That is, all citations must be Shepardized to make sure that there are no superseding statutes or overruling cases that would undermine the authority of the materials cited.

It also involves confirming that all legal authority is properly cited, according to Harvard Bluebook standards (or whatever citation style book prevails in a particular jurisdiction). In addition, all jump cites (point pages) must be checked to confirm that the quote (or other material) cited is actually found on that page. Finally, all direct quotes must be checked to make sure they are quoted accurately.

See also **Shepardizing**.

215

**CLA**

> The designation offered through the National Association of Legal Assistants upon successful completion of a (now) two-and-one-half day examination.

**CLE**

> Acronym for continuing legal education, now required by most state bar organizations.

**coding**

> Document coding refers to abstracting pertinent pieces of information from each document for indexing in a document retrieval database. One of the most important things a litigation support manager does is design the database structure, which is based upon what pieces of information the attorneys believe will need to be searched.
>
> Examples of such pertinent pieces of information include: 1) the date of the document; 2) the author; 3) the corporate entity author, if any; 4) document type such as letter, contract, or financial statement; 5) the recipient of the document, etc. These pieces of information are usually "coded" onto a "coding form" or directly into a computer format.
>
> Once these key items (called "fields") are indexed in the computer, they can be retrieved by searches. For example, if an attorney wanted all letters written by Smith during 1984 and sent to Jones, all documents matching those criteria could be retrieved from the database.
>
> See also **abstract, ALS,** and **litigation support manager.**

**complex litigation**

> Large-scale litigation, defined by a number of different situations. Usually refers to large document cases (500,000 documents or more). Can also refer to multi-district litigation, class action lawsuits, multiple-party actions, cases with a number of cross claims, or many technical factual or legal issues. Bankruptcy cases involving major corporations—and a result, thousands of creditors—are deemed complex litigation.

## conflict of interest

Conflicts of interest can arise in a number of situations. The most common situation in which conflicts arise is if a law firm **accepted a new client** that would put the firm in conflict with an already existing client. An obvious conflict would be to accept as a client the defendant in a law suit in which the firm was already representing the plaintiff.

Another common situation is for a firm to hire an attorney or legal assistant who has had such a close involvement in a matter on the opposite side of a firm's existing client that the firm could possibly be **disqualified from continuing to represent** its client in the matter. Checking for conflicts in the employment of legal professionals has gained in importance with the growing tendency of attorneys to change firms. In addition, now that legal assistants have become much more involved in the practices of many firms, checking for conflicts of interest by firms when they hire **both attorneys and legal assistants** has become more common. Sometimes the conflict is too direct or there is no efficient way to alleviate the conflict, so the attorney or legal assistant cannot be hired.

In some cases, an **ethical wall** (sometimes called a "**Chinese wall**"), can be erected around the person with the conflict, allowing the new firm to hire that person. In **ethical wall** situations, the person with the conflict is diligently screened from all conversation, documentation and knowledge about the matter involved in the conflict. The person **behind the Chinese wall** must also be very diligent in reminding others in the firm not to discuss the matter, even in casual conversation, whenever he or she is around.

## contract attorney

A relatively new phenomenon, a contract attorney is an associate in a law firm who has either been considered and rejected for partnership, or one who has chosen not to be considered at all. This new position has grown out of firms' need to keep a large group of skilled attorneys in order to handle the legal work, but not at the cost of reducing partnership draws significantly. It is also a choice of many attorneys with families or other interests outside the practice of law.

See also **income partner** and **partnership track**.

## corporate maintenance

The duties of a corporate paralegal in updating corporate minute books, preparing minutes of board meetings and ensuring that the corporation files all timely documents.

## court administrator

The judiciary is a career path for some legal assistants. While the monetary benefits may not equal that of firms and corporations, the hours, flexibility, and holidays can be attractive. Typically court administrators work **directly for a judge**, in contrast to the "clerk" position, typically people hired by a state or federal agency.

## court runner

A messenger who "runs" to the courthouse to file and/or retrieve documents. In large firms, court runners are on staff. Court runners use bicycles or motorcycles to cut through the traffic.

## cut and paste

Used in a number of contexts to describe the "cannibalization" of an existing document to modify that document or create a new document. Without access to computerized word processing, one physically cuts the material to be borrowed and placed elsewhere, and then pastes (or tapes) that passage in the new document.

Some word processing programs use cut and paste terminology to describe the act of blocking (or marking) certain passages and moving them to another place in the document or to a new document. Occasionally, attorneys will use the phrase "cut and paste" to describe using earlier legal research memorialized in legal memoranda or briefs, and applying it to similar factual situations.

See also **work product files**.

## - D -

**dBase**

A relational database program used by many law firms for building and managing document retrieval databases.

**depo**

Abbreviation for **deposition**.

**deposition digesting**

See **deposition summarizing**.

**deposition summarizing**

A very necessary skill for all paralegals working in litigation practices. A properly summarized deposition means an attorney should only have to read summary pages instead of the complete deposition in order to understand the facts involved in the deponent's testimony.

Being able to accurately summarize depositions requires sensitivity to the nuances of language, knowledge of evidence rules and a thorough understanding of the issues involved in the particular litigation. Methods for summarizing vary widely, from handwriting the summary, dictating while reading through the deposition, or writing the summary directly on a computer. Testimony from simple fact witnesses is easiest to summarize; testimony from medical, economic or other technical expert witnesses is both the most tedious and difficult to summarize.

The degree of summarization allowed is determined by how the summaries will be used. For instance, if the summaries will be used only by the attorney who took or defended the deposition in order to find particular passages, the summary can be quite concise. On the other hand, if the summary will be used to educate others about the facts of the case, more detail will be necessary.

### DisplayWriter

A word processing system which runs on a dedicated hardware package, not on a personal computer.

### DOA

In addition to being a shorthand term for "dead on arrival," this also is the abbreviation for Director of Administration, the top managerial position in a law firm. Usually non-lawyer, most administrators have strong backgrounds in finance, accounting or computers. They frequently have advanced degrees in business administration.

### docket control

See **calendar** and **tickler files**.

### document clerk

A support position to paralegals, sometimes called a paralegal assistant or case clerk. A document clerk ordinarily handles the more routine and clerical tasks, such as organizing, filing, numbering and indexing documents.

See also **paralegal assistant**.

**document control**

Refers to various methods of identifying rooms, files, file drawers, file folders that must be reviewed for possible production during discovery; marking the documents selected with a unique identifier for later identification; and establishing a document archive system either through a master document set or by some film or image system for later retrieval.

See also **imaging**.

**document production**

Can refer solely to a specific response to a "demand to produce documents" in a litigation matter as a part of the discovery process. On a broader scale, document production refers to the technique of establishing document control and managing an organized production (or receipt) of documents.

See also **Bates stamping** and **document control**.

**draft**

To write an original document, whether pleading, legal memoranda or correspondence. Sometimes confused with filling out legal forms.

**draw**

A partner's share in the profits of the firm. See also **partnership track**.

- E -

**equity partner**

A partner who has "bought into" the partnership, either by actually paying for a valuated portion of the firm, or by having such a valuation deducted from the partner's draw. An equity partner is an owner of the firm.

See also **partnership track**.

**ethical wall**

See **conflict of interest**.

**executive committee**

A law firm committee composed of partners who are the power brokers in a firm. This committee is usually not involved in day-to-day decisions of running the firm, but does decide all significant issues, such as partner draws, major equipment purchases, practice diversification, etc.

See also **management committee**.

**exempt**

Exempt employees are those who are determined to be exempt from federal (and/or state) overtime laws because of their professional status, specialized training or executive level administrative responsibilities. Some law firms classify all legal assistants as exempt employees, while other firms reserve that status for senior paralegals only.

See also **nonexempt**.

**expert witness**

A person with expertise in any field, who may be needed to testify about certain aspects of a matter involving his or her expertise. Frequently, the expert will be retained to review certain documents or physical evidence and provide an opinion and/or a written report of the findings and conclusions drawn. Such experts often are deposed concerning their findings and can be called to testify. Almost all experts charge substantially for their time to review the evidence, testify at deposition and at trial.

One task frequently delegated to paralegals is to maintain a firm's expert witness list, with information on the cost of retaining such experts and the results of the expert's testimony. If the firm has a particular specialty area where experts are frequently retained, the firm's expert witness list should also include information on experts who have frequently been used by the opposing side.

- F -

**facilities management**

The operation of photocopy and messenger services by an outside service, but within the law firm. Usually contracted to the outside service for a term of years. The benefit from using such services vary, but law firms most typically choose this approach as a method of lowering overhead costs.

**file room**

Office in a law firm dedicated to storage of legal records. In larger firms, with more sophisticated recordkeeping requirements, the room becomes a separate department, often called the **records center** or **records department**.

See also **records center**.

**firm marketing**

The person responsible for law firm marketing may be responsible for generating publicity about the firm, writing and distributing press releases, putting together firm brochures and resumes, establishing in-house continuing legal education (especially with regard to new practice areas, and client development techniques), monitoring department productivity and activity, and recommending strategies for expertise emphasis within the firm. Also known as "practice development" in some firms.

**form files**

Generally used to refer to files of court-mandated forms or other types of forms (such as standard leases, power of attorney forms, etc.). Particularly necessary in jurisdictions in which litigation is form-driven. Also important in real estate and corporate practices.

Can also refer to an attorney's (or firm's) general "work product" files, which may consist of copies of all documents previously drafted by the attorney, separated into subject matter areas. Such form files are maintained in order to save time on producing new documents.

See also **cut and paste** and **work product**.

## - G -

**general counsel**

Refers to all attorneys who are employed directly by corporations to staff the company's legal department. Also refers to the top lawyer position in a corporation, hence the combined title "general counsel and vice president of legal affairs."

See also **outside counsel**.

## - H -

**headhunter**

Term used to describe people who work for search firms, typically specializing in searches for attorneys, but also now including legal assistants. If a search firm is looking for a 5-year-plus litigation legal assistant with computerized litigation support expertise, the process of calling people to find out if someone is interested in this position can be termed "head hunting."

**hiring committee**

A law firm committee established to approve or disapprove potential candidates, usually for attorney positions. Sometimes this committee is called the **recruiting committee**, and combines normal attorney and paralegal hiring with summer clerk recruiting.

With attorneys now changing law firms more often, and given the growing experience levels of paralegals, checking for conflicts of interest have become more important for attorneys and paralegals. This function is sometimes performed by the hiring committee.

See also **conflict of interest**.

-I-

**imaging**

A relatively new technology, somewhat similar to microfilming, that involves digitally scanning documents into a CD-ROM format in order to create "images" of the original document. Viewed on a high resolution monitor, document images are much sharper than microfilm and can also be enhanced by digital technology. For instance, poorly reproduced handwritten notes in the corner of a document can be filled in by extrapolating from the writing that is clearly visible.

This technology allows for attorney notes, abstracted records and other add-ons to accompany the imaged document. In using a document retrieval database with an imaged document system, the document numbers found by the search of document fields can also be used to display the imaged documents at the same time. With microfilm, once a document search in the database is completed, the documents must be located—one by one—and then printed for the attorney's review.

See also **microfilm/microfiche**.

**income partner**

A partner who is not made an equity partner, and therefore does not share in the profits of the firm. An income partner is not considered an owner of the firm.

See also **partnership track**.

**InMagic**

Personal computer-based software for document retrieval. Used initially by law firm libraries for maintaining information on the firm's collection, it has been widely used in building litigation document databases.

**intake**

The process of interviewing potential clients to determine if their needs match the services provided by the firm. Also describes initial interviews of new clients to determine the pertinent facts of the case.

Both steps are usually performed by paralegals, and typically apply to plaintiff-oriented firms. For example, in a personal injury case, the paralegal would elicit information concerning when the accident occurred, whether there were any witnesses and what the client's out-of-pocket medical expenses have been to date.

**issue coding**

The process of picking out pertinent issues designated by an attorney from depositions, documents or other sources. Can be as simple as highlighting specific words or portions of a document for an attorney's review. This can also refer to picking out certain subject matters and placing such information in a document retrieval database. Sometimes issues are denoted by **key words** and can be coded as such.

- L -

**LAMA** (pronounced "lahm'-ah")

The Legal Assistant Management Association, an organization open only to legal assistant (or paralegal) managers. LAMA sponsors an annual conference, collects data for and publishes an authoritative salary survey and also publishes newsletters. The national organization sponsors and provides support to local chapters.

**LEXIS**

Database developed to provide easy access to legal reference materials; published by Mead Data Central, Inc. Using boolean search logic (i.e., search for "assumption" and "risk" but not "injury"), the database makes available all legal authority—both case law and statutes— published by West Publishing Company. A key feature used by legal assistants is "Auto-Cite," which provides a quick method for cite checking legal authorities.

See also **cite checking, NEXIS** and **WestLaw.**

**law librarian**

Law librarians are skilled database users and legal researchers. Mid-sized to large firms usually have full-time law librarians; these positions may require a master's degree in library science (MLS). Smaller firms may use paralegals and/or legal secretaries to serve as part-time librarians. In this case, the position is primarily one of ensuring the books and other legal materials are updated periodically.

**legal administrator**

Administrators are responsible for the financial affairs of the firm. They oversee billing, collections, capital expenditure research, and like matters. In smaller firms the administrator may also handle personnel matters such as interviewing, hiring, firing, grievance handling, and managing income levels. This position requires an undergraduate degree and perhaps a master's degree in business, with special emphasis in finance.

**legal assistant manager**

Typically this is a position found in larger firms. Legal assistant managers act as a liaison between management and the legal assistants, responsible for hiring, supervision, review and dismissal, if necessary, as well as budgetary responsibilities. They may also assign case work to ensure work distribution, quality and timeliness.

**litigation support consultant**

Paralegals who have computer skills may find a demand for their services as a consultant to firms in litigation support. Consultation areas include analysis of the project, designing a database structure, developing a database building plan, creating coding sheets, and writing report programs. Some firms employ "in-house" consultants.

**litigation support manager**

Most often refers to the manager in a law firm who is in charge of computerized litigation support. This person will either manage litigation cases directly, or will work with outside vendors. A large part of the job involves consulting with the firm's attorneys about whether a certain case will require automation, and if so, how to design the document retrieval database.

In the past, before personal computers became much more integral to the practice of law, firms were leery of automating litigation matters, reserving this for cases involving 50,000 documents or more. This has changed as a result of software programs becoming easier to use, and with attorneys' realization that even small document cases can benefit from the speed and thoroughness that computer searches offer.

Can also refer to a manager from an outside litigation consulting company.

See also **ALS**.

- M -

**management committee**

A law firm committee usually composed solely of partners, sometimes made up of all practice group section or department heads. In some firms, may function as decision-maker of day-to-day issues. Sometimes called **administrative committee**.

See also **executive committee**.

**managing partner**

> The key partner in a firm responsible for overall decision-making. The position is similar to a chief executive officer or president of a corporation.

> Historically, the position of managing partner was simply accorded to the firm's most senior partner. The current trend however, often found in large firms, is to make the position an elected one, usually for a defined term of three to five years.

**microfilm/microfiche**

> The product—in film form—of taking "pictures" of documents and reducing them to a format requiring magnification. Microfilm comes in rolls of film that can be searched automatically on an automated microfilm reader. Microfiche comes in sheets of film that are viewed on stationary fiche readers.

> The benefits of reducing vast quantities of documents to microfilm or fiche start with the obvious one of reducing storage costs. Another benefit is the preservation of all pages of a document in the order in which they were (hopefully) produced and filmed. The likelihood of document "misfiles" is also substantially reduced (unless the film or fiche is itself misplaced, of course).

> See also **imaging**.

- N -

**NALA** (pronounced "nah'-la")

> The National Association of Legal Assistants, which is an umbrella organization for regional and/or specialty paralegal associations.

> See also **NFPA**.

### National Law Journal

A national weekly newspaper about law and law firms, with articles about new or changing areas of law, along with summaries of key decisions in state and federal courts, divided into practice areas. A fairly traditional publication widely read by many attorneys.

### NEXIS

A general news database created by West Publishing Company, as a companion database to LEXIS. Features include daily news summaries and headlines from key newspapers. This is a good database for finding fairly obscure publications, in addition to all major news stories and magazine articles on a particular topic.

See also **LEXIS**.

### NFPA (pronounced "nif'-pah")

The National Federation of Paralegal Associations. Many regional or specialty paralegal organizations belong to this national, umbrella organization.

See also **NALA**.

### nonexempt

Nonexempt employees are those who, because of their classification primarily as support staff, are entitled to payment of overtime. Persons in these positions are considered **not** to be exempted from federal (and state) overtime laws, because the jobs do not ordinarily **and primarily** require the exercise of independent judgment and initiative.

See also **exempt**.

### - O -

**of counsel**

>An attorney associated with a law firm who is neither an employee nor a partner. Frequently, an of counsel's compensation is geared to his or her own client base, and is not dependent on, or part of, the firm's general compensation system.

**outside counsel**

>Used by members of corporate legal departments to describe attorneys associated with a law firm that handles all or a part of the corporation's legal business.

### - P -

**P.I.**

>Abbreviation for personal injury.

**paralegal assistant**

>Generally an assistant to a paralegal, typically in a litigation practice. The position, which is relatively new, is also sometimes called case clerk or document clerk.

>See also **document clerk.**

**paralegal coordinator**

>Usually more a supervisory than managerial position, the coordinator's primary responsibility is for paralegal work load management, both as a resource for attorneys needing paralegal assistance and to ensure fairly divided work loads among paralegals on staff.

>See also **paralegal manager.**

**paralegal manager**

A law firm management position with varying degrees of responsibility for hiring performance reviews, salary administration, budgets and work assignments. This managerial position is also sometimes called **legal assistant manager.**

See also **LAMA** and **paralegal coordinator.**

**paralegal program**

This term has two usages. It can be used to refer to the paralegal department in a law firm or corporation. Most paralegal "programs" feature a vertical career path and are fairly specialized.

The second usage refers to a program of study to learn the paralegal profession.

**paralegal services company**

Some entrepreneurial legal assistants have started their own companies, providing temporary and permanent employees to law firms and corporations. Some of these paralegals continue to "place themselves" in assignments; others manage paralegals to fill client requests.

**partnership track**

The time period during which associates are evaluated and considered for partnership. Sometimes the partnership track is associated with an **"up or out" policy,** in which associates who are not asked to join the partnership upon completion of the typical evaluation period are instead asked to leave the firm. The evaluation period has lengthened in the past five years, from a track of seven years to 10 or more years.

In addition, the positions of equity partner and income partner have been established to allow firms to make some attorneys partners in name only, without the expense of including them in a share of the firm's profits. In some firms, being made an income partner starts a **second partnership track,** one in which the attorney is evaluated for equity partnership.

An equity partner shares in the profits of the firm, in which shares (or draws) are ordinarily determined by seniority in terms of number of years as a partner. A partner's business-getting (or "rainmaking") expertise is also considered, and is sometimes weighted more heavily than seniority or quality of legal scholarship.

See also **contract attorney** and **rainmaking**.

**PLI**

Practising Law Institute, an organization which sponsors numerous seminars and publishes accompanying materials. Known for practical, how-to approaches, PLI also publishes quite useful materials for legal assistants.

**practice management committee**

A law firm committee responsible for the day-to-day management of the firm's business. In most law firms, except for the very smallest, committees flourish as a method of management.

See also **executive committee** and **management committee**.

**pro bono administrator**

Community service is important to many law practices. Some larger firms hire one individual to coordinate these activities firm-wide.

- Q -

**Quorum Systems**

A division of Control Data Corporation, one of the larger computerized litigation support vendors.

## - R -

**rainmaking**

A "rainmaker" in a law firm is an attorney, usually a partner, who has great skill at attracting, soliciting and keeping clients. This ability is highly prized and handsomely rewarded.

See also **partnership track.**

**RBase**

Relational database software package which is used in personal computer environments for building litigation databases.

**records manager**

A law firm managerial position typically with responsibility for: 1) establishing procedures for setting up new client and matter files, 2) how documents are to be filed within those files, 3) where the files will be located, 4) who will keep them current, and 5) when closed files will be sent to storage and/or destroyed. Frequently, a firm's records manager also has responsibility for: 6) performing conflict checks for potential new clients, 7) conducting searches of the firm's own internal records when required for lawsuits involving the firm, and 8) generally ensuring that all advances in records management technology are applied to the management of the department when appropriate.

With the advent of **imaging** and **bar coding** technology, this position has become much more computer dependent. The position of records manager is generally considered on the career path for experienced paralegals.

See also **file room, imaging** and **work product.**

**recruiting coordinator/administrator**

A law firm management position that usually works with the firm administrator and the recruiting or hiring committee to hire new attorneys. Usually coordinates the summer clerk interviewing and entertainment program.

**recruiting season**

The time of year when a law firm conducts interviews—usually on law school campuses—as a method of recruiting new associates. Frequently, follow-up interviews at the firm's offices are arranged for the most promising candidates.

Because the competition for the top law school graduates is keen, the candidates often "interview" the firm as much as the firm interviews the candidates.

See also **summer clerk/associate**.

**redact**

To delete text from a document by either covering up the text with self-adhesive corrective tape (which comes in several widths), or by marking over the text with a black marking pen. The purpose of redacting is to delete material that is privileged or otherwise exempted from production during discovery (or use at trial).

**redlining**

To highlight the changes in different versions of the same document by underlining all changed words, sentences, paragraphs, etc. Frequently used to track changes in drafts of contracts, real estate offerings and other complicated agreements.

There are several computer software programs that can quickly perform this task, provided the previous and current documents that must be compared are in computer-readable format. One such program is called "CompareRite." WordPerfect also has a compare feature.

See also **blacklining**.

**Redwell**

One of many terms referring to those indispensable light cardboard, expandable file folders, usually brown in color. Also called **Redropes** (after the manufacturer), **redwelds,** and other terms with "red" in the name.

See also **cedar file**.

**reporter**

A collection of written opinions by a court (or court system) which are reported via publication in book form. There are numerous "reporters" for state and federal courts.

Shorthand references to reporters abound, such as "Fed Second," which is the verbalization of "F.2d," the citation form for federal courts of appeal opinions published by West. "Fed Supp" is the shorthand verbalization of "F.Supp.," which is the citation form for federal district court opinions. Each specialized area of practice has its own reporters and shorthand references.

- S -

**service center**

A photocopy, mail room and message center. Sometimes these operations are separated into different areas. Most large firms have "convenience" service centers located on each floor.

**Shepardizing**

Both a publication **name** (*Shepard's Citations*) and the **act** of confirming the currency of case law and statutory citations by checking all subsequent citations of particular cases or statutes. The manual system involves looking for citations through as many as three or four separate volumes. *Shepard's Citation's* information has also been computerized and is available through the Lexis and WestLaw databases, in addition to VeraLex, a database published by Bancroft Whitney.

**small firm**

Usually defined as a law firm of 25 attorneys or fewer.

**Summation**

A personal computer-based software program used for document retrieval. It can be used as a full-text retrieval system as well as for document abstracts.

**summer clerks**

Also known as **summer associates,** a summer clerk is a law school student who works for a law firm during the summer break, usually so both parties can learn more about each other in making potential employment decisions. Students at the top schools have typically been hotly recruited by firms.

- T -

**tickler file**

Describes a manual calendaring and docketing system. Such files frequently consist of numerous multipart forms, containing certain date deadlines, along with client/case information. These forms are filed in date order and then pulled as the date for the reminder approaches.

Although useful for small firms, large firms find that these systems must be computerized to be efficient and effective. Sometimes, however, even firms with computerized systems use a manual system as a backup.

See also **calendar**.

**transactional work**

Refers to legal work involving "deals"—or transactions—such as those found in real estate, entertainment or corporate practices. Considered a specialty area for legal assistants by some firms.

**trial prep** (for **trial preparation**)

Trial preparation generally describes the phase before trial which may include putting together witness notebooks; preparing witnesses to testify; collecting key pleadings, deposition summaries and other key documents for trial notebooks; finalizing the exhibit list and putting together the exhibit documents into notebooks; and designing and producing graphic exhibits such as charts.

See also **war room**.

**trustee**

Acting as a bank trust department trustee has been one excellent avenue for paralegals with expertise in probate and estate planning.

## - W -

**war room**

A "war room" is a room or office set aside for use as: 1) a document depository; 2) a deposition and deposition exhibits library; 3) the place where the computer(s) used in building and gaining access to a litigation support database; 4) the place where legal assistants and document clerks work in preparing a case for trial, because all significant pleadings, documents and exhibits are kept there; 5) all of the above. Such places are called "war rooms" because that is where the strategies for the battles to fight and win the case are planned and carried out.

See also **trial prep**.

**Westlaw**

An on-line legal research database built by West Publishing Company. Features "InstaCite" function for quick cite checking.

See also **cite checking** and **LEXIS**.

**WordPerfect**

Personal computer software now generally accepted as the standard word processing program used by law firms and legal departments in corporations. Written by WordPerfect Corp. (a company located in Orem, Utah), the latest version of WordPerfect is 5.1, which came out in 1989. This software operates in either a stand-alone computer or network environment.

**word processing center**

A center or department in a law firm dedicated to word processing long or complicated documents. Usually staffed by people highly skilled in computerized word processing. Word processors do **not** ordinarily perform legal secretarial functions, but are exposed to as much, if not more, of the stress that comes with producing legal documents on a deadline.

**work product**

> This term has a specific definition in the evidence rules, because attorney work product is protected by attorney-client privilege. While what actually deemed "work product" in any particular circumstance can be the subject of protracted argument, generally "work product" means all documents authored by an attorney, usually not for public consumption.
>
> Work product also has a broader meaning in the sense of all documents from which useful material can be copied or "cannibalized" for the creation of new documents. Many firms are coding the work product of their attorneys, and then indexing that information in a computer database for later retrieval and use in creating new documents.
>
> In the context of this second usage, paralegals who are experienced in building document retrieval databases can find themselves involved in building a work product database for the firm, which can be a very interesting project. However, because the work is ongoing, the project will sometimes be transferred to the firm's library staff who are usually not operating under a billable hours requirement.
>
> See also **cut and paste** and **form files**.

**WP 5.1**

> The latest version of the popular word processing program released by WordPerfect Corporation. See also **WordPerfect**.

**- Y -**

**year-end**

> A modifier used in law firms to describe the review and bonus awarding time period. Can refer to either the calendar or fiscal year end.
>
> **Year-end reviews** in calendar-year-based law firms are usually conducted in October. **Year-end bonuses** in calendar-year-based firms are usually awarded in the middle of December. A few firms have started giving what were called year-end bonuses in July, in order to avoid associations with religious holidays.

# Legal Assistant & Paralegal School List

If you're considering attending a legal assistant school or paralegal program, what follows is a listing of a number of schools, separated into states and, within each state, by city. This list has been compiled from several sources: the American Bar Association (which also provided information on accreditation status); the National Federation of Paralegal Associations; the National Association of Legal Assistants; and finally, from a number of very helpful educators.

Even if you're not planning to attend a school (or have graduated already), the following schools list can also be helpful for those **needing placement assistance**. This is especially true if you're moving to a new city or different part of the country. Almost all schools have placement departments, and while sometimes these services are reserved for graduates only, this is not always the case. You can ask the schools to add you to their mailing list for placement circulars. You can also make valuable networking contacts through the schools. The schools know the local paralegal associations and can certainly tell you about other groups in the legal field and when they meet. Remember to ask for information on prevailing salaries and benefits, and other particulars about the paralegal profession in that area. Perhaps the hottest field in that location is environmental law—you can be sure the paralegal schools will know that information.

Every effort has been made to include all schools currently offering training—either certificates or degrees—in legal assistant or paralegal studies. Because of the rapid growth of formal education programs for paralegals, however, it is possible that some schools have been missed. It is also possible that some of the listed schools have changed names or are no longer offering paralegal courses. Any schools not on the list are invited to contact the Publisher for inclusion in the next edition of this book.

This list is also for informational purposes only, and is **not** intended as an endorsement of any particular school or program.

## ALABAMA

### Birmingham

Faulkner University, Birmingham
2211 Magnolia Avenue
Birmingham, AL 35205

Miles College
Paralegal Studies
P.O. Box 3800
Birmingham, AL 35208

National Academy for Paralegal
Studies, Inc.
1572 Montgomery Hwy., Ste. 100
Birmingham, AL 35216

* Samford University
Division of Paralegal Studies
Birmingham, AL 35229

Southern Institute
Department of Paralegal Studies
2015 Highland Avenue South
Birmingham, AL 35205

University of Alabama, Birmingham
UAB Special Studies
917 11th Street, South
Birmingham, AL 35294

### Decatur

John C. Calhoun State Community College
Paralegal Program
P.O. Box 2216
Decatur, AL 35602-2216

### Florence

Faulkner University, Florence
1001 Florence Boulevard
Florence AL 35630

### Hanceville

Wallace State Community College
Highway 31, North
Hanceville, AL 35077

### Huntsville

Faulkner University, Huntsville
2650 Jordan Lane
Huntsville, AL 35810

### Mobile

Faulkner University, Mobile
1050 Government Street
Mobile, AL 36604

* ABA Final Approval.     **ABA Provisional Approval

242

Spring Hill College
Legal Studies Program
Social Science Division
Mobile, AL 36608

University of South Alabama
Division of C.E. & Evening Studies
307 University Boulevard
Mobile, AL 36688

**Montgomery**

\* Auburn University
Legal Assistant Education
Department of Justice & Public Safety
Montgomery, AL 36193

Community College of the Air Force
Maxwell Air Force Base
745 Selfridge
Maxwell AFB
Montgomery, AL 36113

Faulkner University, Montgomery
5345 Atlanta Highway
Montgomery, AL 36193

Huntington College
Continuing Education
1500 East Fairview Avenue
Montgomery, AL 36106

**Rainsville**

Northeast Alabama State Junior College
P.O. Box 159
Rainsville, AL 35986

**ALASKA**

**Anchorage**

Alaska Business College
Paralegal Education Department
800 East Diamond Boulevard
Suite 3-350
Anchorage, AK 99515

Charter College
4791 Business Park Boulevard
Number 6
Anchorage, AK 99503

University of Alaska, Anchorage
Paralegal Certificate Program
School of Public Affairs, Justice
3211 Providence Drive
Anchorage, AK 99508

**Juneau**

University of Alaska, Juneau
Paralegal Studies Program
School of Business
Bill Ray Center
1108 F Street
Juneau, AK 99801

**ARIZONA**

**Mesa**

Lamson Junior College
Legal Assistant Program
1980 West Main
Mesa, AZ 85201

\* ABA Final Approval.    \*\*ABA Provisional Approval

**Phoenix**

Lawson College
1313 North Second Street
Phoenix, AZ 84004

Paralegal Institute (The)
1315 W. Indian
School Drawer 33903
Phoenix, AZ 85067

* Phoenix College
Legal Assistant Program
1202 W. Thomas Road
Phoenix, AZ 85013

* Sterling School (The)
Legal Assistant Program
801 E. Indian School Road
Phoenix, AZ 85014

* The American Institute
Paralegal Studies Program
1300 North Central Avenue
Phoenix, AZ 85004

**Tempe**

Arizona State University
Paralegal Program
Center for Executive Development
College of Business
Tempe, AZ 85287-4306

**Tucson**

Apollo College
Legal Assistant Program
13 West Westmore Road
Tucson, AZ 85705

* Pima Community College
Downtown Campus
1255 N. Stone Avenue
Tucson, AZ 85703

**ARKANSAS**

**Ft. Smith**

West Ark Community College
Legal Assistant Program
Grand Avenue
Ft. Smith, AR 72764

West Arkansas Community College
Division of Business
P.O. Box 3649
Ft. Smith, AR 72913

**North Little Rock**

The Institute for Paralegal Training at
South Central
Career College
4500 W. Commercial Drive
North Little Rock, AR 72116

**CALIFORNIA**

**Bakersfield**

California State University, Bakersfield
Extended Studies
9001 Stockdale Highway
Bakersfield, CA 93311-1099

* ABA Final Approval.    **ABA Provisional Approval

244

CSB Plus
Attorney Assistant
Certificate Program
Extended Studies and
Regional Programs
9001 Stockdale Highway
Bakersfield, CA  93311-1099

**Brea**

Southern California College of
Business Law
595 W. Lambert Road
Brea, CA  92621

**Carson**

California State University,
Dominguez Hills
Public Paralegal Cert. Program
School of Social and Behavioral Sciences
Carson, CA  90747

Phillips Junior College
Suite 110
One Civic Center
Carson, CA  90745

**Chico**

California State University, Chico
Department of Political Science
Paralegal Certificate Program
Chico, CA  95929-0455

**Citrus Heights**

Career Community College of Business
Paralegal Program
7219 Escalante Way
Citrus Heights, CA  95610

**Costa Mesa**

Orange Coast College
2701 Fairview Road
Costa Mesa, CA  92626

**Culver City**

West Los Angeles College
4800 Freshman Drive
Culver City, CA  90230

**Cupertino**

De Anza College
Legal Assistant Program
21250 Stevens Creek Blvd.
Cupertino, CA  95014

**Davis**

* University of California, Davis
University Extension
Legal Assisting Certificate Program
Davis, CA  95616

**Encino**

University of LaVerne
College of Law
5445 Balboa Boulevard
Encino, CA  91316

**Eureka**

College of the Redwoods
Business Division
7351 Tompkins Hill Road
Eureka, CA  95501-9302

---

* ABA Final Approval.     **ABA Provisional Approval

**Fountain Valley**

* Coastline Community College
11460 Warner Avenue
Fountain Valley, CA 92708

**Fresno**

Fresno City College
1101 E. University Avenue
Fresno, CA 93741

San Joaquin College of Law
Paralegal Program
3385 E. Shields
Fresno, CA 93726

**Fullerton**

Fullerton College
Legal Assistant Program
406 N. Adams Avenue
Fullerton, CA 92632

**Hayward**

California State University, Hayward
Paralegal Certificate Program
Division of Extended Education
Hayward, CA 94542

**Imperial**

Imperial Valley College
P.O. Box 158
Imperial, CA 92251

**Irvine**

* University of California, Irvine
University Extension
Program in Legal Assistantship
P.O. Box AZ
Irvine, CA 92716

**La Jolla**

* University of California, San Diego
Legal Assistant Training Program
9500 Gilman Drive, UCSD Ext. 0176
La Jolla, CA 92093

**LaVerne**

University of LaVerne
1950 Third Street
LaVerne, CA 91750

**Long Beach**

California State University, Long Beach
Extension
1250 Bellflower Blvd.
Long Beach, CA 90840

Metropolitan Business College
2390 Pacific College
Long Beach, CA 90806

**Los Angeles**

* California State University, Los Angeles
Certificate Program for the Legal Assistant
5151 State University Drive
Los Angeles, CA 90032

Los Angeles City College
Law Department
855 North Vermont Avenue
Los Angeles, CA 90029

* ABA Final Approval.     **ABA Provisional Approval

246

Los Angeles Southwest College
Legal Assistant Program
1600 W. Imperial Highway
Los Angeles, CA 90047

* UCLA Extension
Attorney Assistant Training Program
10995 LeConte Ave., Suite 517
Los Angeles, CA 90024

University of Southern California
Paralegal Program
Law Center - University Park
Los Angeles, CA 90089-0071

* University of West Los Angeles
School of Paralegal Studies
12201 Washington Place
Los Angeles, CA 90066

**Mission Viejo**

* Saddleback College
Legal Assistant Program
28000 Marguerite Parkway
Mission Viejo, CA 92692

**Moraga**

* Saint Mary's College
Paralegal Program
P.O. Box 3052
Moraga, CA 94575

**Northridge**

Phillips Junior College
8520 Balboa Boulevard
Northridge, CA 91325

**Norwalk**

* Cerritos College
11110 East Alondra Blvd.
Norwalk, CA 90650

**Oakland**

Merritt College
12500 Campus Drive
Oakland, CA 94619

Saint Mary's College
500 12th Street, Suite 220
Oakland, CA 94512

**Oxnard**

Oxnard College
4000 South Rose Avenue
Oxnard, CA 93033

**Panorama City**

Catherine College
Paralegal Program
8155 Van Nuys Blvd.
Panorama City, CA 91402

**Pasadena**

Pasadena City College
Business Department
1570 E. Colorado Blvd.
Pasadena, CA 91106

Watterson College
1165 E. Colorado Blvd.
Pasadena, CA 91106

* ABA Final Approval.     **ABA Provisional Approval

**Redwood City**

Canada College
4200 Farm Hill Boulevard
Redwood City, CA 94061

**Riverside**

Phillips College
Inland Empire Campus
4300 Central Avenue
Riverside, CA 92506

University of California, Riverside
University Extension
Certificate in Legal Assistantship
Riverside, CA 92521-0112

**Rohnert Park**

Sonoma State University
Attorney Assistant Program
Office of Extended Education
1801 E. Cotati Avenue
Rohnert Park, CA 94928

**Sacramento**

American River College
4700 College Oak Drive
Sacramento, CA 95841

MTI Western Business College
Legal Assistant Program
2731 Capital Avenue
Sacramento, CA 95816

University of Northern California
Paralegal School
816 H Street, Suite 108
Sacramento, CA 95814

Western Institute of Procedural Law
2731 Capitol Avenue
Sacramento, CA 95816

**San Bernardino**

California State University, San Bernardino
Paralegal Program
Political Science Department
5500 University Parkway
San Bernardino, CA 92407

Metropolitan Technical Institute &
Business College
Legal Technician Program
1963 No. E Street, Suite A
San Bernardino, CA 92405

San Bernardino Valley College
Legal Administration Program
701 South Mt. Vernon Avenue
San Bernardino, CA 92403

**San Bruno**

Skyline College
Paralegal Program
3300 College Drive
San Bruno, CA 94066

**San Diego**

Muir Technical Programs
Paralegal Program
4304 Twain Avenue
San Diego, CA 92120

* University of San Diego
Lawyer's Assistant Program
Room 318, Serra Hall
Alcala Park
San Diego, CA 92110

* ABA Final Approval.     **ABA Provisional Approval

248

**San Fernando**

Los Angeles Mission College
Paralegal Program
1212 San Fernando Road
San Fernando, CA  91340-2294

**San Francisco**

City College of San Francisco
A.A. & Certificate Legal
Assistant Programs
50 Phelan Avenue
San Francisco, CA  94112

San Francisco State University
Extended Education - Paralegal Studies
1600 Holloway Avenue
San Francisco, CA  94132-1789

Unilex College
Paralegal Division
995 Market Street
San Francisco, CA  94103

University of San Francisco
Paralegal Studies Program
Lone Mountain Campus, Room 105
San Francisco, CA  94117-1080

**San Jose**

San Jose State University
Legal Assistant Studies/Continuing
Education
One Washington Square
San Jose, CA  95192

**San Luis Obispo**

California Polytechnic State University,
San Luis Obispo
Extended Education Department
San Luis Obispo, CA  93407

**San Marcos**

Watterson College
336 Rancheros Drive, Suite C
San Marcos, CA  92069

**San Rafael**

Dominican College of San Rafael
San Rafael, CA  94901

**Santa Ana**

* Rancho Santiago College
Seventeenth at Bristol
Santa Ana, CA  92706

**Santa Barbara**

University of California, Santa Barbara
Extension
Program in Legal Assistantship
Santa Barbara, CA  93106

**Santa Clara**

Santa Clara University
Institute for Paralegal Education
Lawhouse
Santa Clara, CA  95050

**Santa Clarita**

American Paralegal Institute
21704 Golden Triangle Road
Suite 314
Santa Clarita, CA  91350

* ABA Final Approval.    **ABA Provisional Approval

**Santa Cruz**

University of California, Santa Cruz
Extension
Program in Legal Assistantship
740 Front Street, Suite 155
Santa Cruz, CA 95060

**Saratoga**

West Valley College
Office of Community Development
14000 Fruitvale Avenue
Saratoga, CA 95070

**Sherman Oaks**

Watterson College
5121 Van Nuys Boulevard
Sherman Oaks, CA 91403

**So. Lake Tahoe**

Lake Tahoe Community College
Legal Assistant Certificate
2659 Lake Tahoe Blvd.
P.O. Box 14445
So. Lake Tahoe, CA 95702

**Stockton**

Humphreys College
6650 Inglewood Drive
Stockton, CA 92507

**Torrance**

* El Camino College
Legal Assistant Program
16007 Crenshaw Boulevard
Torrance, CA 90506

**Van Nuys**

Merit College
7101 Sepulveda Boulevard
Van Nuys, CA 91405-2997

**Visalia**

* College of the Sequoias
Paralegal Program
915 South Mooney Blvd.
Visalia, CA 93227

**Whittier**

* Rio Hondo Community College
Paralegal Program
3600 Workman Mill Road
Whittier, CA 90608

**Woodland Hills**

American Paralegal Institute
22837 Ventura Blvd., #203
Woodland Hills, CA 91364

**COLORADO**

**Colorado Springs**

Pikes Peak Community College
5675 S. Academy Blvd., Box 19
Colorado Springs, CO 80906

**Denver**

Community College of Denver
Auraria Campus
Serv. Occup. Div., Room CA-313
1111 West Colfax
Denver, CO 80204

* ABA Final Approval. **ABA Provisional Approval

250

\* Denver Paralegal Institute
Gen'l Prac. Legal Asst. Program
1401 19th Street
Denver, CO 80202

Metropolitan State College
Legal Assistant Program
1006 11th Street
Denver, CO 80204

National Academy for Paralegal
Studies, Inc.
950 S. Cherry St., Suite 1000
Denver, CO 80222

University of Denver
College of Law
Program of Advanced Professional
Development
200 W. 14th Avenue
Denver, CO 80204

**Littleton**

\* Arapahoe Community College
Legal Assistant Program
5900 S. Santa Fe Drive
Littleton, CO 80120

**Pueblo**

University of Southern Colorado
School of Liberal Arts
2200 Bonforte Boulevard
Pueblo, CO 81001

**CONNECTICUT**

**Branford**

Branford Hall School of Business
Paralegal Diploma Program
9 Business Park Drive
Branford, CT 06405

**Bridgeport**

\* University of Bridgeport
Law Center/Legal Assistant Prog.
303 University Avenue
Bridgeport, CT 06601

**Fairfield**

Fairfield University
North Benson Road
CNS-9
Fairfield, CT 06430

\* Sacred Heart University
5151 Park Avenue
Fairfield, CT 06432

**Hamden**

\* Quinnipiac College
Legal Studies Department
Mount Carmel Avenue
Hamden, CT 06518

**Hartford**

\* Hartford College for Women
Legal Assistant Program
50 Elizabeth Street
The Counseling Center
Hartford, CT 06105

**Manchester**

* Manchester Community College
Legal Assistant Program
60 Bidwell Street
Manchester, CT 06040

**Norwalk**

* Norwalk Community College
Legal Assistant Program
333 Wilson Avenue
Norwalk, CT 06854

**Southington**

Briarwood College
Legal Assistant/Paralegal Program
2279 Mount Vernon Road
Southington, CT 06489

**Stamford**

Connecticut Institute for Paralegal
Studies, Inc.
441 Summer Street
Stamford, CT 06901

**Waterbury**

* Mattatuck Community College
Legal Assistant Program
750 Chase Parkway
Waterbury, CT 06708

Post College
Legal Assistant Program
800 Country Club Road
Waterbury, CT 06708

**West Haven**

University of New Haven
Paralegal Studies
300 Orange Avenue
West Haven, CT 06516

**Yalesville**

National Academy for Paralegal
Studies, Inc.
339 Main Street
P.O. Box 4102
Yalesville, CT 06492

**DELAWARE**

**Dover**

* Wesley College
Paralegal Studies Program
Dover, DE 19901

**Georgetown**

Delaware Technical and Community
College
Southern Campus
Legal Assistant Technology
Georgetown, DE 19947

**Wilmington**

Brandywine College
of Widener University
P.O. Box 7139, Concord Pike
Wilmington, DE 19803

* ABA Final Approval.    **ABA Provisional Approval

National Academy for Paralegal
Studies, Inc.
300 Delaware Avenue, 10th Floor
P.O. Box 25046
Wilmington, DE 19801

* University of Delaware
Legal Assistant Education Program
2800 Pennsylvania Avenue
Wilmington, DE 19806

* Widener University
Institute for Professional Development
706 Market Street Mall
Law and Education Center
Wilmington, DE 19801

## DISTRICT OF COLUMBIA

Antioch School of Law
Paralegal Program
1624 Crescent Place N.W.
Washington, D.C. 20009

* George Washington University
Center for Continuing Education and
Workshops
801 22nd Street N.W., Suite T409
Washington, D.C. 20052

* Georgetown University
Legal Assistant Program
School for Summer and Continuing
Education
Washington, D.C. 20057

Institute of Law and Aging
Paralegal Training Program
National Law Center, Suite T401
George Washington University
801 22nd Street N.W.
Washington, D.C. 20052

University of the District of Columbia
1331 H Street N.W.
Washington, D.C. 20005

## FLORIDA

### Boca Raton

Florida Atlantic University
Institute for Legal Assistants
Division of Continuing Education
Boca Raton, FL 33431

Southern Career Institute
164 W. Royal Palm Road
P.O. Box 2158
Boca Raton, FL 33432

### Bradenton

Manatee Junior College
Legal Assistant Program
P.O. Box 1849
Bradenton, FL 33507

### Clearwater

St. Petersburg Junior College
Legal Assistant Program
Clearwater Campus
Coachman, Road & Drew
Clearwater, FL 33515

### Coral Gables

University of Miami
Institute for Paralegal Studies
P.O. Box 248005
Coral Gables, FL 33124

* ABA Final Approval. **ABA Provisional Approval

253

## Ft. Lauderdale

Barry University
Legal Assistant Institute
Ft. Lauderdale, FL  33310

Charron Williams College
Legal Assistant Program
6289 West Sunrise Blvd.
Ft. Lauderdale, FL  33313

Fort Lauderdale College
Legal Assistant Studies Program
100 E. Broward Boulevard
Ft. Lauderdale, FL  33301

Jones College
Ft. Lauderdale Campus
6289 W. Sunrise Boulevard
Ft. Lauderdale, FL  33313

Legal Career Institute
Paralegal Program
5225 West Broward Blvd.
Ft. Lauderdale, FL  33317

## Ft. Meyers

Edison Community College
P.O. Box 06210
Ft. Meyers, FL  33906-6210

## Gainesville

* Santa Fe Community College
Legal Assistant Program
3000 N.W. 83rd Street
Gainesville, FL  32601-1530

## Jacksonville

American Institute for Paralegal
Studies, Inc.
Southeast Regional Office
5700 St. Augustine Road
Jacksonville, FL  32207

Jones College, South Campus
Paralegal Degree and Diploma Programs
3428 Beach Boulevard
Jacksonville, FL  32207

University of North Florida
Paralegal Program
P.O. Box 17074
Jacksonville, FL  33245-7074

## Lake Worth

Palm Beach Junior College
4200 Congress Avenue
Lake Worth, FL  33461

## Lakeland

Jones College, Lakeland Campus
Paralegal Degree and Diploma Programs
2620 Kathleen Road
Lakeland, FL  33809

## Longwood

PRS Career Academy, Inc.
Legal Studies Program
2648 West Highway 434
Longwood, FL  32779

* ABA Final Approval.    **ABA Provisional Approval

254

## Miami

* Broward Community College
Legal Assistant Program
3501 S.W. Davie Road, Bldg. 9
Miami, FL 33314

Jones College
Paralegal Degree and Diploma Programs
Miami Campus
255 S.W. 8th Street
Miami, FL 33130

* Miami-Dade Community College
Legal Assistant Program
Mitchell Wolfson New World Center
300 N.E. 2nd Avenue
Miami, FL 33132

## Miami Shores

Barry University
Legal Assistant Institute
11300 N.E. Second Avenue
Miami Shores, FL 33161

## Naples

Barry University
Legal Assistant Institute
Naples, FL 33941

## Ocala

Central Florida Community College
P.O. Box 1388
Ocala, FL 32670

## Orlando

Orlando College
Paralegal Program
925 South Orange Avenue
Orlando, FL 32806

* Southern College
Legal Assistant Program
5600 Lake Underhill Road
Orlando, FL 32807

University of Central Florida
Allied Legal Services Program
P.O. Box 25000
Orlando, FL 32816

Valencia Community College
East Campus
P.O. Box 3028
Orlando, FL 32802

## Palm Beach

Palm Beach Junior College, North
3160 PGA Boulevard
Palm Beach, FL 33410

## Pensacola

Pensacola Junior College
Legal Assistant Program
1000 College Boulevard
Pensacola, FL 32504

University of West Florida
Legal Administration Program
Department of Political Science
11000 University Parkway
Pensacola, FL 32514

* ABA Final Approval.     **ABA Provisional Approval

**Riviera Beach**

Legal Career Institute
Paralegal Program
7289 Garden Road
Riviera Beach, FL 33404

**Sarasota**

Sarasota Voc./Tech. Center
Legal Assistant Program
4748 Beneva Road
Sarasota, FL 34231

**St. Petersburg**

St. Petersburg Junior College
Legal Assistant Program
P.O. Box 13489
Division of Business
St. Petersburg, FL 33733

**Tampa**
Hillsborough Community College
P.O. Box 30030
Tampa, FL 33620

Paralegal Careers, Inc.
1211 N. Westshore
Suite 100
Tampa, FL 33607

Tampa College
Paralegal Program
3924 Coconut Palm Drive
Tampa, FL 33619

**GEORGIA**

**Athens**

** Athens Area Technical Institute
Paralegal Studies Program
U.S. Highway 29 North
Athens, GA 30610

**Atlanta**

American Institute for Paralegal
Studies, Inc.
First Atlanta Tower, Suite 2400
Atlanta, GA 30383

Atlanta Paralegal Institute
1393 Peachtree Street, N.E.
Atlanta, GA 30309

Morris Brown College
Legal Assistant Program
643 Martin Luther King Jr. Dr.
Atlanta, GA 30314

* National Center for Paralegal Training
Lawyer's Assistant Program
3414 Peachtree Road N.E., Suite 528
Atlanta, GA 30326

**Douglasville**

Academy for Paralegal Studies
8493 Campbellton Street
Douglasville, GA 30133

**Gainesville**

Gainesville College
Legal Assistant Program
Mundy Mill Road
Gainesville, GA 30501

* ABA Final Approval.     **ABA Provisional Approval

**HAWAII**

**Honolulu**

* Kapiolani Community College
Legal Assistant Program
620 Pensacola Avenue
Honolulu, HI 96814

**IDAHO**

**Moscow**

University of Idaho
College of Law
Paralegal Program
Moscow, ID 83840

**Pocatello**

National Academy for Paralegal
Studies, Inc.
2043 E. Center
Pocatello, ID 83205

**ILLINOIS**

**Carbondale**

* Southern Illinois University at
Carbondale
Paralegal Studies Program
Carbondale, IL 62901

**Chicago**

MacCormac Junior College
327 South LaSalle Street
Chicago, IL 60604

* Roosevelt University
Lawyer's Assistant Program
430 So. Michigan Avenue
Chicago, IL 60605

Uptown Learning Center
Legal Assistant Training Program
1220 West Wilson
Chicago, IL 60640

**Elmhurst**

MacCormac Junior College
615 No. West Avenue
Elmhurst, IL 61761

**Normal**

Illinois State University
Legal Studies Program
Schroeder 306
Political Science Dept.
Normal, IL 61761

**Oakbrook Terrace**

American Institute for Paralegal
Studies, Inc.
One South 450 Summit Avenue
Suite 230
Oakbrook Terrace, IL 60181

**Palatine**

* William Rainey Harper College
Legal Technology Program
1200 W. Algonquin Road
Palatine, IL 60067-7398

**Peoria**

Midstate College
Paralegal Services
244 S.W. Jefferson, Box 148
Peoria, IL 61602

**South Holland**

* South Suburban College
Paralegal/Legal Assistant Program
15800 S. State Street
South Holland, IL 60473

**Springfield**

* Sangamon State University
Legal Studies Program
LSP PAC 429
Springfield, IL 62794-9243

**Wilmette**

* Loyola University
Institute for Paralegal Studies
Mallinckrodt Campus
1041 Ridge Road
Wilmette, IL 60091

Mallinckrodt College
Legal Assistant Program
1041 Ridge Road
Wilmette, IL 60091

**INDIANA**

**Evansville**

* University of Evansville
Legal Paraprofessional Program
1800 Lincoln Avenue
Evansville, IN 47722

**Indianapolis**

Butler University
Legal Assistant Program
4600 Sunset
Indianapolis, IN 46208

Indiana Central University
1400 E. Hanna Avenue
Indianapolis, IN 46227

Lockyear College
Legal Assistant Program
1200 Waterway Boulevard
Indianapolis, IN 46202

**Muncie**

* Ball State University
Legal Assistant & Legal Admn.
Muncie, IN 47306

**South Bend**

American Institute for Paralegal
Studies, Inc.
52582 U.S. 31 No.
South Bend, IN 46637

Indiana University at South Bend
Paralegal Studies Certificate
1700 Meshawaka Avenue
South Bend, IN 46634

**Terre Haute**

Indiana State University
Conferences & Non-Credit Pgms.
Alumni Center, Room 240
Terre Haute, IN 47809

* ABA Final Approval.   **ABA Provisional Approval

## Vincennes

* Vincennes University
Paralegal Program
1002 North 1st Street
Vincennes, IN 47591

## IOWA

### Cedar Rapids

* Kirkwood Community College
6301 Kirkwood Boulevard, S.W.
P.O. Box 2068
Cedar Rapids, IA 52406

### Davenport

Marycrest College
1607 West 12th Street
Davenport, IA 52804

### Des Moines

* Des Moines Area Cmty. College
Legal Asst. Pgm., Urban Campus
1100 7th Street
Des Moines, IA 50314

### Estherville

Iowa Lakes Community College
Legal Assistant Program
300 South 18th Street
Estherville, IA 51334

### Sioux City

National Academy for Paralegal
Studies, Inc.
627 Frances Building
Sioux City, IA 51101

## KANSAS

### Great Bend

Barton County Community College
Legal Assisting
Great Bend, KS 67530

### Hutchinson

Hutchinson Community College
Legal Assistant Program
1300 North Plum
Hutchinson, KS 67501

### Olathe

National Academy for Paralegal
Studies, Inc.
105 South Kansas
Olathe, KS 66061

### Overland Park

* Johnson County Community College
Paralegal Program
12345 College at Quivera
Overland Park, KS 66210

The Brown Mackie College
Legal Assistant Program
8000 W. 110th Street
Overland Park, KS 66210

### Topeka

Washburn University of Topeka
Legal Assistant Program
17th & College
Topeka, KS 66621

* ABA Final Approval.      **ABA Provisional Approval

**Wichita**

Southern Technical College
Legal Assisting Program
2015 South Meridan
Wichita, KS 67213

* Wichita State University
Legal Assistant Program
College of Business Admin.
Wichita, KS 67208

**KENTUCKY**

**Frankfort**

National Academy for Paralegal
Studies, Inc.
P.O. Box 1291
Frankfort, KY 40602

**Lexington**

Institute for Paralegal Studies at
Sullivan College
2659 Regency Road
Lexington, KY 40503

**Louisville**

* Institute for Paralegal Studies
at Sullivan College
3101 Bardstown Road
Louisville, KY 40205

Sullivan Jr. College of Business Institute
for Paralegal Studies
3101 Bardstown Road
Louisville, KY 40205

* University of Louisville
Paralegal Program
106 Ford Hall
Political Science Dept.
Louisville, KY 40292

**Midway**

* Midway College
Paralegal Studies Program
Midway, KY 40347

**Morehead**

Morehead State University
College of Arts and Sciences
Paralegal Program
Morehead, KY 40351

**Richmond**

* Eastern Kentucky University
Paralegal Programs
McCreary 113
Richmond, KY 40475-3122

**LOUISIANA**

**Baton Rouge**

Louisiana State University
Paralegal Studies Program
361 Pleasant Hall - LSU
Baton Rouge, LA 70803

**Lafayette**

Univ. of Southwestern Louisiana
University College
P.O. Box 43370
Lafayette, LA 70504-3370

* ABA Final Approval.    **ABA Provisional Approval

**Marrero**

Phillips Junior College
Paralegal Studies Program
5001 West Bank Expressway
Marrero, LA 70072

**Metairie**

Institute for Legal Studies
3501 N. Causeway Boulevard
Suite 900
Metairie, LA 70002

**New Orleans**

Phillips Junior College
Paralegal Studies Program
822 South Clearview Avenue
New Orleans, LA 70123

* Tulane University
University College Paralegal Studies
Program
6823 St. Charles Avenue
New Orleans, LA 70118

University of New Orleans
Paralegal Institute
Metropolitan College
344 Camp Street, Suite 512
New Orleans, LA 70130

**Shreveport**

Louisiana State University in Shreveport
Paralegal Institute
Div. of Cont. Education &
Special Programs
Shreveport, LA 71115

**Thibodaux**

Nicholls State University
Legal Assistant Studies
P.O. Box 2089
Thibodaux, LA 70310

**MAINE**

**Bangor**

Beal College
Paralegal Program
629 Main Street
Bangor, ME 04401

University of Maine
University College Legal Technology
Program
Katahdin Hall
210 Texas Avenue
Bangor, ME 04401

**Portland**

University of Southern Maine
Dept. of Community Programs
USM Intown Center
68 High Street
Portland, ME 04101

**Rockland**

National Academy for Paralegal
Studies, Inc.
P.O. Box 1028
Rockland, ME 04841

* ABA Final Approval.    **ABA Provisional Approval

**Waterville**

National Academy for Paralegal
Studies, Inc.
RFD 3, Box 2470
Waterville, ME 04901

**MARYLAND**

**Arnold**

Anne Arundel Community College
Paralegal Studies Program
101 College Parkway
Careers Bldg., Room 234
Arnold, MD 21012

**Baltimore**

Community College of Baltimore, Harbor
Paralegal Program
Lombard Street at Market Place
Baltimore, MD 21202

* Dundalk Community College
7200 Sollers Point Road
Baltimore, MD 21222

**Bel Air**

Harford Community College
Adult Occupational Education
401 Thomas Run Road
Bel Air, MD 21014

**College Park**

University of Maryland
University College
College Park Campus
College Park, MD 20742

**Eudowood**

National Academy for Paralegal
Studies, Inc.
P.O. Box 20148
Eudowood, MD 21284

**Largo**

Prince George's Cmty. College
Paralegal Program
301 Largo Road
Largo, MD 20772-2199

**Stevenson**

* Villa Julie College
Paralegal Program
Green Spring Valley Road
Stevenson, MD 21153

**Takoma Park**

Montgomery College
Legal Assistant Program
Takoma Park, MD 20912

**MASSACHUSETTS**

**Amherst**

Hampshire College
Amherst, MA 01002

**Beverly**

North Shore Community College
3 Essex Street
Beverly, MA 02193

* ABA Final Approval.     **ABA Provisional Approval

262

## Boston

Boston State College
Paralegal Program
625 Huntington Avenue
Boston, MA 02115

Boston University
Metropolitan College
Legal Assistant Program
755 Commonwealth Avenue
Boston, MA 02215

Kathryn Gibbs School
Legal Assistant Program
5 Arlington Street
Boston, MA 02116

Newbury College
Paralegal Program
921 Boylston Street
Boston, MA 02115

Suffolk University
College of Liberal Arts & Sciences
Lawyer's Assistant Certificate
Beacon Hill
Boston, MA 02114-4280

University of Massachusetts - Boston
Center for Legal Education Serv.
Downtown Center
Boston, MA 02125

## Burlington

Middlesex Community College
Paralegal Studies Program
Terrace Hall Avenue
Burlington, MA 01803

## Chicopee

* Elms College
Paralegal Institute
Chicopee, MA 01013

## Dedham

Northeastern University
Paralegal Program
Center for Continuing Education
370 Common Street
Dedham, MA 02026

## Haverhill

* Northern Essex Community College
Paralegal Studies Program
Elliot Street
Haverhill, MA 01830

## Longmeadow

Bay Path Junior College
Legal Assistant Program
588 Longmeadow Street
Longmeadow, MA 01106

## Newton Centre

Mount Ida College
Paralegal Studies Program
777 Dedham Street
Newton Centre, MA 02159

## Paxton

* Anna Maria College
Paralegal Program
Sunset Lane
Paxton, MA 01612-1198

* ABA Final Approval.     **ABA Provisional Approval

**Waltham**

* Bentley College
Institute of Paralegal Studies
Beaver & Forest Streets
Waltham, MA 02254

**Weston**

Regis College
Legal Studies Program
235 Wellesley Street
Weston, MA 02193

**Weymouth**

National Academy for Paralegal
Studies, Inc.
53 Winter Street
Weymouth, MA 02189

**Worcester**

Assumption College
Paralegal Studies
Center for Continuing & Professional
Education
500 Salisbury Street
Worcester, MA 01609

Becker Junior College
Paralegal Studies Program
61 Sever Street
Worcester, MA 01609

**MICHIGAN**

**Allendale**

Grand Valley State College
School of Public Service
College Landing
467 Mackinac Hall
Allendale, MI 49401

**Battle Creek**

* Kellogg Community College
Legal Assistant Program
450 North Avenue
Battle Creek, MI 49016

**Big Rapids**

* Ferris State University
Legal Assistant Program
Big Rapids, MI 49307

**Dearborn**

Henry Ford Community College
5101 Evergreen Road
Dearborn, MI 48128

**Dearborn Heights**

Henry Ford Community College
22586 Ann Arbor Trail
Dearborn Heights, MI 48127

**Detroit**

Mercy College of Detroit
Legal Asst./Legal Admn. Program
8200 W. Outer Drive
Detroit, MI 48219

* ABA Final Approval.     **ABA Provisional Approval

Michigan Paralegal Institute
65 Cadillac Square
Suite 3200
Detroit, MI 48226

* University of Detroit Mercy
Legal Asst./Legal Admn. Programs
8200 W. Outer Drive
Detroit, MI 48219

**Farmington Hills**

Oakland Community College
Orchard Ridge Campus
27055 Orchard Lane Road
Farmington Hills, MI 48018

**Flint**

Mott Community College
1401 E. Court Street
Flint, MI 48503

**Lansing**

* Lansing Community College
Legal Assistant Program
Criminal Justice & Law Center
419 N. Capitol Avenue
P.O. Box 40010
Lansing, MI 48901-7210

**Livonia**

* Madonna College
36600 Schoolcraft Road
Livonia, MI 48150

**Port Huron**

St. Clair County Cmty. College
323 Erie Street
Port Huron, MI 48060

**Rochester**

Michigan Christian College
800 West Avon Road
Rochester, MI 48063

* Oakland University
Diploma Program for Legal Assistants
Div. of Continuing Education
Rochester, MI 48063

**Sault Ste. Marie**

Lake Superior State College
A.S. & B.A. Legal Asst. Programs
Social Science Department
Sault Ste. Marie, MI 49783

**Southfield**

American Institute for
Paralegal Studies, Inc.
Southfield Regional Office
Honeywell Center, Suite 225
17515 W. Nine Mile Road
Southfield, MI 48075

**Warren**

* Macomb Community College
South Campus
14500 Twelve Mile Road
Warren, MI 48093

**Ypsilanti**

* Eastern Michigan University
Legal Assistant/Paralegal Program
Ypsilanti, MI 48197

* ABA Final Approval.    **ABA Provisional Approval

## MINNESOTA

### Inver Grove Hgts.

* Inver Hills Community College
Legal Assistant Program
8445 College Trail
Inver Grove Hgts., MN  55076

### Minneapolis

* Minnesota Legal Assistant Inst.
12450 Wayzata Boulevard
Minneapolis, MN  55343

* North Hennepin Community College
Legal Assistant Program
7411 85th Avenue North
Minneapolis, MN  55445

### Moorhead

Moorhead State University
Legal Assistant Program
11th Street South
Moorhead, MN  56560-9980

### St. Paul

* Hamline University
Legal Assistant Program
1536 Hewitt Avenue
St. Paul, MN  55104-1284

### Winona

* Winona State University
Paralegal Program
Minne Hall
Winona, MN  55987

## MISSISSIPPI

### Columbus

* Mississippi University for Women
Paralegal Program
Div. of Business and Economics
College Street
Columbus, MS  39701

### Hattiesburg

* University of Southern Mississippi
Paralegal Studies
P.O. Box 5108 Southern Station
Hattiesburg, MS  39401

### Jackson

University of Mississippi
Paralegal Studies Program
Universities Center
1855 Eastover Drive, Suite 101
Jackson, MS  39211

### Raymond

Hinds Community College
Paralegal Technology Program
Raymond, MS  39154

### Senatobia

Northwest Mississippi Jr. College
Legal Assistant Program
300 North Panola Street
Senatobia, MS  38668

* ABA Final Approval.    **ABA Provisional Approval

**Tupelo**

University of Mississippi
Tupelo Campus
Paralegal Studies Program
655 Eason Boulevard
Tupelo, MS 38801

**MISSOURI**

**Cape Girardeau**

Southeast Missouri State University
900 Normal
Cape Girardeau, MO 63701

**Fulton**

* William Woods College
Paralegal Studies Program
Fulton, MO 65252

**Kansas City**

* Avila College
Legal Assistant Program
11901 Wornall Road
Kansas City, MO 64145

Concorde Career Institute
Legal Assistant Program
P.O. Box 26610
Kansas City, MO 64196

Penn Valley Community College
Legal Technology Program
3201 S.W. Tfwy.
Kansas City, MO 64111

Rockhurst College
Paralegal Studies
1100 Rockhurst Road
Kansas City, MO 64110

**Liberty**

William Jewell College
Paralegal Program
Evening Division
Liberty, MO 64068

**Springfield**

Drury Evening College
Continuing Education Division
Legal Assistant Studies
900 North Benton Avenue
Springfield, MO 65802

Rutledge College
Legal Assistant Program
625 North Benton
Springfield, MO 65806

**St. Joseph**

* Missouri Western State College
4525 Downs Drive
St. Joseph, MO 64507

Platt Junior College
Legal Assistant Program
3131 Frederick Avenue
St. Joseph, MO 64506-2911

**St. Louis**

Marysville College
13550 Conway Road
St. Louis, MO 63110

* ABA Final Approval.    **ABA Provisional Approval

Mid-America Paralegal Institute
8008 Carondelet, Suite 211
St. Louis, MO 63105

National Academy for Paralegal
Studies, Inc.
11907 Manchester Road
St. Louis, MO 63131

St. Louis Community College at Meramec
11333 Big Bend
St. Louis, MO 63122

St. Louis Community College at
Florissant Valley
3400 Perhall Road
St. Louis, MO 63135

* Webster University
Legal Studies Program
470 East Lockwood Avenue
St. Louis, MO 63119-3194

**MONTANA**

**Billings**

Rocky Mountain College
Legal Assistant Program
1511 Poly Drive
Billings, MT 59102-1796

**Great Falls**

College of Great Falls
Paralegal Studies
1301 20th Street South
Great Falls, MT 59405

**Missoula**

Missoula Voc. Tech. Center
Legal Assisting Cert. Program
909 South Avenue West
Missoula, MT 59801

**NEBRASKA**

**Lincoln**

Lincoln School of Commerce
Legal Studies Program
1821 K Street
P.O. Box 82826
Lincoln, NE 68501

Nebraska Wesleyan College
Legal Assistant Program
Lincoln, NE 68504

**Omaha**

* College of St. Mary
Paralegal Studies Program
1901 South 72nd Street
Omaha, NE 68124

* Metropolitan Community College
Legal Asst./Paralegal Program
P.O. Box 3777
Omaha, NE 68103-0777

Nebraska College of Business
Legal Assistant Program
3636 California Street
Omaha, NE 68131

VTI Career Institute of Omaha
Legal Assistant Program
32nd Avenue and Dodge Streets
Omaha, NE 68131

* ABA Final Approval.     **ABA Provisional Approval

## NEVADA

### Las Vegas

Las Vegas Business College
Legal Assistant Program
2917 West Washington Avenue
Las Vegas, NV 89107

### North Las Vegas

Clark County Community College
Legal Assistant Program
3200 East Cheyenne Avenue
North Las Vegas, NV 89030

### Reno

Reno Business College
Paralegal Program
140 Washington Street
Reno, NV 89503

## NEW HAMPSHIRE

### Dover

McIntosh College
Legal Assistant Program
23 Cataract Avenue
Dover, NH 03820

### Durham

University of New Hampshire
Paralegal Studies Program
24 Rosemary Lane
Durham, NH 03824

### Manchester

National Academy for Paralegal
Studies, Inc.
97 West Merrimack Street
Manchester, NH 03101

Notre Dame College
Legal Assistant Program
2321 Elm Street
Manchester, NH 03104

### Nashua

* Rivier College
Baccalaureate and Certificate
Paralegal Studies
Nashua, NH 03060

## NEW JERSEY

### Bridgewater

Taylor Business Institute
250 Route 28
Post Office Box 6875
Bridgewater, NJ 08807

### Cherry Hill

South Jersey Paralegal School
302 Sherry Way
Cherry Hill, NJ 08034

### East Orange

Upsala College
Paralegal Program
Beck Hall, 203
East Orange, NJ 07019

---

* ABA Final Approval.    **ABA Provisional Approval

**Edison**

* Middlesex County College
Legal Studies Department
155 Mill Road
P.O. Box 3050
Edison, NJ 08818-3050

**Laurel Springs**

American Institute for Paralegal
Studies, Inc.
75 South Brookline Drive
Laurel Springs, NJ 08021

**Lincroft**

Brookdale Community College
765 Newman Springs Road
Lincroft, NJ 07738

**Linden**

Institute of Paralegal Studies
453 North Wood Avenue
Linden, NJ 07036

**Madison**

* Fairleigh Dickinson University
Paralegal Studies Program
285 Madison Avenue
Madison, NJ 07940

**Mahwah**

National Academy for Paralegal
Studies, Inc.
One Lethbridge Plaza, Suite 23
P.O. Box 835
Mahwah, NJ 07430

**Mays Landing**

Atlantic Community College
Paralegal Program
Mays Landing, NJ 08330-9888

**Millburn, NJ**

Law Center for Paralegal Studies
374 Millburn Avenue
Suite 200
Millburn, NJ 07041

**Paramus**

Bergen Community College
400 Paramus Road
Paramus, NJ 07652

Plaza School
Garden State Plaza
Route 17 & Route 4
Paramus, NJ 07652

**Passaic Park**

First School for Careers
Paralegal Division
110 Main Avenue
Passaic Park, NJ 07055

**Pemberton**

Burlington County College
CA 267
Pemberton-Brown Mills Road
Pemberton, NJ 08068

---

* ABA Final Approval.     **ABA Provisional Approval

**Sommerville**

Raritan Valley Community College
Legal Assisting Program
P.O. Box 3300
Sommerville, NJ 08876

**Toms River**

Ocean County College
Legal Assistant Technology Program
Toms River, NJ 08753

**Trenton**

* Mercer County Community College
Legal Assistant Program
P.O. Box B
Trenton, NJ 08690

**Upper Montclair**

* Montclair State College
Department of Legal Studies
Paralegal Studies Program
Upper Montclair, NJ 07043

**Vineland**

* Cumberland County College
Legal Technology Program
P.O. Box 517
Vineland, NJ 08360

**Waldwick**

Juris-Tech
The Paralegal School
100 West Prospect
Waldwick, NJ 07463

**NEW MEXICO**

**Albuquerque**

Albuquerque Tech./Voc. Institute
Legal Assistant Program
4700 Morris, N.E.
Albuquerque, NM 87111

University of Albuquerque
St. Joseph's Place, N.W.
Albuquerque, NM 87105

**Shiprock**

Navajo Community College
Legal Advocates Training Pgm.
P.O. Box 580
Shiprock, NM 87420

**NEW YORK**

**Albany**

American Career Schools, Inc.
130 Ontario Street
Albany, NY 12206

Junior College of Albany
140 New Scotland Avenue
Albany, NY 12208

**Binghamton**

Broome Community College
Paralegal Assistant Program
P.O. Box 1017
Binghamton, NY 13902

* ABA Final Approval.    **ABA Provisional Approval

271

## Bronx

* Bronx Community College
University Ave. & West 181 St.
Bronx, NY 10453

* Lehman College of the City University of
New York
Paralegal Studies Program
Office of Continuing Education
Bedford Park Blvd., West
Bronx, NY 10468

## Brooklyn

Brooklyn College
Paralegal Program
1212 Boylan Hall
Brooklyn, NY 11210

* Long Island University
Brooklyn Center
Paralegal Studies Program
University Plz. - LLC 302
Brooklyn, NY 11201-5372

* New York City Technical College
of the City Univ. of New York
300 Jay Street
Room N-422
Brooklyn, NY 11201-2983

## Buffalo

Erie Community College
Paralegal Unit
121 Ellicott Street
Buffalo, NY 14209

## Central Islip

American Career Schools, Inc.
1707 Veterans Highway
Central Islip, NY 11722

New York Institute of Technology
Paralegal Studies Program
Building 66 - Room 131
Carleton Avenue
Central Islip, NY 11722

## Corning

Corning Community College
Paralegal Assistant Program
Spencer Hill Road
Corning, NY 14830

## Dobbs Ferry

Mercy College
Paralegal Studies Program
Dept. of Law, Criminal Justice
555 Broadway
Dobbs Ferry, NY 10522

## Flushing

* Queens College/CUNY
Continuing Education Program
Paralegal Studies
Flushing, NY 11367

## Garden City, L.I.

* Adelphi University
University College
Center for Career Programs
Lawyer's Assistant Program
Garden City, L.I., NY 11530

* ABA Final Approval.     **ABA Provisional Approval

\* Nassau Community College
Paralegal Program
Stewart Avenue
Garden City, NY 11530-6793

**Greenvale**

\* Long Island University
C.W. Post Campus
Paralegal Studies Program
Greenvale, NY 11548

**Hamburg**

\* Hilbert College
Legal Assistant Program
5200 South Park Avenue
Hamburg, NY 14075

**Hartsdale**

American News Institute Programs
110 Central Park Avenue South
Hartsdale, NY 10530

**Herkimer**

Herkimer County Cmty. College
Paralegal Program
Herkimer, NY 13350

**Jamaica (Queens)**

St. John's University
Legal Assistant Program
Grand Central & Utopia Pkwy.
Jamaica (Queens), NY 11439

**Loch Sheldrake**

Sullivan County Cmty. College
Paralegal Program
Loch Sheldrake, NY 12759

**Manhattan Beach**

Kingsborough Community College
City University of New York
Office of Continuing Education
Paralegal Studies Program
Manhattan Beach, NY 11235

**New Rochelle**

Iona College
Legal Assistant Program
715 North Avenue
New Rochelle, NY 10801

**New York City**

Baruch College
Paralegal Certificate Program
17 Lexington Avenue
Box 409
New York, NY 10010

Hunter College
Paralegal Program
Center for Lifelong Learning
695 Park Avenue
New York, NY 10021

International Career Institute
Paralegal Program
120 West 30th Street
New York, NY 10001

\* ABA Final Approval.     \*\*ABA Provisional Approval

Marymount Manhattan College
Paralegal Studies Program
221 East 71st Street
New York, NY 10021

* New York University
Institute of Paralegal Studies
11 West 42nd Street
New York, NY 10036

Paralegal Institute
132 Nassau Street
New York, NY 10038

The New School
Paralegal Studies
66 West 12th Street
New York, NY 10011

The Sobelsohn School
Paralegal Program
352 Seventh Avenue
New York, NY 10001

**Poughkeepsie**

* Marist College
Paralegal Program
North Road
Poughkeepsie, NY 12601-1381

**Purchase**

* Manhattanville College
Paralegal Program
Office of Special Programs
Purchase, NY 10577

**Sanborn**

Niagara County Community College
Legal Assistant Program
3111 Saunders Settlement Road
Sanborn, NY 14132

**Schenectady**

Schenectady County Cmty. College
Paralegal Program
78 Washington Avenue
Schenectady, NY 12305

**Seldon**

* Suffolk County Cmty. College
A.A.S. Legal Assistant Program
533 College Road
Seldon, NY 11784

**Sparkill**

Long Island University
Rockland Campus
Route 340
Sparkill, NY 10976

**Staten Island**

The City University of New York
St. George Campus
130 Stuyvesant Place
Staten Island, NY 10301

**Suffern**

National Academy for Paralegal
Studies, Inc.
P.O. Box 517
Suffern, NY 10901

* ABA Final Approval.    **ABA Provisional Approval

274

Rockland Community College
Legal Assistant Program
145 College Road
Suffern, NY 10901

**Syracuse**

* Syracuse University College
Legal Assistant Program
610 East Fayette Street
Syracuse, NY 13244-6020

**White Plains**

* Mercy College
White Plains Extension Center
Paralegal Studies Program
White Plains, NY 10601

**Yonkers**

* Elizabeth Seton College
Legal Assistant Program
1061 North Broadway
Yonkers, NY 10701

**NORTH CAROLINA**

**Asheville**

Cecils Jr. College of Business
1567 Patton Avenue
Asheville, NC 28806

**Boone**

Appalachian State University
Department of Criminal Justice and
Political Science
Boone, NC 28606

**Charlotte**

Central Piedmont Cmty. College
Paralegal Technology Program
1201 Elizabeth Avenue
P.O. Box 35009
Charlotte, NC 28235

**Fayetteville**

* Fayetteville Tech. Cmty. College
Paralegal Technology Program
P.O. Box 5236
Fayetteville, NC 28303

**Greensboro**

Greensboro College
Applied Arts & Social Sciences
815 West Market Street
Greensboro, NC 27401-1875

**Greenville**

Pitt Technical Institute
Paralegal Program
P.O. Drawer 7007
Greenville, NC 27834

**Jacksonville**

Coastal Carolina Cmty. College
Paralegal Technology Program
444 Western Boulevard
Jacksonville, NC 28540

**Lexington**

Davidson County Cmty. College
P.O. Box 1287
Intersection of Old Greensboro
Road & Interstate 40
Lexington, NC 27292

* ABA Final Approval.    **ABA Provisional Approval

## Morehead City

* Carteret Community College
Paralegal Technology Program
3505 Arendell Street
Morehead City, NC 28557-2989

## Raleigh

* Meredith College
Legal Assistant Program
3800 Hillsborough Street
Raleigh, NC 27607-5298

## Sanford

Central Carolina Tech. Institute
Department of Community Colleges
1105 Kelly Drive
Sanford, NC 27330

## Sylva

Southwestern Technical Institute
P.O. Box 95
Sylva, NC 28779

## NORTH DAKOTA

### Bismarck

National Academy for Paralegal
Studies, Inc.
116 North Fourth Street
Bismarck, ND 58502

### Devils Lake

University of North Dakota
Lake Region
Legal Assistant Program
Devils Lake, ND 58301

## OHIO

### Akron

Hammel College
885 E. Buchtel
Akron, OH 44305

### Cincinnati

* University of Cincinnati
University College
Legal Assistant Program
Mail Location #207
Cincinnati, OH 45221

### Cleveland

American Retraining Center
Paralegal Program
1900 Euclid Avenue, Suite 801
Cleveland, OH 44115

* Dyke College
Paralegal Education Programs
112 Prospect Avenue
Cleveland, OH 44115

### Columbus

American Institute for Paralegal
Studies, Inc.
2999 E. Dublin-Granville Road
Suite 217
Columbus, OH 43229

* Capital University Law Center
Legal Assistant Program
665 South High Street
Columbus, OH 43215

* ABA Final Approval.     **ABA Provisional Approval

276

Ohio Paralegal Academy
209 South High Street
Suite 507
Columbus, OH 43215

**Dayton**

* Sinclair Community College
Legal Assisting Program
444 West Third Street
Dayton, OH 45402

**Mount St. Joseph**

College of Mount St. Joseph
Legal Assistant Program
Suburban Cincinnati
Mount St. Joseph, OH 45051

**Springfield**

Clark Technical College
Box 570
Springfield, OH 45501

**Toledo**

* University of Toledo
Legal Assisting Technology
Scott Park Campus
2801 W. Bancroft Street
Toledo, OH 43606

**West Chester**

National Academy for Paralegal
Studies, Inc.
9319 Cincinnati-Columbus Road
West Chester, OH 45069

**Wooster**

Paralegal Institute of the Western Reserve
Academy
Silver Building, Suite 201
Public Square
Wooster, OH 44691

**Zanesville**

Muskingum Area Technical College
Paralegal Program
1555 Newark Road
Zanesville, OH 43701


**OKLAHOMA**

**Bartlesville**

Tri-County Area Vocational/
Technical School
6101 Nowata Road
Bartlesville, OK 74006

**Claremore**

Rogers State College
Will Rogers & College Hill
Claremore, OK 74017-2099

**Midwest City**

* Rose State College
Legal Assistant Pgm./Bus. Div.
6420 Southeast 15th
Midwest City, OK 73110

---

* ABA Final Approval.    **ABA Provisional Approval

**Norman**

* University of Oklahoma
Paralegal Program, CLE Law Ctr.
300 Timberdell, Room 314
Norman, OK 73019

**Oklahoma City**

American Institute for Paralegal
Studies, Inc.
530 N.W. 33rd Street
Oklahoma City, OK 73118

* Oklahoma Junior College of Business &
Technology
Paralegal/Legal Asst. Program
3232 Northwest 65
Oklahoma City, OK 73116

**Tahlequah**

Northeastern State University
Paralegal Studies Program
Criminal Justice Department
Tahlequah, OK 74464

**Tulsa**

** Oklahoma Junior College of Business &
Technology
Paralegal Department
7370 East 71st Street
Tulsa, OK 74133

* Tulsa Junior College
Business Service Division
909 South Boston Avenue
Tulsa, OK 74119

**OREGON**

**Portland**

Bradford School
Legal Assisting Program
921 SW Washington
Portland, OR 97205

College of Legal Arts
Legal Assistant Studies Program
University Center Building
527 Southwest Hall, Suite 415
Portland, OR 97201

Portland Community College
Legal Assistant Program
Department of Government Serv.
12000 Southwest 49th Avenue
Portland, OR 97219

**Oregon City**

National Academy for Paralegal
Studies, Inc.
Barclay Building, Suite 209
701 Main Street
Oregon City, OR 97045

**Salem**

Oregon State Department of Education
942 Lancaster Drive, N.E.
Salem, OR 97310

* ABA Final Approval.    **ABA Provisional Approval
278

# PENNSYLVANIA

## Abington

Penn State University
Ogontz Campus, Cont. Educ.
1600 Woodland Road
Abington, PA  19001

## Allentown

* Cedar Crest College
Paralegal Studies Program
100 College Drive
Allentown, PA  18104-6169

## Bethlehem

Northampton Co. Area Cmty. College
Legal Assistant Cert. Program
3835 Green Pond Road
Bethlehem, PA  18017

## Chester

* Widener University
Institute for Prof. Development
Room 135, Kapelski Center
Chester, PA  19013

## Dunsmore

Penn State University
Worthington Scranton Campus
120 Ridge View Drive
Dunsmore, PA  18512

## Erie

* Gannon University
Lawyer's Assistant Program
University Square
Erie, PA  16541

Penn State University
Behrend College, Cont. Educ.
Station Road
Erie, PA  16563

## Fogelsville

Penn State University, Allentown
Continuing Education
Academic Building
Fogelsville, PA  18051

## Harrisburg

Academy of Med. Arts & Business
Paralegal Programs
279 Boas Street
Harrisburg, PA  17102

* Harrisburg Area Cmty. College
Legal Assistant Program
3300 Cameron Street Road
Harrisburg, PA  17110

## Hazelton

Penn State University
Hazleton Campus, Cont. Educ.
Highacres
Hazelton, PA  18201

## Huntingdon Valley

American Institute for Paralegal
Studies, Inc.
Pennsylvania Regional Office
LeMont Plaza
609 County Lane Road
Huntingdon Valley, PA  19006

* ABA Final Approval.    **ABA Provisional Approval

279

**Indiana**

Indiana Univ. of Pennsylvania
Paralegal Program
School of Business
Indiana, PA 15705

**Labrobe**

St. Vincent College
Paralegal Certificate Program
Career Development Center
Labrobe, PA 15650-2690

**Lehman**

Penn State University
Wilkes-Barre Campus, Cont. Educ.
Lehman, PA 18627

**McKeesport**

Penn State University
McKeesport Campus, Cont. Educ.
University Drive
McKeesport, PA 15132

**Media**

Penn State University
Delaware Campus, Cont. Educ.
25 Yearsley Mill Road
Media, PA 19063

**Middletown**

Penn State University
Capital College, Cont. Educ.
Route 230
Middletown, PA 17057

**Monroeville**

Community College of Alleghany County
Boyce Campus
595 Beatty Road
Monroeville, PA 15146

**Mont Alto**

Penn State University
Mont Alto Campus, Cont. Educ.
Mont Alto, PA 17237

**Montoursville**

Penn State University
Williamsport Area, Cont. Educ.
420 Broad Street
Montoursville, PA 17754

**Philadelphia**

Career Institute (The)
1825 JFK Boulevard
Philadelphia, PA 19103

Katherine Gibbs School
Paralegal Program
Land Title Building
100 South Broad Street
Philadelphia, PA 19110

* Peirce Junior College
Paralegal Studies Program
1420 Pine Street
Philadelphia, PA 19103

* The Philadelphia Institute
1926 Arch Street
Philadelphia, PA 19103

**Pittsburgh**

Allegheny Community College
808 Ridge Avenue
Pittsburgh, PA  15212

* Duquesne University
Paralegal Program
711 Rockwell Hall
Pittsburgh, PA  15282

Penn State
The Pittsburgh Center
337 Fourth Avenue
Pittsburgh, PA  15222

Robert Morris College
Legal Assistant Cert. Program
Fifth Avenue at Sixth
Pittsburgh, PA  15219

University of Pittsburgh
Legal Studies Program
435 Cathedral of Learning
Pittsburgh, PA  15260

Western School of Health
& Business Careers
221-25 Fifth Avenue
Pittsburgh, PA  15222

**Reading**

Penn State University
Berks Campus, Cont. Educ.
Tulpehocken Road, RD 5
P.O. Box 2150
Reading, PA  19608

**Scranton**

* Marywood College
Legal Assistant Program
Scranton, PA  18509

**Sharon**

Penn State University
Shenango Valley Campus, Cont. Educ.
147 Shenango Avenue
Sharon, PA  16146

**Summerdale**

* Central Pennsylvania Bus. School
Division of Legal Studies
College Hill Road
Summerdale, PA  17093-0309

**Uniontown**

Penn State University
Fayette Campus, Cont. Educ.
P.O. Box 519 - Route 119N
Uniontown, PA  15401

**University Park**

Penn State University
State College Area, Cont. Educ.
109 Grange Building
University Park, PA  16802

Pennsylvania State University
Continuing Education
601 Business Admn. Bldg.
University Park, PA  16802

**Villanova**

* Villanova University
Paralegal Program
Villanova, PA  19085

* ABA Final Approval.    **ABA Provisional Approval

**Wayne**

Main Line Paralegal Institute
100 E. Lancaster
Wayne, PA 19087

**Wilkes Barre**

King's College
Legal Assistant Program
Department of Criminal Justice
Wilkes Barre, PA 18711

**York**

Penn State University
York Campus, Cont. Educ.
1031 Edgecomb Avenue
York, PA 17403

**PUERTO RICO**

**Caparra Terrace**

Universidad de Ponce
Legal Assistant Program
Avenida De Diego 700
Caparra Terrace, PR 00920

**Ponce**

Universidad de Ponce
Legal Assistant Program
P.O. Box 648
Ponce, PR 00733

**RHODE ISLAND**

**Bristol**

Roger Williams College
Paralegal Studies
Old Ferry Road
Bristol, RI 02809

**Newport**

Salve Regina-The Newport College
Legal Assistant Program
Newport, RI 02840

**Providence**

Johnson & Wales University
Office Careers Institute
8 Abbott Park Place
Providence, RI 02903

**SOUTH CAROLINA**

**Beaufort**

Beaufort Technical College
Paralegal Program
P.O. Box 1288 - Ribaut Road
Beaufort, SC 29902

**Charleston**

Trident Technical College
P.O. Box 10367
Charleston, SC 29411

Watterson College
Paralegal Studies Program
1064 Gardner Road, Suite 105
Charleston, SC 29407

* ABA Final Approval.      **ABA Provisional Approval

## Columbia

Columbia Junior College
Prof. Ctr. for Paralegal Studies
829 Gervais Street
Columbia, SC 29201

* Midlands Technical College
P.O. Box 2408
Columbia, SC 29202

## Conway

Horry-Georgetown Tech. College
Paralegal Program
P.O. Box 1966 - Highway 501 E.
Conway, SC 29526

## Greenville

* Greenville Technical College
Paralegal Department
P.O. Box 5616 Station B
Greenville, SC 29606-5616

## Rock Hill

National Academy for Paralegal
Studies, Inc.
P.O. Box 3588
Rock Hill, SC 29731

## SOUTH DAKOTA

### Sioux Falls

National Academy for
Paralegal Studies, Inc.
226 N. Phillips Avenue, #204
Sioux Falls, SD 57102

## Yankton

Yankton College
Legal Assistant Program
12th & Douglas
Yankton, SD 57078

## TENNESSEE

### Bristol

Bristol College
Bristol College Drive
Bristol, TN 37620

### Cleveland

* Cleveland State Cmty. College
Legal Assistant Program
P.O. Box 3570
Cleveland, TN 37320-3570

### Jackson

Jackson State College
Office of Continuing Education
P.O. Box 2467
Jackson, TN 38302-2467

### Knoxville

University of Tennessee
Paralegal Training Program
608 Stokely Management Center
Knoxville, TN 37996-0565

### Memphis

Memphis State University
Department of Business Admn.
Memphis, TN 38152

* ABA Final Approval.    **ABA Provisional Approval

National Academy for Paralegal
Studies, Inc.
5100 Wheelis Drive, Suite 100
Memphis, TN 38117

State Technical Institute
Legal Assistant Program
5983 Macon Cove
Memphis, TN 38134-7693

**Milligan College**

Milligan College
Legal Assistant Program
Milligan College, TN 37682

**Nashville**

Edmondson Junior College
Legal Assistant Program
1166 Murpheesboro
Suite 200
Nashville, TN 37217

* Southeastern Paralegal Institute
2416 21st Avenue, South
Third Floor
Nashville, TN 37212

**TEXAS**

**Arlington**

University of Texas, Arlington
Paralegal Program
Dept. of Political Science
Arlington, TX 76019

**Austin**

Durham Nixon-Clay Business Coll.
119 West Eighth Street
P.O. Box 1626
Austin, TX 78767

University of Texas, Austin
Legal Assistant Program
P.O. Box 7879
Austin, TX 78713-7879

**Baytown**

* Lee College
511 South Whiting Street
Baytown, TX 77520-4703

**Beaumont**

Lamar University
Continuing Education
P.O. Box 10008
Beaumont, TX 77710

**Canyon**

West Texas State University
Department of History and
Political Science
Canyon, TX 79016

**Commerce**

East Texas State University
Dept. of Political Science
Commerce, TX 75428

* **ABA Final Approval.**    **\*\*ABA Provisional Approval**

## Corpus Christi

Del Mar College
Legal Assistant Program
Baldwin & Ayers
Corpus Christi, TX 78404

## Dallas

El Centro College
Legal Assistant Program
Main and Lamar
Dallas, TX 75202

Legal Assistant/Paralegal Pgm.
4849 Greenville Avenue, Suite 200
Dallas, TX 75206

* Southeastern Paralegal Institute
Legal Assistant Program
5440 Harvest Hill, Suite 200
Dallas, TX 75230

* Southern Methodist University
Legal Asst. Certificate Program
SMU Box 275
Dallas, TX 75275

## Denison

Grayson County College
Legal Assistant Program
6101 Grayson Drive
Denison, TX 75020

## Denton

Texas Woman's University
Dept. of History and Government
P.O. Box 23974
Denton, TX 76204

## El Paso

El Paso County Cmty. College
Legal Assistant Program
P.O. Box 20500
El Paso, TX 79998

## Grand Prairie

Video Technical Institute (VTI)
Institute for Paralegal Studies
2505 N. Highway 360 - Suite 420
Grand Prairie, TX 75053

## Houston

Career Institute
3015 Richmond Avenue
Houston, TX 77098

Houston Cmty. College System
Legal Assistant Program
4701 Dixon Street
Houston, TX 77007

North Harris County College
Legal Assistant Program
2700 W. W. Thorne, Suite W115
Houston, TX 77075

* Southwestern Paralegal Institute
Basic Legal Assistant Studies
2211 Norfolk, Suite 420
Houston, TX 77098-4096

Texas Para-Legal School, Houston
608 Fannin, Suite 1903
Houston, TX 77002

* ABA Final Approval.    **ABA Provisional Approval

University of Houston at Clear Lake City
Legal Studies Program
P.O. Box 20
2700 Bay Area Blvd.
Houston, TX 77058

**Hurst**

Tarrant County Jr. College
Northeast Campus
828 Harwood Road
Hurst, TX 76054

**Kilgore**

Kilgore College
Legal Assisting Program
1100 Broadway
Kilgore, TX 75662

**McKinney**

Collin Co. Cmty. College Dist.
Legal Assistant Program
2200 West University
McKinney, TX 75070

**Odessa**

Odessa College
Legal Assistant Program
201 W. University
Odessa, TX 79764

**San Antonio**

San Antonio College
Legal Assistant Program
1300 San Pedro Avenue
San Antonio, TX 78284

**San Marcos**

Southwest Texas State University
Lawyer's Assistant Program
Evans Liberal Arts Building
San Marcos, TX 78666

**Woodland**

Woodland Paralegal Institute
5 Grogans Park, Suite 200
Woodland, TX 77381

**UTAH**

**Orem**

* Utah Valley Community College
Legal Assistant Program
1200 South 800 West
Orem, UT 84058

**Salt Lake City**

* Westminster College
of Salt Lake City
1840 South 1300 East
Salt Lake City, UT 84105

**VERMONT**

**Burlington**

Champlain College
P.O. Box 670
Burlington, VT 05402

* ABA Final Approval.     **ABA Provisional Approval

**Montpelier**

Woodbury College
Paralegal Studies Program
659 Elm Street
Montpelier, VT 05602

**VIRGINIA**

**Alexandria**

* Northern Virginia Cmty. College
Legal Assistant Program
3001 N. Beauregard
Alexandria, VA 22311

**Arlington**

* Marymount University
Paralegal Studies Program
2807 North Glebe Road
Arlington, VA 22207-4299

**Big Stone Gap**

Mountain Empire Cmty. College
Legal Assistant Program
Drawer 700
Big Stone Gap, VA 24219

**Bristol**

* Virginia Intermont College
Paralegal Studies Program
Bristol, VA 24201

**Falls Church**

Para-Legal Institute
7700 Leesburg Pike, Suite 305
Falls Church, VA 22043

**Ferrum**

Ferrum College
Legal Assistant Program
Ferrum, VA 24088

**Hampton**

Thomas Nelson Community College
Legal Assistant Program
P.O. Box 9407
Hampton, VA 23670

**Harrisonburg**

* James Madison University
Department of Political Science
Paralegal Studies Program
Harrisonburg, VA 22807

**Lynchburg**

Central Virginia Cmty. College
3506 Wards Road
Lynchburg, VA 24502

National Academy for Paralegal
Studies, Inc.
1022 Court Street
P.O. Box 1359
Lynchburg, VA 24505

**Norfolk**

American Institute for
Paralegal Studies, Inc.
500 E. Main Street
Suite 628
Norfolk, VA 23514

* ABA Final Approval.    **ABA Provisional Approval

**Richmond**

* J. Sargeant Reynolds Cmty. Coll.
Parham Road Campus
P.O. Box C-32040
Richmond, VA  23261-2040

University of Richmond
University College
Evening School
Richmond, VA  23173

**Roanoke**

Virginia Western Cmty. College
3095 Colonial Avenue, S.W.
Roanoke, VA  24038

**Staunton**

Elizabeth Brant School
Staunton, VA  24401

**Virginia Beach**

Tidewater Community College
Legal Assistant Program
1700 College Crescent
Virginia Beach, VA  23456

**WASHINGTON**

**Bellevue**

American Institute for Paralegal
Studies, Inc.
1700 Security Pacific Plaza
777 108th Avenue, N.E.
Bellevue, WA  98004

Bellevue Community College
3000 Landerholm Circle, S.E.
Bellevue, WA  98009-2037

City University
Legal Studies Programs
16661 Northup Way
Bellevue, WA  98008

**Ellensburg**

Central Washington University
Program in Law & Justice
Ellensburg, WA  98926

**Longview**

Lower Columbia College
Legal Assistant Program
1600 Maple
Longview, WA  98632

**Lynnwood**

* Edmonds Community College
Legal Assistant Program
20000 68th Avenue West
Lynnwood, WA  98036

**Midway**

* Highline Community College
Legal Assistant Program
Community College District 9
Midway, WA  98031

**Port Orchard**

Metropolitan Business College
2501 SE State Highway 160
Port Orchard, WA  98366

* ABA Final Approval.    **ABA Provisional Approval

**Seattle**

National Academy for Paralegal
Studies, Inc.
P.O. Box 21873
Seattle, WA 98111-3873

Univ. of Washington, Extension
Paralegal Studies Program
5001 25th Avenue, NE GH-21
Seattle, WA 98195

**Spokane**

Spokane Community College
Legal Assistant Program
North 1810 Greene Street
Spokane, WA 99207

**Tacoma**

Pierce College
Paralegal Studies Program
9401 Farwest Drive SW
Tacoma, WA 98498

**WEST VIRGINIA**

**Fairmont**

Fairmont State College
Legal Assistant Program
Division of Social Science
Fairmont, WV 26554

**Huntington**

* Marshall University
Community College
Legal Assistant Program
Huntington, WV 25701

**Wheeling**

National Academy for
Paralegal Studies, Inc.
100 Carmel Road
Wheeling, WV 26003

**WISCONSIN**

**Cleveland**

* Lakeshore Technical College
Legal Assistant Program
1290 North Avenue
Cleveland, WI 53015

**Eau Claire**

* Chippewa Valley Tech. College
Legal Assistant Program
620 W. Clairmont Avenue
Eau Claire, WI 54701

**Kenosha**

Carthage College
Paralegal Program
2001 Alford Drive
Kenosha, WI 53140-1994

**Mequon**

Concordia University, Wisconsin
Paralegal Degree Program
12800 North Lake Shore Drive
Mequon, WI 53092-9652

* ABA Final Approval.    **ABA Provisional Approval

**Milwaukee**

American Institute for
Paralegal Studies, Inc.
710 N. Plakington Avenue
Suite 500
Milwaukee, WI 53203

\* Milwaukee Area Technical College
Legal Assistant Program
700 West State Street
Milwaukee, WI 53233

**WYOMING**

**Casper**

Casper College
Legal Assistant Program
125 College Drive
Casper, WY 82601

**Cheyenne**

Laramie County Community College
Legal Assistant Program
1400 E. College Drive
Cheyenne, WY 82007

# Appendix C

# Legal Assistant & Paralegal Associations List

## UNITED STATES

**American Association of Law Libraries**
c/o Judy Genesen
53 W. Jackson Boulevard, Suite 940
Chicago, IL 60604

**American Association for Paralegal Education**
c/o Sandra L. Sabanske
P.O. Box 40244
Overland Park, KS 66212

**American Bar Association**
c/o Jill Wine-Banks
750 N. Lake Shore Drive
Chicago, IL 60611

**Association of Legal Administrators**
c/o Jan Waugh
175 E. Hawthorne Parkway
Suite 325
Vernon Hills, IL 60061-1428

**American Academy of Legal Assistants**
1022 Paul Avenue, N.E.
Norton, VA 24273

**American Paralegal Association**
P.O. Box 35233
Los Angeles, CA 90035

**Legal Assistant Management Association**
P.O. Box 40129
Overland Park, KS 66204

**National Association for Independent Paralegals**
c/o Catherine Elias-Jermany
585 Fifth Street West
Sonoma, CA 95476

**National Association of Law Firm Marketing Administrators**
60 Rivere Drive, Suite 500
Northbrook, IL 60062

**National Association for Law Placement**
1666 Connecticut Avenue, Suite 450
Washington, D.C. 20009

**National Association of Legal Assistants**
1601 S. Main Street, Suite 300
Tulsa, OK 74119

**National Association of Legal Secretaries**
2250 E. 73rd Street, Suite 550
Tulsa, OK 74136

**National Federation**
of Paralegal Associations
104 Wilmot Road, Suite 201
Deerfield, IL 60015-5195

**National Legal Assistant**
**Conference Center**
2444 Wilshire Blvd., Suite 301
Santa Monica, CA 90403

**National Notary Association**
23012 Ventura Boulevard
P.O. Box 4625
Woodland Hills, CA 91365-4624

**National Paralegal Association**
c/o Jeffrey Valentine,
Executive Director
P.O. Box 406
Solebury, PA 18963

**National Shorthand Reporters**
**Association**
118 Park Street, S.E.
Vienna, VA 22180

**Professional Legal Assistants, Inc.**
P.O. Box 31951
Raleigh, NC 27690-0315

**CANADA**

**Alberta Association of Legal Assistants**
MacKimmie Mathews
700, 401 9th Avenue, S.W.
P.O. Box 2010
Calgary, AB, CANADA T2P 2M2

**Canadian Association of Legal Assistants**
Phillips & Vineberg
5 Place Ville Marie, Suite 700
Montreal, Quebec, CANADA H3B 2G2

**Canadian Association of Legal Assistants**
c/o Dayle M. Brends
Ogilvy, Renault
1981, Avenue McGill College
Montreal, CANADA PQ H3A 3C1

**Institute of Law Clerks of Ontario**
Suite 502, 425 University Avenue
Toronto, ON M5G 1T6
CANADA

**Legal Education Society of Alberta**
2005 IPL Tower
10201 Jasper Avenue
Edmonton, Alberta, CANADA T5J 3N7

**ALABAMA**

**Birmingham**

* Alabama Association
 of Legal Assistants
Kim Babb, NALA Liaison
Sirote, Permutt,
P.O. Box 55727
Birmingham, AL 35255

* National Association of Legal Assistants, Inc.
** National Federation of Paralegal Associations, Inc.
292

* Legal Assistant Society
  of Southern Institute
  Paralegal Program-Southern Institute
  2015 Highland Avenue South
  Birmingham, AL 35205

**Mobile**

** Mobile Association
  of Legal Assistants
  c/o Mary Beth Bradley, President
  P.O. Box 1852
  Mobile, AL 36633

**Montgomery**

* Alabama Association
  of Legal Assistants
  Pam Gray, CLA, President
  Capell, Howard
  P.O. Box 2069
  Montgomery, AL 36197

**ALASKA**

**Anchorage**

** Alaska Association
  of Legal Assistants
  P.O. Box 101956
  Anchorage, AK 99510-1956

** Alaska Legal Assistants
  Association
  P.O. Box 1956
  Anchorage, AK 99510

**Fairbanks**

* Fairbanks Association
  of Legal Assistants
  Billie Kline, President
  P.O. Box 73503
  Fairbanks, AK 99707

* Fairbanks Association
  of Legal Assistants
  Barbara A. Johnson, NALA Liaison
  101 Oak Drive
  Fairbanks, AK 99709

**Juneau**

** Juneau Legal Assistants
  Association
  P.O. Box 22336
  Juneau, AK 99802

**ARIZONA**

**Flagstaff**

** Northern Arizona Paralegal
  Association
  Department of Law Enforcement
  & Paralegal Studies
  Northern Arizona University
  Box 15005
  Flagstaff, AZ 86011

**Mesa**

* Arizona Paralegal Association
  Irene Morris, CLA, NALA Liaison
  Kern and Wolley
  1201 S. Alma School Road
  Suite 15500
  Mesa, AZ 85210

* National Association of Legal Assistants, Inc.
** National Federation of Paralegal Associations, Inc.

* Southeast Valley Association
  of Legal Assistants
Sandy Slater, President
423 N. Country Club, Suite 50
Mesa, AZ 85201

**Phoenix**

** Arizona Association
  of Professional Paralegals
P.O. Box 25111
Phoenix, AZ 85002

* Arizona Paralegal Association
Patricia G. Elliott, CLAS, President
Holloway & Thomas, P.C.
2700 North Central Ave., Suite 1500
Phoenix, AZ 85004

* Legal Assistants
  of Metropolitan Phoenix
Alexis D. Quiroz, CLA, President
c/o Snell & Wilmer
1430 Valley Bank Center
Phoenix, AZ 85073-3100

* Legal Assistants
  of Metropolitan Phoenix
Beverly Kane, NALA Liaison
Myers, Barnes & Jenkins
Renaissance Square, Suite 1200
2 North Central Avenue
Phoenix, AZ 85004

**Tucson**

* Tucson Association
  of Legal Assistants
Barbara Tidd, CLA, President
1319 S. Lynx Drive
Tucson, AZ 85713

* Tucson Association
  of Legal Assistants
Charlene A. Videen, CLA, NALA Liaison
Plaza Palomino, Suite 301
2960 N. Swan Road
Tucson, AZ 85712

**ARKANSAS**

**Little Rock**

* Arkansas Association
  of Legal Assistants
Cathie Cox, CLA, President
Wright, Lindsey & Jennings
2200 Worthen Bank Bldg.
Little Rock, AR 72201

* Arkansas Association
  of Legal Assistants
Alice Cook, CLA, NALA Liaison
Mitchell Law Firm
1000 Savers Federal Bldg.
Little Rock, AR 72201

**CALIFORNIA**

**Camarillo**

* Ventura County Association
  of Legal Assistants
Cynthia Adams, NALA Liaison
291 Lantana Street
Camarillo, CA 93010

* National Association of Legal Assistants, Inc.
** National Federation of Paralegal Associations, Inc.

## Fremont

\* Paralegal Association
 of Santa Clara County
Donna Rowson, President
1864 Mohican Ct.
Fremont, CA 94539

## Fresno

\*\* San Joaquin Association
 of Legal Assistants
P.O. Box 1306
Fresno, CA 93715

## Los Angeles

\*\* Los Angeles Paralegal
 Association
P.O. Box 241928
Los Angeles, CA 90024

## Modesto

\*\* Central Valley Paralegal
 Association
c/o Frances M. Foxen
Thayer, Harvey, Hodder & Gregerson
City Mall 948 Eleventh Street
Suite 20
P.O. Box 3465
Modesto, CA 95353

## Napa

\*\* NAPA Valley Association
 of Legal Assistants
Wagner Hamilton & Associates
1836 2nd Street
Napa, CA 94559

## Newport Beach

\*\* Orange County Paralegal
 Association
P.O. Box 8512
Newport Beach, CA 92658-8512

## Oxnard

\* Ventura County Association
 of Legal Assistants
Sheree Thompson, President
1210 Escalon Drive
Oxnard, CA 93030

## Redwood City

\*\* Paralegal Association
 of San Mateo
c/o Linda Vetter
250 Wheeler Avenue
Redwood City, CA 94061

## Riverside

\*\* Inland Counties Paralegal
 Association
P.O. Box 292
Riverside, CA 92502-0292

## Sacramento

\*\* Sacramento Association
 of Legal Assistants
P.O. Box 453
Sacramento, CA 95812-0453

---

\* National Association of Legal Assistants, Inc.
\*\* National Federation of Paralegal Associations, Inc.

**San Diego**

** San Diego Association
 of Legal Assistants
P.O. Box 87449
San Diego, CA  92138-7449

**San Francisco**

** California Alliance
 of Paralegal Association
114 Sansome St., Suite 644
San Francisco, CA  94104

** Coalition for Paralegal
 and Consumer Rights
1714 Stockton Street
Suite 400
San Francisco, CA  94133

** San Francisco Association
 of Legal Assistants
P.O. Box 26668
San Francisco, CA  94126-6668

**San Jose**

* Paralegal Association
 of Santa Clara County
Jo Floch, NALA Liaison
129 Parkwell Court
San Jose, CA  95138-1633

**San Luis Obispo**

** Central Coast Legal
 Assistants
P.O. Box 93
San Luis Obispo, CA  93406

**San Rafael**

** Marin County Association
 of Legal Assistants
P.O. Box 13051
San Rafael, CA  94913-3051

**Santa Barbara**

* Legal Assistants Association
 of Santa Barbara
Lynn Mollie, CLA, President
Henderson & Angle
530 E. Montecito Street
Santa Barbara, CA  93103

* Legal Assistants Association
 of Santa Barbara
Kit Johnson, NALA Liaison
P.O. Box 2280
Santa Barbara, CA  93120-2280

**Santa Rosa**

** Redwood Empire Legal
 Assistants
P.O. Box 1498
Santa Rosa, CA  95402

**Visalia**

** Sequoia Paralegal
 Association
P.O. Box 93278-3884
Visalia, CA  93278

* National Association of Legal Assistants, Inc.
** National Federation of Paralegal Associations, Inc.

## COLORADO

### Colorado Springs

* Legal Assistants
 of Colorado
Alma Rodrigues, CLA, President
4150 Novia Drive
Colorado Springs, CO 80911

### Denver

** Rocky Mountain Legal
 Assistants Association
P.O. Box 304
Denver, CO 80201

## CONNECTICUT

### Bridgeport

** Connecticut Association
 of Paralegals-Fairfield County
P.O. Box 134
Bridgeport, CT 06601

### Hartford

** Central Connecticut Association
 of Legal Assistants
P.O. Box 230594
Hartford, CT 06123-0594

### New Haven

** Connecticut Association
 of Paralegals-New Haven
P.O. Box 862
New Haven, CT 06504-0862

### New London

** Legal Assistants
 of Southeastern Connecticut
P.O. Box 409
New London, CT 06320

## DELAWARE

### Wilmington

** Delaware Paralegal
 Association
P.O. Box 1362
Wilmington, DE 19899

## DISTRICT OF COLUMBIA

** National Capital Area
 Paralegal Association
1155 Connecticut Ave., N.W.
Washington, D.C. 20036

## FLORIDA

### Bay Harbor Islands

* Dade Association
 of Legal Assistants
Lori Allen, CLA,
 NALA Liaison
9720 W. Bay Harbor Dr., #3
Bay Harbor Islands, FL 33154

---

* National Association of Legal Assistants, Inc.
** National Federation of Paralegal Associations, Inc.

## Bradenton

* Florida Legal
  Assistants, Inc.
Nancy A. Martin, CLA,
  President
P.O. Box 503
Bradenton, FL 34206

* Florida Legal
  Assistants, Inc.
Sharon K. Cohron, CLA, CFLA
7819 2nd Avenue West
Bradenton, FL 34209

## Daytona Beach

* Volusia Association
  of Legal Assistants
Mary Joan Harrington,
  NALA Liaison
Cobb, Cole & Bell
P.O. Box 191
Daytona Beach, FL 32015

## Ft. Lauderdale

** Broward County Paralegal
  Association
c/o Leigh M. Williams
Ruden, Barnett, McClosky
P.O. Box 1900
Ft. Lauderdale, FL 33302

## Jacksonville

* Jacksonville Legal
  Assistants
Teresa Arington,
  President
7751 Belfort Parkway
Bldg. 200
Jacksonville, FL 32216

* Jacksonville Legal
  Assistants
Mary F. Greenhill, CLA,
  NALA Liaison
2301 Independent Square
Jacksonville, FL 32202

## Miami

* Dade Association
  of Legal Assistants
Priscella Meyer, President
700 Brickell Avenue
Miami, FL 33133

## Orlando

* Orlando Legal
  Assistants
Roxane MacGillivray, CLA,
  President
Akerman, Senterfitt & Eidson
P.O. Box 231
Orlando, FL 32802

* National Association of Legal Assistants, Inc.
** National Federation of Paralegal Associations, Inc.

* Orlando Legal
  Assistants
Cathy Perry, CLAS,
  NALA Liaison
Civil Litigation Specialist
c/o Florida Bar Foundation
80 N. Orange Ave., Suite 102
Orlando, FL  32801-1023

**Ormond Beach**

* Volusia Association
  of Legal Assistants
Rosemary E. Hallman, CLA,
  President
Ledford, Mayfield & Ogle
P.O. Box 4118
Ormond Beach, FL  32175-4118

**Pensacola**

* Pensacola Legal Assistants
Deborah Johnson, President
Levin, Middlebrooks & Mabie
226 S. Palafox Street
Pensacola, FL  32581

* Pensacola Legal Assistants
Darla Hartigan, CLA,
  NALA Liaison
1817 East Lloyd Street
Pensacola, FL  32503

**GEORGIA**

**Atlanta**

** Georgia Association
  of Legal Assistants
P.O. Box 1802
Atlanta, GA  30301

**HAWAII**

**Honolulu**

** Hawaii Association
  of Legal Assistants
P.O. Box 674
Honolulu, HI  96809

**IDAHO**

**Boise**

* Idaho Association
  of Legal Assistants
Joanne Kimey, President
P.O. Box 1254
Boise, ID 83701

* Idaho Association
  of Legal Assistants
Signa Treat, CLA,
  NALA Liaison
P.O. Box 1254
Boise, Idaho 83701

**ILLINOIS**

**Bloomington**

* Central Illinois Paralegal
  Association
Deb Monke, CLA, NALA Liaison
1312 E. Empire Street
Bloomington, IL  61701

* National Association of Legal Assistants, Inc.
** National Federation of Paralegal Associations, Inc.

**Chicago**

** Illinois Paralegal
 Association
P.O. Box 857
Chicago, IL  60690

**Downers Grove**

** Independent Contractors
 Association of Illinois
6400 Woodward Avenue
Downers Grove, IL  60516

**Normal**

* Central Illinois
 Paralegal Association
Melanie Baker, President
1700 N. School, #88
Normal, IL  61761

**Peoria**

** Peoria Paralegal
 Association
c/o Sharon Moke
1308 Autumn Lane
Peoria, IL  60604

**INDIANA**

**Evansville**

* Indiana Legal Assistants
Dorothy French, CLA,
 President
Newman, Trockman
P.O. Box 3047
Evansville, IN  47730

**Indianapolis**

** Indiana Paralegal
 Association
P.O. Box 44518,
 Federal Station
Indianapolis, IN  46204

**Merrillville**

* Indiana Legal Assistants
Randall Forsythe,
 NALA Liaison
Katz, Brenman & Angel
7895 Broadway, #R-5
Merrillville, IN  46410

**South Bend**

** Michiana Paralegal
 Association
P.O. Box 11458
South Bend, IN  46634

**IOWA**

**Ames**

** Iowa Association
 of Legal Assistants
c/o D. Diane Smith
310 Strawberry Lane
Ames, IA  50010

**Cedar Rapids**

** Paralegals of Iowa, Ltd.
P.O. Box 1943
Cedar Rapids, IA  52406

* National Association of Legal Assistants, Inc.
** National Federation of Paralegal Associations, Inc.

## KANSAS

### Topeka

** Kansas Legal
  Assistants Society
P.O. Box 1675
Topeka, KS  66601

### Wichita

* Kansas Association
  of Legal Assistants
Ronda R. Hoover, CLAS,
  President
Hinkle, Eberhart & Elkouri
301 N. Main, Suite 2000
Wichita, KS  67201

* Kansas Association
  of Legal Assistants
Jami D. Buck, CLA,
  NALA Liaison
Foulston & Siefkin
700 Fourth Financial Center
Wichita, KS  67202

## KENTUCKY

### Lexington

** Lexington Paralegal
  Association
c/o Edwina Gilmore
P.O. Box 574
Lexington, KY  40586

### Louisville

** Louisville Association
  of Paralegals
P.O. Box 962
Louisville, KY  40201

## LOUISIANA

### Baton Rouge

** Baton Rouge
  Paralegal Association
P.O. Box 306
Baton Rouge, LA  70821

### Haughton

* Northwest Louisiana
  Paralegal Association
Nancy M. Constanzi, CLA,
  NALA Liaison
217 Mill Creek Lane
Haughton, LA  71037

### Lafayette

** Lafayette Paralegal
  Association
c/o Lynn Panoff
P.O. Box 2775
Lafayette, LA  70502

### Lake Charles

** Louisiana State
  Paralegal Association
c/o Wanda V. Courmier
P.O. Box 1743
Lake Charles, LA  70602

* National Association of Legal Assistants, Inc.
** National Federation of Paralegal Associations, Inc.

** Southwest Louisiana
  Association of Paralegals
P.O. Box 1143
Lake Charles, LA 70602

**New Orleans**

** New Orleans Paralegal
  Association
P.O. Box 30604
New Orleans, LA 70190

**Shreveport**

* Northwest Louisiana
  Paralegal Association
Cheryl Mahaffey, CLA,
  President
610 Marshall Street
Suite 212
Shreveport, LA 71101

**MAINE**

**Augusta**

* Maine Association
  of Paralegals
Michele Fossett,
  NALA Liaison
Law Office of Linda Gifford
78 Winthrop Street
Augusta, ME 04330

**Kittery**

* Maine Association
  of Paralegals
Lawrence Yerxa, President
McEachern & Thornhill
P.O. Box 360
Kittery, ME 03904

**Portland**

** Maine Association
  of Paralegals
Southern Maine Chapter
P.O. Box 7554 DTS
Portland, ME 04112

**MARYLAND**

**Baltimore**

** Baltimore Association
  of Legal Assistants
P.O. Box 13244
Baltimore, MD 21201

**MASSACHUSETTS**

**Boston**

** Massachusetts
  Paralegal Association
P.O. Box 423
Boston, MA 02102

**Springfield**

** Western Massachusetts
  Paralegal Association
c/o Nancy J. Wessel
Richard J. Ianello
95 State Street
Springfield, MA 01103

* National Association of Legal Assistants, Inc.
** National Federation of Paralegal Associations, Inc.

**Worcester**

** Central Massachusetts
Paralegal Association
P.O. Box 444
Worcester, MA 01614

**MICHIGAN**

**Birmingham**

* Legal Assistants
Association of Michigan
Cora S. Webb, President
P.O. Box 12316
Birmingham, MI 48012

**Charlevoix**

* Legal Assistants
Association of Michigan
Vicki V. Voisin, CLA,
NALA Liaison
Simpson & Moran, P.C.
202 Clinton Street
Charlevoix, MI 49720

**MINNESOTA**

**Minneapolis**

** Minnesota Association
of Legal Assistants
Grain Exchange Building
P.O. Box 15165
Minneapolis, MN 55415

**Rochester**

* Minnesota Paralegal
Association
Tracy Blanshan,
President
Kennedy Law Office
724 SW First Avenue
Rochester, MN 55902

* Minnesota Paralegal
Association
Muriel Hinrichs,
NALA Liaison
O'Brien, Ehrick, Wolf,
Deaner & Maus
611 Marquette Bank Bldg.
Rochester, MN 55903

**St. Cloud**

** St. Cloud Area
Legal Services
c/o Mary Yeager
P.O. Box 896
St. Cloud, MN 56302

**MISSISSIPPI**

**Gulfport**

** Gulf Coast Paralegal
Association
942 Beach Drive
Gulfport, MS 39507

* National Association of Legal Assistants, Inc.
** National Federation of Paralegal Associations, Inc.

**Hattiesburg**

* Society for Paralegal
  Studies
Univ. of Southern Mississippi
Laura Lilly, President
S.S. Box 5108
Hattiesburg, MS 39406-5108

* Society for Paralegal
  Studies
Univ. of Southern Mississippi
Ronald G. Marquardt,
  Staff Liaison
S.S. Box 5108
Hattiesburg, MS 39406-5108

**Jackson**

* Mississippi Association
  of Legal Assistants
Connie M. Cavanaugh,
  President
Wise, Carter, Child & Caraway
P.O. Box 651
Jackson, MS 39205

* Mississippi Association
  of Legal Assistants
Suellen Johnson Reilly,
  NALA Liaison
Watkins, Ludlam & Stennis
P.O. Box 427
Jackson, MS 39205-0427

** Paralegal Association
  of Mississippi
P.O. Box 22887
Jackson, MS 39205

**MISSOURI**

**Kansas City**

** Kansas City Association
  of Legal Assistants
P.O. Box 13223
Kansas City, MO 64199

**St. Louis**

* St. Louis Association
  of Legal Assistants
Carol Young, President
P.O. Box 9690
St. Louis, MO 63122

** Gateway Paralegal
  Association
c/o Karen L. Arico
Southwestern Bell Corp.,
  Legal Dept.
One Bell Center, Room 3521
St. Louis, MO 63101-3099

**Springfield**

** Southwest Missouri
  Paralegal Association
c/o Marie E. Smith
517 East Seminole
Springfield, MO 65807

* National Association of Legal Assistants, Inc.
** National Federation of Paralegal Associations, Inc.

## MONTANA

### Billings

** Montana Paralegal
  Association
c/o Clare Young
P.O. Box 693
Billings, MT  59103-0693

### Great Falls

** Big Sky Paralegal
  Association
P.O. Box 2753
Great Falls, MT  59403

## NEBRASKA

### Omaha

* Nebraska Association
  of Legal Assistants
Linda A. Walker, CLA,
  President & NALA Liaison
McGill, Gotsdiner, Workman
  & Lepp, P.C.
10010 Regency Circle, Suite 300
Omaha, NE  68114

## NEVADA

### Las Vegas

* Clark County Organization
  of Legal Assistants, Inc.
Robin S. Orwiler, CLA, President
Edwards, Hunt, Hale & Hansen, Ltd.
415 S. 6th Street, Suite 300
Las Vegas, NV  89101

### Reno

* Sierra Nevada Association
  of Paralegals
Carol A. Hunt, President
P.O. Box 40638
Reno, NV 89504

* Sierra Nevada Association
  of Paralegals
Merrilyn Marsh, CLA,
  NALA Liaison
Belding, Harris & Hodge
417 W. Plumb Lane
Reno, NV  89509

## NEW HAMPSHIRE

### Exeter

* Paralegal Association
  of New Hampshire
Betty Jean Bailey, CLA,
  NALA Liaison
Tyco Laboratories, Inc.
One Tyco Park
Exeter, NH  03833

### Manchester

* Paralegal Association
  of New Hampshire
Frances Dupre, President
c/o Wiggin & Nourie
P.O. Box 808
Manchester, NH  03105

* National Association of Legal Assistants, Inc.
** National Federation of Paralegal Associations, Inc.

## NEW JERSEY

### Clifton

\* The Legal Assistants
  Association of New Jersey, Inc.
Diane B. Mitchell, CLA,
  NALA Liaison
38 Cottage Lane
Clifton, NJ 07012

### Dayton

\*\* New Jersey Legal
  Assistants Association
Central Jersey Paralegal Div.
P.O. Box 403, U.S. Hwy 130
Dayton, NJ 08810

### Haddonfield

\*\* South Jersey
  Paralegal Association
P.O. Box 355
Haddonfield, NJ 08033

### Mercerville

\*\* Paralegal Association
  of Central Jersey
93 Princeton Court
Mercerville, NJ 08619

### Montclair

\* The Legal Assistants
  Association of New Jersey, Inc.
Dorothy Deignan Perretti,
  President
Dwyer, Connell & Lisbona
427 Bloomfield Avenue
Montclair, NJ 07043

### New Brunswick

\*\* Central Jersey Paralegal
  Association
c/o Barbara McManus
Rutgers, The State Univ.
  of New Jersey
Office of Employment
  & Labor Counsel
60 College Avenue
New Brunswick, NJ 08903

### Westmont

\*\* Paralegal Association
  of Burlington
County College
P.O. Box 2222
216 Haddon Avenue
Westmont, NJ 08108

## NEW MEXICO

### Albuquerque

\*\* Legal Assistants
  of New Mexico
c/o Jacque Walston
The Modnoll Firm
500 45th Street
Albuquerque, NM 87103

## NEW YORK

### Binghamton

\*\* Southern Tier
  Association of Paralegals
P.O. Box 2555
Binghamton, NY 13902

\* National Association of Legal Assistants, Inc.
\*\* National Federation of Paralegal Associations, Inc.

## Buffalo

** Western New York
  Paralegal Association
P.O. Box 207
Niagara Square Station
Buffalo, NY 14202

## Deer Park

** Long Island Paralegal
  Association, Inc.
P.O. Box 31
Deer Park, NY 11729

## Glen Falls

** Adirondack Paralegal
  Association
c/o Maureen T. Provost
Bartlett, Pontiff, Stewart,
  Rhodes & Judge, P.C.
One Washington Street
Box 2168
Glen Falls, NY 12801-0012

## New York City

** Manhattan Paralegal
  Association
200 Park Avenue,
  Suite 303 East
New York, NY 10166

## Rochester

** Paralegal Association
  of Rochester, Inc.
P.O. Box 40567
Rochester, NY 14604

## Wappingers Falls

** Legal Professionals
  of Dutchess County
c/o Terri Thorley
51 Maloney Road
Wappingers Falls, NY 12590

## White Plains

** Westchester County Paralegal
  Association
c/o Connie Vincent
Law Offices of David E. Worby, P.C.
Two Lyons Place
White Plains, NY 10601

** Westrock Paralegal
  Association
c/o Debby Ybarra
Box 101
95 Mamaroneck Avenue
White Plains, NY 10601

## NORTH CAROLINA

## Camp Lejeune

* Coastal Carolina
  Paralegal Club
Elisabeth Alvarez-Fager,
  President
5634 Delaware Avenue
Camp Lejeune, NC 28542

---

* National Association of Legal Assistants, Inc.
** National Federation of Paralegal Associations, Inc.

## Charlotte

* North Carolina Paralegal
  Association, Inc.
Mary F. Haggerty, CLA,
  NALA Liaison
Parker, Poe, Adams & Bernstein
4201 Congress St.
Suite 145
Charlotte, NC 28209

## Fayetteville

** Cumberland County
  Paralegal Association
P.O. Box 1358
Fayetteville, NC 28302

## Goldsboro

* North Carolina Paralegal
  Association, Inc.
T. William Tewes, Jr., CLA,
  President
Law Offices of Robert E. Fuller, Jr.
P.O. Box 1121
Goldsboro, NC 27533-1121

** Triad Paralegal
  Association
Drawer U
Greensboro, NC 27402

## Jacksonville

* Coastal Carolina Paralegal
  Club
Col. Robert Switzer,
  NALA Liaison
444 Western Boulevard
Jacksonville, NC 28546

## Raleigh

** Raleigh Wake
  Paralegal Association
P.O. Box 1427
Raleigh, NC 27602

## NORTH DAKOTA

### Bismarck

* Western Dakota Association
  of Legal Assistants
Vicki Kunz, CLA,
  NALA Liaison
Wheeler, Wolf
P.O. Box 2056
Bismarck, ND 58502

### Fargo

* Red River Valley
  Legal Assistants
Jeanine Rodvold, CLA,
  President
Conmy, Feste, Bossart
400 Norwest Center
Fargo, ND 58126

### Grand Forks

* Red River Valley
  Legal Assistants
Kathy Stradley, CLA,
  NALA Liaison
P.O. Box 5156
Grand Forks, ND 58026-5156

* National Association of Legal Assistants, Inc.
** National Federation of Paralegal Associations, Inc.

**Minot**

* Western Dakota Association
  of Legal Assistants
Janice Eslinger, CLA,
  President
McGee, Hankla
P.O. Box 998
Minot, ND  58702

**OHIO**

**Akron**

** Northeastern Ohio
  Paralegal Association
c/o Joanne Vetter
265 South Main Street
Akron, OH  44308

**Cincinnati**

** Cincinnati Paralegal
  Association
P.O. Box 1515
Cincinnati, OH  45201

**Cleveland**

** Cleveland Association
  of Paralegals
P.O. Box 14247
Cleveland, OH  44114

**Columbus**

** Legal Assistants
  of Central Ohio
P.O. Box 15182
Columbus, OH  43215-0182

**Dayton**

** Greater Dayton
  Paralegal Association
P.O. Box 515
Mid City Station
Dayton, OH  45402

**Toledo**

* Toledo Association
  of Legal Assistants
Cynthia L. Patterson, CLAS,
  President
Owens-Corning Fiberglas
Fiberglas Tower, OLEC-3
Toledo, OH  43659

* Toledo Association
  of Legal Assistants
Joyce A. Haas, CLA,
  NALA Liaison
Spengler, Nathanson, Heyman,
  McCarthy & Durfee
1000 National Bank Building
Toledo, OH  43604

**OKLAHOMA**

**Beaver**

* Student Association
  of Legal Assistants
Rogers State College
Leslie Fuller, President
RR3, Box 12-A
Beaver, OK  73932

* National Association of Legal Assistants, Inc.
** National Federation of Paralegal Associations, Inc.

## Enid

* Oklahoma Paralegal
  Association
Denise Newsom, CLA,
  President
McKnight & Gasaway
P.O. Box 1108
Enid, OK 73702

## Norman

* Rose State Paralegal
  Association
Marisa Ann Bruner,
  President
1811 Wren, #3
Norman, OK 73069

## Oklahoma City

* Oklahoma Paralegal
  Association
Sherie Adams, CLAS,
  NALA Liaison
Fuller, Tubb & Pomeroy
800 BOK Plaza
201 S. Robert S. Kerr Avenue
Oklahoma City, OK 73102-4292

## Tulsa

* TJC Student Association
  of Legal Assistants
Judy Tucker
TJC-Legal Assistant Program
909 S. Boston, Room 429
Tulsa, OK 74119

* Tulsa Association
  of Legal Assistants
Stephanie Mark, CLAS
Hall, Estill
4100 BOK Tower
Tulsa, OK 74172

## OREGON

### Eugene

* Pacific Northwest Legal
  Assistants
Jana Bauman, CLA,
  President
Swanson & Walters
975 Oak, Suite 220
Eugene, OR 97401

### Portland

** Oregon Legal Assistants
  Association
P.O. Box 8523
Portland, OR 97207

* Pacific Northwest Legal
  Assistants
Ginger M. Hoffman, CLA,
  NALA Liaison
c/o Jeffrey P. Foote
1020 SW Taylor, Suite 800
Portland, OR 97205

* National Association of Legal Assistants, Inc.
** National Federation of Paralegal Associations, Inc.

## PENNSYLVANIA

### Erie

** Paralegal Association of
  Northwestern Pennsylvania
P.O. Box 1504
Erie, PA  16507

### Harrisburg

** Central Pennsylvania
  Paralegal Association
P.O. Box 11814
Harrisburg, PA  17108

* Keystone Legal Assistant
  Association
Catrine Nuss, President
3021 Guineveer Drive, Apt. B4
Harrisburg, PA  17110

### Lancaster

** Lancaster Area Paralegal
  Association
c/o Rosemary Merwin
Gibble, Kraybill & Hess
41 East Orange Street
Lancaster, PA  17602

### Philadelphia

** Paralegal Association
  of Pierce Junior College
c/o Pierce Junior College
1420 Pine Street
Philadelphia, PA  19102

** Philadelphia Association
  of Paralegals
1411 Walnut Street, Suite 200
Philadelphia, PA  19102

### Pittsburgh

** Pittsburgh Paralegal
  Association
P.O. Box 1053
Pittsburgh, PA  15230

### Pottstown

** Pennsylvania Business Institute
  Paralegal Association
13 Armand Hammer Boulevard
Pottstown, PA  19464

### Reading

** Berks County Paralegal
  Association
c/o Daniella Johnson
Roland & Schlegal
P.O. Box 902
Reading, PA  19603-0902

### Scranton

** Sigma Pi Mu-Legal
  Assistant Division
c/o Marywood College
Social Sciences Department
P.O. Box 704
Scranton, PA  18509

---

* National Association of Legal Assistants, Inc.
** National Federation of Paralegal Associations, Inc.

## Sugarloaf

** Northeastern Pennsylvania
Association of Legal Assistants
c/o Brenda K. Harvey
Hourigan, Kluger, Spohrer & Quinn
Conyngham-Drums Road
Route 1, Box 464
Sugarloaf, PA  18249-9737

## Summerdale

* Keystone Legal Assistant
Association
Peggy Clements, CLA,
NALA Liaison
Campus on College Hill
Summerdale, PA  17093

## West Hazelton

** Wilkes-Barre Area Group
c/o Tom Albrechta
6 East Green Street
West Hazelton, PA  18201

## PUERTO RICO

## San Juan

** Puerto Rico Association
of Legal Assistants
c/o Hedily Schmidt
GPO Box 4225
San Juan, PR  00936

## RHODE ISLAND

## Providence

** Rhode Island Paralegal
Association
P.O. Box 1003
Providence, RI  02901

## SOUTH CAROLINA

## Charleston

** Charleston Association
of Legal Assistants
c/o Stacie Rose
Stuart Feldman, Esq.
P.O. Box 429
Charleston, SC  29402

## Columbia

** Columbia Legal Assistants
Association
c/o Barbara G. McGui
McNair Law Firm, P.A.
P.O. Box 11390
Columbia, SC  29211

** Carolina Paralegal
Association
c/o Anna Chason
7437 Highview Road
Columbia, SC  29204

* National Association of Legal Assistants, Inc.
** National Federation of Paralegal Associations, Inc.

**Florence**

** Paralegal Association
   of the Pee Dee
c/o Martha Knight
P.O. Box 5592
Florence, SC  29502

**Greenville**

* Greenville Association
   of Legal Assistants
Amanda A. Folk, CLA,
   President
Bozeman, Grayson, Smith
   & Price
301 College Street
Suite 400
Greenville, SC  29601

* Greenville Association
   of Legal Assistants
Diane R. Thompson,
   NALA Liaison
Office of the City Attorney
P.O. Box 2207
Greenville, SC  29602

**SOUTH DAKOTA**

**Black Hawk**

* South Dakota Legal
   Assistants Association, Inc.
Cindy Johnson, CLA, President
8801 Woodland Drive
Black Hawk, SD  57718

**Rapid City**

* South Dakota Legal
   Assistants Association, Inc.
Debra Niemi, NALA Liaison
P.O. Box 2670
Rapid City, SD  57709

**TENNESSEE**

**Chattanooga**

** Southeast Tennessee
   Paralegal Association
c/o Calecta Veagles
P.O. Box 1252
Cattanooga, TN  37401

* Tennessee Paralegal
   Association
Sandra H. Hughes, President
Legal Department
American National Bank
P.O. Box 1638
Chattanooga, TN  37401

**Cleveland**

** Cleveland State Community
   College Legal Assistant
   Association
P.O. Box 3570
Cleveland, TN  37311

**Memphis**

** Memphis Paralegal
   Association
P.O. Box 3646
Memphis, TN  38173-0646

* National Association of Legal Assistants, Inc.
** National Federation of Paralegal Associations, Inc.

* Tennessee Paralegal
  Association
Martha Wedgeworth, CLA,
  NALA Liaison
Neely, Green, Fargarson
  & Brooke
P.O. Drawer 3543
Memphis, TN  38173

**Nashville**

** Middle Tennessee
  Paralegal Association
P.O. Box 198006
Nashville, TN  37219

**TEXAS**

**Amarillo**

* Texas Panhandle Association
  of Legal Assistants
Nancy Stephens, CLA, President
Smith, Jarrell & Associates
P.O. Box 15525
Amarillo, TX  79105

* Texas Panhandle Association
  of Legal Assistants
Faith Pemberton, CLA,
  NALA Liaison
Miller & Herring
P.O. Box 2330
Amarillo, TX  79105

** Texas Panhandle Association
  of Legal Assistants
c/o Nancy Stephens
P.O. Box 1127
Amarillo, TX  79105-1127

**Andrews**

* Legal Assistant
  Association/Permian Basin
Jana G. Clift, CLA,
  NALA Liaison
300 North Main
Andrews, TX  79714

**Austin**

* Capital Area Paralegal
  Association
Chris Hemingson, CLA,
  President
Pope, Hopper, Roberts
  & Warren, P.C.
111 Congress, Suite 1700
Austin, TX  78701

* Capital Area Paralegal
  Association
Linette Edwards, CLAS,
  NALA Liaison
Jones, Day, Reavis & Pogue
301 Congress Avenue
Suite 1200
Austin, TX  78701

** Legal Assistants Division
  of the State Bar of Texas
P.O. Box 12487
Austin, TX  78711

**Beaumont**

* Southeast Texas Association
  of Legal Assistants
Janie Boswell, CLAS, President
P.O. Box 813
Beaumont, TX  77704

* National Association of Legal Assistants, Inc.
** National Federation of Paralegal Associations, Inc.

* Southeast Texas Association
  of Legal Assistants
Patricia A. Rios,
  NALA Liaison
P.O. Box 813
Beaumont, TX 77704

**Brownfield**

* West Texas Association
  of Legal Assistants
Eyvonne Crenshaw Palmer, CLAS,
  President
P.O. Box 1283
Brownfield, TX 79316

**Carrollton**

** Dallas Association
  of Legal Assistants
P.O. Box 117885
Carrollton, TX 75011-7885

**Corpus Christi**

* Nueces County Association
  of Legal Assistants
Joyce Hoffman, President
Edwards & Terry
P.O. Drawer 480
Corpus Christi, TX 78403

* Nueces County Association
  of Legal Assistants
Evelyn Just, CLA,
  NALA Liaison
800 Bayview Federal Building
Corpus Christi, TX 78474

**Dallas (see Carrollton)**

**El Paso**

* El Paso Association
  of Legal Assistants
Sandra Olson, CLA, President
Scott, Hulse, Marshall
Texas Commerce Bank
El Paso, TX 79901

* El Paso Association
  of Legal Assistants
Rosella A. Aguayo, CLA,
  NALA Liaison
Mayfield & Perrenot
First City Bank Building
Fifth Floor
El Paso, TX 79901

**Fort Worth**

** Fort Worth Paralegal
  Association
P.O. Box 17021
Ft. Worth, TX 76102

**Houston**

** Houston Legal Assistants
  Association
P.O. Box 52241
Houston, TX 77052

**Longview**

* Northeast Texas Association
  of Legal Assistants
Genee McFadden, CLA, President
3704 Kriss Drive
Longview, TX 75604

* National Association of Legal Assistants, Inc.
** National Federation of Paralegal Associations, Inc.

\* Northeast Texas Association
of Legal Assistants
Carol Klotz, CLA,
 NALA Liaison
Central Abstract & Title Co.
P.O. Box 1869
Longview, TX  75606

**Lubbock**

\* West Texas Association
of Legal Assistants
Gloria G. Lytle, CLA,
 NALA Liaison
Crenshaw, Dupree & Milam
P.O. Box 1499
Lubbock, TX  79408-1499

**Madison**

\*\* Legal Assistants Professional
Association (Brazos Valley)
c/o Linda Manning,
 Acting President
P.O. Box 925
Madison, TX  77864

**Midland**

\* Legal Assistant
Association/Permian Basin
Cecile Wiginton, CLA,
 President
P.O. Box 913
Midland, TX  79702

**San Antonio**

\*\* Alamo Area Professional
Legal Assistants, Inc.
P.O. Box 524
San Antonio, TX  78292

**Texarkana**

\* Texarkana Association
of Legal Assistants
Debbie H. Brower, CLA,
 President
Holman, Arnold & Cranford
2222 Hampton Rd.
P.O. Box 5367
Texarkana, TX  75505-5367

\* Texarkana Association
of Legal Assistants
Linda Vickers, CLA,
 NALA Liaison
Arnold & Arnold
P.O. Box 1858
Texarkana, TX  75504

**Tyler**

\*\* Tyler Area Association
of Legal Assistants
P.O. Box 1178
Tyler, TX  75711

**Wichita Falls**

\* Wichita County Student
 Association
Kathy M. Parker Adams
Continuing Education
Midwestern State University
3400 Taft
Wichita Falls, TX  76308

\* National Association of Legal Assistants, Inc.
\*\* National Federation of Paralegal Associations, Inc.

* Wichita County Student
  Association
Kris Tilker
Continuing Education
Midwestern State University
3400 Taft
Wichita Falls, TX 76308

## UTAH

### Orem

** Law Society
c/o Legal Assistant Program
Utah Valley Community
  College
1200 South 800 West
Orem, UT 84058

### Salt Lake City

* Legal Assistants
  Association of Utah
Michele B. Rehermann,
  President
P.O. Box 112001
Salt Lake City, UT 84147-2001

* Legal Assistants
  Association of Utah
Deanna Spillman, CLAS,
  NALA Liaison
3810 South Centennial Road
Salt Lake City, UT 84044

## VIRGINIA

### Harrisonburg

** Shenandoah Valley
  Paralegal Association
c/o Nancy Bryant
P.O. Box 88
Harrisonburg, VA 22801

### Newport News

* Peninsula Legal
  Assistants, Inc.
Diane Morrison, CLA,
  President
Jones, Blechman, Woltz
  & Kelly, P.C.
P.O. Box 12888
Newport News, VA 23612

* Peninsula Legal
  Assistants, Inc.
Novelie Genell Fisk, CLAS,
  NALA Liaison
Jones, Blechman, Woltz
  & Kelly, P.C.
P.O. Box 12888
Newport News, VA 23612

* Tidewater Association
  of Legal Assistants
Kimberly C. Heath,
  NALA Liaison
Jones, Blechman, Woltz
  & Kelly
6000 Thimble Shoals Boulevard
Newport News, VA 23606

* National Association of Legal Assistants, Inc.
** National Federation of Paralegal Associations, Inc.

**Norfolk**

* Tidewater Association
  of Legal Assistants
Claire S. Isley, CLA,
  President
Willcox & Savage, P.C.
1800 Sovran Center
Norfolk, VA  23510

**Richmond**

* Richmond Association
  of Legal Assistants
Vicki M. Roberts, President
McGuire, Woods, Battle
  & Boothe
One James Center
5th Floor
901 E. Cary Street
Richmond, VA  23219

* Richmond Association
  of Legal Assistants
Kimberly R. Jones,
  NALA Liaison
Signet Bank/VA
P.O. Box 25970
Richmond, VA  23260-5970

**Roanoke**

** Roanoke Valley
  Paralegal Association
P.O. Box 1018
Roanoke, VA  24005

**VIRGIN ISLANDS**

**St. Thomas**

* Virgin Islands
  Paralegals
Eloise Mack, President
P.O. Box 6276
St. Thomas, VI  00804

* Virgin Islands
  Paralegals
Betty L. King,
  NALA Liaison
P.O. Box 9121
St. Thomas, VI  00801

**WASHINGTON**

**Richland**

* Columbia Basin College
  Paralegal Association
Peggy Cottrell
Westinghouse Hanford Co.
P.O. Box 1970
Richland, WA  99352

* Columbia Basin College
  Paralegal Association
Kerri A. Wheeler, CLAS,
  Faculty Advisor
Washington Public Power
  Supply System
P.O. Box 968
Richland, WA  99352

* National Association of Legal Assistants, Inc.
** National Federation of Paralegal Associations, Inc.

## Seattle

** Washington Legal
  Assistants Association
2033 6th Avenue
Suite 804
Seattle, WA  98121

## WEST VIRGINIA

### Charleston

* Legal Assistants
  of West Virginia, Inc.
Mary Pat Hanson,
  President
Hunt & Wilson
P.O. Box 2506
Charleston, WV  25329-2506

* Legal Assistants
  of West Virginia, Inc.
Joanna W. Olds, CLA,
  NALA Liaison
Jackson & Kelly
P.O. Box 553
Charleston, WV  25322-0553

### Wheeling

** West Virginia Association
  of Legal Assistants
c/o Ms. Paula Houston
Volk, Frankovitch, Anetakis,
  Recht, Robertson & Hellerstedt
3000 Boury Center
Wheeling, WV  26003

## WISCONSIN

### Milwaukee

** Paralegal Association
  of Wisconsin
P.O. Box 92882
Milwaukee, WI  53202

## WYOMING

### Casper

* Legal Assistants
  of Wyoming
Nancy R. Hole, CLA,
  President
Brown & Drew
Casper Business Center
Suite 800
123 West First Street
Casper, WY  82601

* Legal Assistants
  of Wyoming
Michele D. Doyle,
  NALA Liaison
Williams, Porter, Day
  & Neville
145 S. Durbin, Suite 300
Casper, WY  82601

### Riverton

** Wyoming Legal Assistant
  Association
c/o Roger Thomas
HC 31, Box 2746H
Riverton, WY  82501

* National Association of Legal Assistants, Inc.
** National Federation of Paralegal Associations, Inc.

# APPENDIX D

# Suggested Reading

Aiger, John P., "Putting your Job Interview into Rehearsal," *The New York Times*
(October 16, 1983)

*America's Federal Jobs*, Jist Works, Inc., Indianapolis, Indiana
(1991)

Berkey, Rachel Lane, "Finding Employment," *Legal Assistant Today*
(Spring 1985)

Bolles, Richard N., *What Color is Your Parachute?*, Ten Speed Press,
Berkeley, California (1991)

Catalyst Staff, *Marketing Yourself*, Bantam Books, New York (1980)

Half, Robert, "Essential Skills," *Working Woman* (November 1985)

Half, Robert, *How to Get a Better Job in This Crazy World*, A Plume Book,
New York (1990)

Harrington, Betty Lehan, *Games Mother Never Taught You*,
Warner Books, New York (1977)

Howard, Terry, "Challenging Government Job Opportunities for the Paralegal,"
*Legal Assistant Today* (May/June 1991)

Irish, Richard, *Go Hire Yourself an Employer*, 3rd Edition, Doubleday,
New York (1987)

Jackson, Tom, *Guerrilla Tactics in the New Job Market*, 2nd Edition, Bantam Books,
New York (1991)

Jackson, Tom, *The Perfect Resume*, Anchor Books, Garden City,
    New York (updated edition 1981)

Medley, H. Anthony, *Sweaty Palms: The Neglected Art of Being Interviewed*,
    Ten Speed Press, Berkeley, California (1984)

Molloy, John T., *New Dress for Success*, Warner Books,
    New York (1988)

Molloy, John T., *The Woman's Dress for Success Book*, Warner Books,
    New York (1977)

Petras, Kathryn and Ross Petras, *Jobs '91*, Prentice Hall, New York (1991)

Raye-Johnson, Vanda, *Effective Networking*, Crisp Publications, Palo Alto,
    California (1990)

Rushlow, Ed, *Get a Better Job*, Peterson's Guides, Princeton, New Jersey (1990)

Rust, H. Lee, *Job Search*, Amacom, New York (1991)

Sheele, Adele, *Skills for Success*, Ballantine Books, New York (1979)

Snelling, Robert O. Sr. and Anne M. Snelling, *Jobs*, Simon & Schuster (1989)

Wright, John W., and Edward S. Dwyer, *American Almanac of Jobs and Salaries*,
    Avon Books, New York (1990)

Yates, Martin, *Knock 'Em Dead with Great Answers to Tough Interview Questions*,
    Bob Adams, Inc., Publisher, Holbrook, Massachusetts (1991)

# Afterword

*How To Land Your First Paralegal Job* was written out of a genuine desire to help those of you looking to enter an exciting new career in the legal field. I wanted to write the most comprehensive manual available on the subject. I have shared my most "secret" tips, those that I personally use to launch new paralegals in their journey to a satisfying position.

As the paralegal and legal assistant field changes, new techniques and innovative methods develop, and new opportunities for paralegals arise, this manual will be updated accordingly. My publisher, Estrin Publishing Co., and I would love to hear from you for future editions. **Share your experiences in finding your first paralegal job with us**. Tell us what worked and what didn't. We want your suggestions for improvement. Let us know where you had problems, where you found winning situations.

Although success is never guaranteed, using these techniques **will** enable you to follow in the footsteps of many, many entry and experienced level paralegals who have landed their dream jobs. I hope this book introduces you to a richer, more fulfilling career path. Let me know how you do.

Best of luck. I wish you phenomenal success!

# About the Author

Andrea Wagner's extensive background in both practice and personnel placement in the paralegal field has given her a unique understanding of the legal profession.

A native of Los Angeles, Wagner set her first career sights on the theater, earning her bachelor's degree in theater arts from the University of California at Berkeley. She earned a California Standard Lifetime Teaching Credential in 1972 and spent three years teaching drama in the Roseville Unified School District.

Wagner received a master of arts degree from California State University, Sacramento, in 1979. She became a theater arts instructor at the University of La Verne before entering the paralegal profession.

An honors graduate in the University of West Los Angeles School of Paralegal Studies, Wagner earned her litigation paralegal certificate in 1979.

After working as a litigation legal assistant and an independent paralegal, Wagner became placement director for her alma mater, where she counseled students seeking employment and significantly increased the visibility of the University of West Los Angeles with law firms and corporation.

In 1986, Wagner became executive recruiting director for C.B. Estrin & Associates, one of the largest paralegal placement companies in the country. She held this position until 1990, when she became director of paralegal services for Sorkin & Associates. Currently, Wagner is a career counselor for legal professionals. A former member of the board of directors for the Los Angeles Paralegal Association and president of the University of West Los Angeles Paralegal Alumni Association, Wagner lectures extensively on paralegal placement. She has also written for various publications, including *Legal Assistant Today* magazine.

# Index

**- Y -**

year-end, defined  240
year-end bonus  6, 178, 191, 194
    **see also** interviewing and salary
       negotiations
Yellow Pages  98, 99

# ORDER FORM

**Telephone orders:**    Call Toll Free:  **(800) 358-5897**
*Have your Visa or MasterCard ready.*

**FAX orders:**    **(310) 829-7659**

**Postal orders:**    Estrin Publishing
2811 Wilshire Blvd., Suite 707
Santa Monica, CA  90403
(310) 315-0480

_____  **Yes! I want to know "How to Land Your First Paralegal Job!"  I
understand that I may return it for a full refund—for any
reason, no questions asked.**

_____  Send information regarding the books and publications for for the legal
field from Estrin Publishing.

_____  Send me more information about Estrin Publishing seminars for
paralegals and legal assistants.

_____  Please add my name to the Paralegal Grapevine so that I may receive
more information about the paralegal career.

**Name:** _____

**Address:** _____

**City:** _____  **State:** _____  **Zip:** _____

**Sales tax:**
Please add **8.25%** for books shipped to **California** addresses only.

**Shipping:**
Book rate:  $2.00 for the first book and $1.00 for additional copies.
Regular shipping may take three to four weeks.

Air Mail: $3.50 per book

**Payment:**    [    ] Check    [    ] Visa    [    ] MasterCard

**Name
on Card:** _____  Expiration Date _____

**Card No.:** _____

**Signature:** _____